Labour and Society in Britain and the USA

Volume 1

The Amalgamated Society of Engineers, formed in Great Britain, also established branches in the USA. The frontispiece, kindly supplied by John Smethurst, shows a membership certificate issued to a New Jersey machinist.

Labour and Society in Britain and the USA

Volume 1
Capitalism, Custom and Protest, 1780–1850

NEVILLE KIRK

SCOLAR PRESS

Published by   Ashgate Publishing Company
SCOLAR PRESS   Old Post Road
Gower House   Brookfield
Croft Road   Vermont 05036
Aldershot   USA
Hants GU11 3HR
England

British Library Cataloguing-in-Publication data

Kirk, Neville
    Labour and Society in Britain and the
    USA. – Vol.1: Capitalism, Custom and
    Protest, 1780–1850
    I. Title
    331.1209

Library of Congress Cataloging-in-Publication Data

Kirk, Neville
    Labour and society in Britain and the USA / Neville Kirk.
        p.   cm.
    Includes bibliographical references and index.
    Contents: v. 1. Capitalism, custom, and protest, 1780–1850 – v.
2. Challenge and accommodation, 1850–1939.
    ISBN 1–85928–021–8 (v. 1) ISBN
1–85928–022–6 (v. 2)
    1. Labor movement–Great Britain–History. 2. Labor movement–
United States–History. 3. Working class–Great Britain–History.
4. Working class–United States–History. 5. Protest movements–
Great Britain–History. 6. Protest movements–United States–
History. 7. Capitalism–Great Britain–History. 8. Capitalism–
United States–History. 9. Great Britain–Social conditions.
10. United States–Social conditions. I. Title.
HD8388.K57   1994
305.5′62′094–dc20   93–47283
                        CIP

ISBN 1 85928 021 8

Typeset in 10 point Garamond by Intype, London, and printed in Great Britain at the University Press, Cambridge.

Contents

To Kate and Bob, Dorothy and (in memory of) Edward.

Preface

My interest in comparative labour history stems from my time as an MA student in the Centre for the Study of Social History at Warwick University in 1968–9. Edward Thompson, David Montgomery, Fred Reid, James Hinton and the postgraduate students created a stimulating and challenging intellectual atmosphere in which it was expected that staff and students would both extend and share their knowledge. The results, for both the participants and the university authorities, were unforgettable.

Equally stimulating sojourns in Pittsburgh and at Yale, and my teaching experiences at Manchester Polytechnic (since 1992 Manchester Metropolitan University) and Liverpool Polytechnic (now Liverpool John Moore's University) have further deepened my interest in the social, economic and labour history of Britain and America. Without the advice, patience and encouragement of staff and students in these various institutions and places these books would not have been written.

More immediately, a combination of factors encountered during recent experiences of teaching courses in British and American history – highly motivated and stimulating students, the demanding challenges presented by comparative work, and the dearth of genuinely comparative British and American labour and social history material – finally persuaded me to put pen to paper. Hopefully, the result will be useful to students. And it is to the students at Yale and Manchester Metropolitan University, who demonstrated infinite good humour in the face of my comparative 'experiments', that I owe a major debt of gratitude.

These two companion volumes offer far more in the way of a critical guide to, and synthesis of, the (especially recent) secondary literature relating to British and American workers and their respective social orders and labour movements than an exercise in primary-based research. As such, my studies have heavily depended upon the prior labours of Bruce Laurie, Sean Wilentz, David Montgomery, David Brody, Leon Fink, James Hinton, John Rule, Eddie Hunt, John Belchem, Dorothy Thompson, John Stevenson and many others.

Several people have kindly read parts of the text. I am grateful to John Rule, Mike Rose, Pat Hudson, David Howell and David Montgomery for their considered and encouraging comments. I owe a special vote of gratitude to John Walton who has painstakingly read and commented upon many pages of text. The seminars held by John Walton at

Lancaster, the graduate students at Yale, Mike Rose at Manchester, Ron Noon and Sam Davies at Liverpool, Pat Thane in London, and the Cambridge Social History seminar helped me to focus more sharply my thoughts and organisation. I am, of course, entirely responsible for the actual views and facts expressed in the text.

Several other debts have been accumulated. George Zis kindly granted me a period of two terms' study leave in which to complete the manuscript. Terry Wyke has diligently compiled the indexes. Alec McAulay, Ellen Keeling and their colleagues at Scolar Press provided patient expertise and hard work. And the flanks, if not the peat 'groughs' of Kinder Scout, Brown Knoll, *et al.* have continued to offer the space and solitude in which to run and exercise my thoughts.

Neville Kirk
New Mills
September 1993

Introduction

This introduction presents an overview of the key assumptions, arguments and organisational structures of both this study of pre-1850 workers and society and its companion volume, *Challenge and Accommodation, 1850–1939*. These two books can be read as discrete studies of different periods of labour and social history. But in truth a number of unifying issues, themes and aims inform both volumes. The main purpose of both books is thus to offer the reader an explicitly comparative approach to the study of workers, organised labour and society in modern Britain and North America. Central concern rests with the history of workers and their collective, labour movement organisations and protests from the post-revolutionary period in America and the Industrial Revolution in Britain to the immediate pre-Second World War years in both countries. Organised chronologically and thematically, these books do not, however, present an exhaustive chronological account of labour movement development. Such an account would extend to several volumes and must, in any case, await the publication of a more substantial body of comparative research than at present exists. Rather, I have adopted three less ambitious and more manageable aims: to investigate the key formative influences upon, the main characteristics of, and important debates surrounding the development of organised labour and workers' movements in the two countries; to situate labour movement institutions within their wider social context (of which labour's institutions are an integral part and outside of which they cannot be properly understood);[1] and to trace the interactions between those economic and other 'hard facts of life', which confronted people irrespective of volition, and the conscious, purposeful attempts of workers to shape their own destinies. In these various ways these studies will combine description and analysis, and examine the complex relationships between institutions, movements and wider culture, and human agency and social conditioning. But the general, overriding purpose is to offer comparisons and contrasts both within and across national boundaries.

COMPARATIVE LABOUR HISTORY: DEVELOPMENT, STRENGTHS AND WEAKNESSES

Such comparisons and contrasts are, at least with reference to British and North American labour history, very much in their infancy. Selig Perlman, Hobsbawm, Montgomery and others have urged us to extend our perspectives beyond national boundaries,[2] and general *economic* histories of Britain and the United States do contain useful sections relating to the institutional development of labour.[3] There are, furthermore, a growing number of comparative labour history essays in journals.[4] Yet in terms of both the general international picture and, more specifically, Britain and the United States, there continue to exist major gaps in our knowledge and plentiful scope for the development of new and genuinely comparative initiatives. For example, 'comparative' labour history anthologies are often compilations of discrete, nationally-based case studies: the task of making linkages, of drawing comparisons and contrasts across national boundaries is left mainly to the wit and imagination of the reader.[5] And, as my students have been all too painfully aware, there simply does not exist a comparative, book-length study of labour in Britain and the United States. It is my intention both to provide an introductory study and to contribute towards the wider process of constructing a more explicit and integrated comparative labour history.

As with the comparative method itself, the comparative study of workers in Britain and the United States presents the historian with a challenging blend of opportunities and difficulties. In terms of labour, various nationally based differences between Britain and the United States constitute obstacles to instant comparisons and generalisations. Such differences reside in the chronology and character of industrialisation, in the relative importance and character of the agricultural sector, in contrasting political traditions and structures, and in social structure and values.[6] Similarly, many labour historians have adhered to the notion of American 'exceptionalism', the view that American workers have, as a result of a mixture of factors (the 'gift' of the vote, opportunities for high levels of geographical and occupational mobility, the absence of a homogeneous working class, the profoundly divisive effects of slavery and racism, the deep imprint of capitalist values upon large sectors of the population and so on), lacked the 'true' class consciousness of their European and British counterparts.[7]

Differences, complexities and variations *within* nationally based labour movements and social structures further compound the difficulties of making satisfactory generalisations. Indeed, given the importance of distinctive national traditions and manifold complexities it might, therefore, seem that traditional comparisons are doomed to failure from the outset.

My books will argue otherwise. It will be suggested, for example, that distinctive national traditions coexisted and interacted with similar or common international influences and experiences, and that ties and mutual influences between the post-revolutionary United States and Britain remained strong. The combined and uneven development of full-blown industrial capitalism, proletarianisation, accelerated urbanisation and the diminished relative importance of agriculture, the growing importance of class consciousness, and mounting pressures for greater political democracy and improved living standards – these constituted important examples of broad processes and influences which extended across national boundaries, but which were greatly shaped by distinctive national traditions.

More specifically, the continued importance of the 'Atlantic Economy' during the first half of the nineteenth century, mass emigration from Britain to the United States, and the longer-term influences of language, law and customs of Britain upon America ensured that, for better or worse, relations would remain close throughout the nineteenth century.[8] During the present century the rise of the United States to a position of capitalist hegemony and its continued 'special relationship' with Britain have been factors of major economic, political and cultural significance. It will, furthermore, be suggested that the recent trend in American labour historiography to fundamentally challenge the 'exceptionalism' argument is rooted in firm empirical evidence. At least down to the 1920s British and American workers had far more in common than the conventional wisdom would have us believe. Transnational comparisons which pay due attention to variations in terms of time and place and distinct national traditions are both valid and instructive.

COLLECTIVISM, INDIVIDUALISM AND THE QUESTION OF CLASS

Further difficulties reside in the extent to which we can describe workers' behaviour and values as being predominantly collective and co-operative or individualistic and competitive in character; and the degree to which it is appropriate to attach the label of class to such values and behaviour. These are difficulties which exist both within and across national boundaries. Given their centrality to labour history in general and this book in particular, it is useful to alert the reader immediately as to my views on these matters.

In *The Fall of the House of Labor* David Montgomery has clearly

identified the dangers of seeing the American working class as a fixed
and unified collective body. Montgomery declares:

> To write about the working class is to discuss many disparate
> individuals. At any moment in the American past the researcher
> encounters such a variety in personal aspirations, talents, and sense
> of self among working people as to defy stereotypes. Moreover,
> socially prescribed differences in gender, race, religion and national-
> ity have influenced various workers' behavior in powerfully differ-
> ent ways. Instead of listening for the 'voice of the working class',
> therefore, we must be attuned to many different voices, sometimes
> in harmony, but often in conflict with one another.[9]

Emphases upon internal differences and divisions have characterised
the approaches of many labour historians to the study of British
workers.[10] Indeed, so strong has been the reaction against the central
importance of class in modern British history (especially in relation to
workers' experiences) during the past decade of Thatcherite triumphs
and labour movement defeats that the class-based, historical-materialist
approach of Thompson, Hobsbawm and others has lost much of its
former dominance in the fields of labour and social history. It is, furthermore, ironic that whilst emphases upon class and class consciousness
have centrally informed recent debates among American labour historians, they have experienced diminished support among influential
sections of the history profession in Britain.[11]

This study will take due account of differences and divisions within
working-class life on both sides of the Atlantic. But it will also argue
that the forces of fragmentation were compelled to confront the strong
impulses towards mutual dependence and support, solidarity and collective action, within working-class experience. Such impulses operated
within both 'objective' reality and consciousness. Indeed, I will go
further, to make the claim that the working people of nineteenth- and
early twentieth-century Britain and the United States were characterised
more by collective and solidarity values and actions than by those of
the acquisitive individualism of the bourgeoisie.

As David Montgomery has observed, diversity is only one side of
the coin of workers' experience. Largely unintended processes simultaneously bring together seemingly unconnected individuals and groups.
Historical interest and skills rest in an exploration of the ways in which
the contradictory thrusts towards unity and fragmentation, difference
and commonality, interact and come to dominate both at specific points
of time and over time. And an exploration of the rich and contradictory
characteristics of late nineteenth-century and early twentieth-century
American workers' lives has revealed to Montgomery the paramount
importance of class:

it remains not only possible but imperative to analyze the American experience of the late nineteenth and early twentieth centuries in terms of conflicting social classes. The human relationships structured by commodity production in large collective enterprises devoted to private gain generated bondings and antagonisms that were, in one form or another, the daily experience of everyone involved . . .

Although the modern experience of class had its origin in the encounter with wage labour . . . class consciousness permeated social intercourse outside the workplace as well as within it. Married women caring for their children in bleak, congested neighbourhoods and facing creditors, charity officials, and the ominous authority of the clergy were reminded of their class as regularly as were their husbands, daughters and sons in the factories. Children learned early the difference between their parents' attire, bearing and patterns of speech and those of the gentlemen and ladies who seemed to move with such grace and ease through the corridors of power and the emporiums of abundance.[12]

Learning to cope with the manifold insecurities and indignities of life led to the conclusion that 'although others might wield social influence as individuals, workers' only hope of securing what they wanted in life was through concerted action': mutualism was preferable to individualism.[13] And, notes Montgomery, being so rooted in daily life, the ethic of mutualism had a wide appeal which extended far beyond the minority ranks of organised labour. Simultaneously, however, class consciousness was 'more than the unmediated product of daily experience. It was also a project.' And central to the success of that project was, observes Montgomery, 'deliberate human agency', especially as seen in the unceasing endeavours of the 'militant minority' of labour activists to construct the organisations and disseminate the ideas dedicated to the 'emancipation of labor'.[14]

Similar emphases upon mutual dependence and support, collectivism, and the largely oppositional and class-based character of working-class culture have characterised the historical-materialist approaches of Raymond Williams, Dorothy and Edward Thompson, Eric Hobsbawm and John Saville to the study of the modern British working class. It is within the broad tradition of historical materialism that this book is to be situated.

At this stage it is sufficient to simply record my reasoned commitment to historical materialism. The detailed implications of this commitment – in terms of its adequacy or otherwise as a method of conceptualisation, description and analysis – will emerge during the course of the book. It is, however, necessary at this point to comment further upon two of the key elements of historical materialism – collectivism and class – which figure so largely in this study.

In terms of collectivism, the reader's attention should be drawn to three observations. First, while highlighting the importance of collectivism and mutality to workers, I do not thereby claim that such patterns of thought and action are either predetermined or unchanging. As Gordon, Edwards and Reich have observed, there are firm structural under-pinnings to working-class collectivism:

> Atomized through labor market competition and faced with the continual threat of surplus labor supplies, workers are driven to strengthen their connections with other workers in order to protect their wages, jobs, and working conditions and in order to advance their own interests. This tendency toward *collective working-class activity* leads not only to labor unions but also to informal resistance on the job and more organized forms of political activity and self-defense off the job.[15]

However, as implied in the above quotation, such underpinnings constitute an impetus towards an expectation, rather than a sufficient guarantee, of collectivism. Collectivism is not solely produced by economic or other kinds of structures. In addition to the latter, we must pay close attention to consciousness and the entire social *ensemble* of forces in order to develop a comprehensive account of collectivism. We should also note that the strength of collectivism varies in terms of time and place.

Second, to highlight collectivism is not to dismiss the importance of individualism, independence and competition. Attention to historical context is of primary importance in evaluating the relative weight and significance of these respective values and practices. Furthermore, we should remember that cultures are not one-dimensional in character, being, for example, neither wholly individualistic nor wholly collectivist. Cultures are complex wholes which combine within themselves a wide range of practices, values and potential meanings. Thus dominant, subor-dinate, oppositional, consensual, complementary and contradictory elements inhabit cultures at specific points in time.[16] The aim is to explore complexities and contradictions, to engage cultural with other factors in order to reveal meanings, and to identify continuous, changing and dominant cultural processes.

To move to a more concrete level of analysis, elements of individual-ism and co-operation can be observed to coexist within a predominantly collective and mutualist culture. For example, many early–mid Victorian artisans and skilled workers were simultaneously committed to the values of self-help, self-respect, independence, 'manliness', individual restraint *and* to the notions of collective improvement and organisation, improvement within rather than escape from the working class, and corporate, even class, pride. And although the balance between individualistic and collective nuances and emphases changed in the post-Chartist years (oppositional and transforming aims becoming less marked), nevertheless there was a continued reliance upon collective means to pursue personal, and family- and community-based goals. This was in stark contrast to the acquisitive individualism preached by large sections of the middle class. And the artisan's 'individualism', geared mainly to coping with the insecurities of working-class life and operating within a collective framework, was not to be confused with the 'rags-to-riches' individualism of the bourgeoisie. In sum, class experience remained significant. Common interclass attachments to words such as independence and individualism could not conceal different, even antagonistic, class-based cultural meanings.[17]

Third, working-class collectivism and mutualism expressed themselves in a variety of ways and directions. There was no absolute or 'true' form of working-class consciousness and behaviour, no universal model against which actual experience could or should be measured. Mutualism was present, among other influences, in the family, neighbourhood and at the levels of daily 'commonsense' and more structured formal ideologies. In Britain a strong sense of 'Us and Them', of allegiance to other workers and mistrust, even hostility, towards non-manual strata, frequently pervaded working-class life and consciousness. In the United States a similar state of affairs existed, albeit within more distinctive and varied ethnic and racial structures. Food riots, attacks on property and machinery, trade unions, co-operative and friendly societies and independent political organisations constituted some of the many ways in which workers acted together.

Worker consciousness could range from a conservative and fatalistic acceptance of the status quo to clearly formulated plans to reform or transform capitalism in labourist and socialist ways. These kinds of consciousness were not necessarily mutually exclusive. The 'commonsense' of everyday life could contain a mix of all three, and much more besides. Nevertheless, reasoned and patterned processes intermingled with the seeming incoherence and contradictions of daily existence. Choice of strategy was greatly influenced by a considered evaluation of the possibilities of its realisation, of the hard realities of power, of the balance of social and political forces, the prospects for change and so forth. Indeed an important task of this study is to identify and explain the adoption of particular strategies at specific points in time. And while I do not posit a natural, linear and unproblematical historical progression from 'primitive' to more 'modern' forms of working-class collectivism and protest, I do suggest that the passing of time witnessed the more extensive adoption of formal collective structures and ideologies among workers on both sides of the Atlantic.

Emphases upon the variety, complexity and irreducibility of working-class collectivism might appear to the reader to be unduly platitudinous, even unnecessary. But my emphases have been inserted as a counterweight to the views of some 'Marxists' that the working class is destined, by the 'laws of history', to 'advance' to the 'true' stage of revolutionary socialist class consciousness, and that anything which deflects from or falls short of this 'true' standard is to be dismissed as 'false', non-class-based consciousness. The weaknesses of such views are, of course, well known and are fully acknowledged in the present study. History does not move in mechanistic, lawed, linear and teleological ways. Working-class consciousness and behaviour must be examined within their specific historical contexts and their own terms of reference rather than against an unreal absolute standard. Different forms of consciousness and behaviour carry equal validity to their respective subjects, and merit critical evaluation by contemporaries, historians and others. To view what actually existed in terms of what ought to have existed is improperly to flatten, misrepresent and devalue the former.

In turning to the issue of class, it should be noted that I have largely followed E. P. Thompson's usage. Having, in my view, admirably withstood the rigours of thirty years of critical examination, Thompson's views concerning class, as first expressed in *The Making of the English Working Class*, offer the historian a stimulating and fruitful way of interrogating the empirical evidence.[18]

'By class', writes Thompson,

> I understand a historical phenomenon, unifying a number of disparate and seemingly unconnected events, both in the raw material of experience and in consciousness. I emphasize that it is a *historical* phenomenon. I do not see class as a 'structure', nor even as a 'category', but as something which in fact happens (and can be shown to have happened) in human relationships.[19]

Class resides, therefore, neither totally in the objective determinations of experience/structure, nor totally in consciousness, but in the historical interactions, between, on the one hand, consciousness and agency and, on the other, structure. Class experience (or structured determination) is, claims Thompson, 'largely determined by the productive relations into which men are born – or enter involuntarily'; and class consciousness is defined as 'the way in which these experiences are handled in cultural terms: embodied in traditions, value-systems, ideas, and institutional forms'.[20]

Whilst endorsing Thompson's emphases upon experience *and* consciousness, I would like to make two additions to his framework of analysis. First, in order to take adequate cognizance of the presence, values and behaviour of women and their relationships *vis-à-vis* men, the notion of gender and gender-based differences, divisions and inequalities must be more explicit interwoven into discussions of class.[21] Second, we should (as Thompson's concrete historical practice demonstrates) locate class experience/structure more firmly in politics, culture, ideology and identify the 'economic' in its widest sense, and not only in production. To argue as such is, as noted by Przeworski, to avoid the false temptation to view only economic relations as objective and all other relations as within the realms of subjectivity.[22] I suggest, in effect, that economics, politics, ideology and culture simultaneously reside within both underlying structure and consciousness. Structure can enjoy an independent existence: but *meaning* is not revealed by structure alone. It is the interaction between structure and consciousness which produces meanings at particular points in time.

As the product of an ongoing engagement between structure and consciousness, class, as emphasised by Thompson, owes as much to agency as conditioning. And, as a historical relationship, class changes over time. Contrary to the suggestions frequently made by historians of varied, often contrasting, persuasions, classes are never completely 'finished' or 'fully made' in either an absolute or linear sense. Neither do classes consist of a monolithic and undifferentiated mass of people, lumped together by *total* unity of experience, values and aims. History, as already noted, does not operate in such linear, mechanistic, uniform and absolute ways. We can record occasions upon which seemingly separate individuals come together in class ways, and thus refer to a process of class 'making'. Conversely, of course, we can also observe processes of fragmentation and conflict, of class 'unmaking'. The point is that neither of these processes is absolute or static: change is of the essence.

In moving to a discussion of the structural underpinnings of class, it is extremely difficult to afford causal priority to a particular structure or aspect of experience. Necessary attention to the variations and complexities of history render absolute (i.e. universal) or purely abstract (concerned solely with logical rigour and consistency) models of structural causation inadequate to the delicate task at hand. Of far greater promise is an approach which offers conditional generalisations (able to meet the demands of conceptual rigour and necessary attention to historical variety, specificity and complexity) and provisional conclusions (subject to change in the light of subsequent research). It will be suggested that this historically based approach recognises the necessity rather than the sufficiency of material determinations (getting a living, feeding, clothing and housing oneself and dependants) of class, and the simultaneous influences of politics, culture and ideology upon class formation. In some contexts it may be demonstrated that one particular structure exerts greater power and influence than the others: but this is a matter of concrete historical demonstration rather than of purely abstract reasoning. In any event, it is the complex ways in which a wide range of influences *interact* to produce (or to deny) class which we must note. Reductionism – whether of the traditional economic or more recent idealist kind (class as the creation of ideas, especially political ideas, and language) – is far too narrow and unsatisfactory a mode of analysis.[23]

In terms of the dimension of class consciousness, four observations should be noted. First, I follow Thompson in suggesting that class consciousness does not precede class experience. People do not enter the historical stage simply possessed or not possessed of this magical quality, 'class consciousness'. Rather, in the course of pursuing a variety of aims within circumstances largely not intended or chosen, people can, and sometimes (but by no means invariably) do, identify common points of interest and come to act, even struggle, together. Class expression – in terms of ideas, value-systems and institutions – emerges from within experiential struggle and debate. Przeworski has expressed this point of view more abstractly:

> economic, political, and ideological conditions jointly structure the realm of struggles that have as their effect the organization, disorganization, or reorganization of classes. Classes must thus be viewed as effects of struggles structured by objective conditions that are simultaneously economic, political, and ideological.

And, continues Przeworski, 'Precisely because class formation is an effect of struggles, outcomes of this process are at each moment of history to some extent indeterminate.'[24]

Second, class consciousness arises when people, as a result of common experiences, 'feel and articulate the identity of their interests as between themselves', and as against other people, 'whose interests are different from (and usually opposed to) theirs'.[25] The expression of an identity of interest among workers signifies that *for a period of time* (as, for example, during the Chartist years) differences and divisions are overshadowed by a deeper sense of class solidarity. But such solidarity is, in turn, frequently fragile, being prone to change and fragmentation over time.

Third, I will argue against both an absolute or 'true' expression of class, and a necessary progression from one stage of class consciousness to another. As with the general case of working-class collectivism, class consciousness can, indeed has, taken a variety of expressions which carry equal validity to their holders. We can thus endorse Thompson's views that, 'No actual class formation in history is any truer or more real than any other', and that, 'class defines itself as, in fact, it eventuates'.[26]

Fourth, in rejecting attempts to force class into an analytical strait-jacket, we must equally be careful not to adopt such a wide and loose usage that class loses its necessary definitional precision and rigour. In this context it is important to identify criteria which, while subject to proper empirical questioning and controls, nevertheless give us a sufficiently rigorous analytical framework within which we can detect not only the presence or absence, but also the extent and depth, of class. I suggest that the criteria of independence, constituency and hostility/conflict constitute useful yardsticks of class feeling and behaviour.

In terms of independence, it is helpful to determine the extent to which workers and their allies (especially small producers and radical intellectuals) either created their own institutions, ideas, value systems, formal ideologies and ways of life, or were rooted within, and largely committed to, a world mainly created and controlled by other social groups and classes. Class-based issues and anti-capitalist thoughts and actions may have been present in the latter case, but, I argue, were generally of far less overall significance than in the world created specifically by workers for workers. For example, non-working-class nineteenth-century Liberals, Conservatives, Republicans and Democrats utilised the languages of class in an effort to enlist worker support for and, in the American case, active participation in, largely middle- and upper-class controlled political parties. In these parties class-based issues of specific concern to manual workers were present but not generally paramount. And such parties' projected public images went far beyond their sympathies towards the working class.[27] Conversely, far more self-consciously class-based appeals and anti-capitalist ideologies were generally characteristic of socialist parties and independent political organisations of labour. In this sense the presence or absence of independent labour politics and the strength of the appeal exerted by such politics were important indications of the force of class.

In relation to the notion of constituency, I suggest that the extent to which class consciousness exists is greatly influenced by the size and character of that body of workers embracing a common identity of interests which in turn overshadows internal differences and divisions.

Finally, to what extent were common interests accompanied by expressions of collective hostility towards, and conflict with, other groups and social classes – as manifested especially in attitudes and behaviour antagonistic towards the interests and beliefs of capitalists?[28] A related question concerns the ways and extent to which the daily 'commonsense' of class expressed itself in more organised and formal political, economic and cultural forms. Did, furthermore, a sense of belonging to the working class *necessarily* imply hostility towards and conflict with other classes?[29] In order to answer such questions we must pay careful attention to the powerful ways in which politics, ideology and culture shaped identity. Economic factors and structures do not, in themselves, adequately reveal meanings and produce identities. And although social reality lies, in part, 'out there', in conditions and constraints beyond choice, yet human choice and influence *simultaneously* both help to constitute and give meaning to social reality. Herein exists the continual dialogue between conditioning and agency.

It was stated much earlier in this introduction that the comparative method of study offers the historian an exciting blend of opportunities and difficulties. Some of the major difficulties have been seen to reside in the extent to which generalisations can be made across national boundaries, and in relation to different chronologies and social structures. We have, furthermore, confronted the obstacles of conceptual and methodological rigour, clarity and adequacy. No difficulty or obstacle has, however, so far proved to be insuperable. Indeed, the positive opportunities provided by the comparative method – in terms of exploring the interplays and tensions between distinctive national, regional and local traditions and similar, sometimes common, transnational processes and structures, and in setting the notions of class, ethnicity, race, gender and so on into engagement within a variety of historical contexts – are truly legion, if simultaneously somewhat daunting in their magnitude and complexity.

STRUCTURE AND ARGUMENTS

These volumes are structured in accordance with the methodological concerns outlined above. Part One of Volume One sets the broad material foundations of the birth and early development of labour movements in both countries, paying specific attention to the process of combined and uneven capitalist development upon labour. Part One is mainly economic in its orientation, centrally focusing upon changes and continuities at work, and in social relations of production during the second half of the eighteenth century and the first half of the nineteenth century. Capitalist transformation embraced, however, not only changes within production but also shifts within the wider economy and society, and in cultural and political life. Part One accordingly incorporates key developments and tensions within the broader culture – and especially the conflicts produced by the impingement of free-market capitalism upon the 'customary' and 'moral-economic' lives of the labouring people – into its framework of analysis.

Part Two deals more substantially with institutions, politics and ideologies. This section's main focus rests upon the character and aims of popular protest and early working-class movements, particularly from the late 1820s to the 1860s. Two major questions are posed. To what extent did class centrally inform popular movements of the 1830s and early 1840s on both sides of the Atlantic? And to what extent and for which reasons did such movements and their social bases of support decline and fragment between the mid 1840s and the 1860s? I present the hypotheses that class was indeed of major importance to both British and American workers during the second quarter of the century; and that a common process of class fragmentation did occur around mid century. At the same time I suggest that class was both more extensive and durable in the British context, and that the shared process of fragmentation assumed peculiarly national characteristics (such as the more pronounced influences of temperance, religious revivalism, racism and nativism in the United States). Furthermore, organised working-class movements in mid-Victorian Britain both made greater institutional advances and were more accepted by the state and (to a lesser extent) employers than their counterparts in America.

By the mid 1870s organised labour in Britain was dominated by skilled and craft workers, was largely cautious and moderate in outlook, and had won recognition from the state and an increasing number of employers. By way of contrast across the Atlantic the hostile actions of employers and the state both rendered the American labour (especially trade-union) movement more of an unwelcome outsider and increased the potential for conflict and labour militancy.

Part One of Volume Two concerns itself with the themes of capitalist development, trade unionism and relations at work, and politics, ideologies and cultures during the period from the 1860s to the waning of post-war militancy during the early 1920s.

Chapter 1 draws the reader's attention to the continuing character of capitalist transformation in both countries. Within this common framework significant national differences emerged. Above all, the process of transformation was more rapid and extensive in the United States. Thus moves to monopoly capitalism, to large units of production, to the closer integration between banking and manufacturing concerns, to technological change, and to the transformation of the labour process by means of Taylorism and other schemes proceeded more quickly in the United States. When allied to the erratic tempo of industrial growth and acute pressures upon capital accumulation between 1873 and 1896, and the diverse and simultaneously mutualistic and increasingly self-

assertive character of the American working class, such factors ensured
that the years between the 1870s and 1920s would constitute a period
of industrial turbulence. In Britain the pace and extent of change was
less marked. The British economy did not 'fail' in any absolute sense
in this period, but the retreat of the 'workshop of the world' into the
safe markets of Empire accentuated conservatism, traditionalism and
empiricism. Likewise, the British working class was far more settled
and homogeneous than its dramatically reconstituted (by immigration
and mobility) American counterpart. Yet continuity and stability were
far from the norm in Britain. The adverse effects of the 'Great
Depression' upon profit margins, mounting competition from the
United States and Germany, and the improvement in living standards
and growing self-confidence of the mass of previously unorganised
workers, were instrumental in a hardening of employer and state attitudes towards organised labour and in effecting important shifts in
working-class movements.

Chapter 2 examines such shifts in relation to trade unionism and
work-place relations. Attention is drawn to the history of bitter and protracted labour struggles in the United States, and to the rich tapestry of
worker and petty producer responses to the growth of monopoly capitalism. Indeed, contrary to the conventional orthodoxy of the Wisconsin
school of labour history, the response of 'pure and simple unionism'
was neither preordained nor totally dominant in the pre-First World
War years. Industrial unionism, revolutionary unionism, and the broad
transforming plans of the Knights of Labor and Populists were aspects
of a wide variety of responses and initiatives which sought to win the
workers' allegiance. Yet by the 1920s the 'pure and simple unionism' of
the American Federation of Labor (AF of L) was hegemonic. And in
terms of the comparative context the United States increasingly appeared
to be a laggard. Trade-union density was much higher in Britain, and
the 'new unionism' of the unskilled and semi-skilled, which had
developed in Britain between the 1870s and 1914, had failed to take
effective and secure root in the United States.

In terms of political developments during the late nineteenth century
and early twentieth century, Chapter 3 demonstrates that the United
States was far less 'exceptional' than is often supposed. Not only did
many American workers adopt radical political means (as seen in support for socialism, independent labour politics, Labor-Populism, and the
Knights of Labor) in order to challenge the capitalist giant, but were
also concerned with the loss of the republican heritage, with the class-
ridden 'Europeanisation' of their country and with the restoration of
'equal rights'. As with 'pure and simple' trade unionism, the increasingly
'non-partisan' political philosophy of the AF of L leadership was domi-

nant rather than unopposed within American labour up to the early 1920s. Further evidence in favour of the anti-exceptionalist position is found in the tenacity of Lib-Labism, the relative weakness of the Labour Party and the minority influence of socialism in pre-1914 Britain. The chapter concludes, however, by suggesting that by the early 1920s national differences had hardened. The decline of radicalism in the United States stood in marked contrast to the rise of Labour in Britain.

Part Two of Volume Two sets out to explain the sharp contrasts which characterised the fortunes of workers and labour movements in both countries during the inter-war years. In Britain a high level of post-war militancy and radicalism was followed by the defeat of the General Strike, declining trade-union membership to the mid 1930s, and generally cautious trade-union leadership. Mass unemployment failed to produce mass revolutionary sentiment, but the Communist Party did achieve significant if limited influence among key groups of workers. The 1920s had witnessed the rise of the Labour Party to a position of national prominence, supported by a seemingly homogeneous and growing cloth-capped constituency. But political hegemony in the inter-war years as a whole, and especially during the 1930s, belonged to the Conservative Party. Only during the 1940s did Labour outstrip its achievements of the late 1920s.

In the United States largely defensive attitudes and actions dominated the labour movement up to the mid 1930s. As noted earlier, by 1923 worker militancy had ebbed from its high post-war levels, trade unionism had been largely excluded from the larger corporations, and AF of L orthodoxy and conservatism were in the driving seat. As observed by Montgomery, the decade from the mid 1920s to the mid 1930s constituted 'a remarkable hiatus in the evolution of the labor movement'. Strike activity fell to an all-time low, radicals were isolated from the mass movement, trade unionism remained largely confined to the craft and skilled sectors, and 'corporate mastery of American life seemed secure'.[30] Yet this exceptionalism was temporary rather than permanent. Widespread industrial 'unrest' and conflict in 1934, the formation of the Committee for Industrial Organisation in 1935, mass support for trade-union principles and struggles among hitherto seemingly docile, fatalistic and divided workers, general disillusionment with *laissez-faire* capitalism, the renewed importance of socialists and communists to workers' struggles, and the alliance between organised labour and the Democratic Party were important indices of the depth and rapidity of change during the second half of the 1930s. To be sure, independent labour politics in America did not develop to anything like the same national extent as in Britain. But even in this case we must be wary of easy 'exceptionalist' generalisation. The British Labour Party's 'rise' during the 1930s was extremely slow and uneven. It could further be argued that wider class and narrower 'labourist' sentiments (the latter articulated through the medium of the Democratic Party) were growing apace in 1930s America.[31]

The Conclusion summarises our findings concerning similarities and differences between workers and labour movements in the two countries. In relation to the class and exceptionalism debate, specific attention is drawn to the significant, if limited, existence and persistence of (largely non-revolutionary forms of) class among workers in both Britain and the United States. It is further argued that class presence and durability were, on balance, more pronounced in Britain – factors which owed much to the more inflexible British political system; to Britain's more homogeneous labour force; and to the more infrequent, less sustained and less successful attempts of British employers and sections of the state to destroy the collective organisations of workers.

The Process of Capitalist Transformation and the Roots of Popular and Working-Class Protest, 1780s–1850s

OVERVIEW, DEFINITIONS AND ARGUMENTS

Between the late eighteenth century and the 1840s popular movements of an increasingly radical and working-class character emerged in Britain and the United States. In the latter country revolutionary republicanism, trade unionism, the various experiments in independent labour politics, the limited but growing appeal of anti-capitalist ideas, widespread opposition to monopolists and speculators, schemes for land and currency reform, slave resistance to, and important, if infrequent, outright revolts against plantation slavery, and the emergence of a distinctively American version of class testified to the quickened pace of popular radicalism, especially during the 1830s.[1] In Britain popular movements in defence of custom and tradition (most notably food riots and 'Church and King' disturbances) increasingly gave way after the first decade of the nineteenth century to an unprecedented and massive upsurge in more self-consciously radical and class-based movements. The long campaign for the vote for adult males, opposition to the harmful effects of unregulated economic growth and technological change (as seen particularly in Luddism), agitation in favour of a cheap radical press, opposition to government and state coercion (especially in Ireland), anti-Poor Law agitation, factory reform, Chartism, trade unionism, and riot and unrest in the agricultural districts of the country – all pointed to a profound and widespread sense of popular unease and anger.[2]

Popular radicalism was undoubtedly stronger in Britain than in the United States before the late 1820s. But the late 1820s and 1830s witnessed the emergence of a mass working-class presence of a radical kind in both countries. Chartism in Britain and general trade unionism in the United States provided striking confirmation of this presence. Indeed, a number of historians, working within discrete, nationally based frameworks, have independently offered us the same conclusion: the development of a marked sense of class consciousness on the part of significant numbers of labouring people on both sides of the Atlantic during the 1830s.[3]

Class consciousness and labour solidarity proved, however, to be fragile and relatively shortlived in character. By the mid 1840s labour radicalism had largely gone underground in the United States. It is true that the late 1840s and the 1850s did witness several attempts to rebuild the collective institutions of labour; and local trade unionism and industrial conflict were especially prominent. Similarly, the various Ten Hours campaigns, popular support for 'Free-Soilism', agrarian reform, and for producer and consumer co-operatives testified to the continued appeal of radicalism. But in truth the institutions of labour and the appeal of the 'movement' were all too precarious and limited from the mid 1840s to the outbreak of the Civil War in 1860. The labour movement was largely confined to a minority of white male skilled workers, and the wider working class was deeply divided by race, gender, ethnicity, skill, culture and politics. Only in the post-bellum period was a truly national labour movement brought into being.[4]

In Britain there occurred a similar, if less profound, loosening of class loyalties and solidarities. It was the case that Chartism did not expire in 1848, that independent working-class political activity continued into the 1860s, and that the (predominantly skilled) trade-union movement and the co-operative and friendly-society movements made steady and, in some cases, spectacular advances during the mid-Victorian years. Conversely, independent labour politics rapidly lost much of their former mass appeal, the labour movement did become more closely identified with a minority of skilled male workers, and there did occur a marked accentuation of all manner of divisions (based upon skill, culture, ethnicity and gender) within the working class. Above all, there was a greater acceptance of the seeming permanence of capitalism than in the Chartist period and, in practice, much greater emphasis upon obtaining limited and gradual reforms and advances within the confines of the existing social system.[5] Thus, whilst class consciousness and radicalism did not entirely disappear in either country (and were, generally speaking, more pronounced in Britain), nevertheless the middle years of the century did witness a common process of class fragmentation and the decline of class-based frontal assaults upon the overall legitimacy of industrial capitalism.

The processes of class 'making' and 'unmaking', briefly outlined above, will be fully explored in Part 2. The purpose of Part 1 is to establish the broad (especially economic) context in which early working-class and popular movements arose. The central argument put forward is that the accelerated development of industrial capitalism from the mid eighteenth century onwards constituted a factor of fundamental importance to the emergence of labour movements. The bulk of this section accordingly concerns itself with the nature and effects of capitalist transformation up to the middle years of the nineteenth century.

We can usefully begin by defining our key concepts – industrial capitalism and capitalist transformation – and advancing our main arguments. We define industrial capitalism as a system of full-blown commodity production geared up to profit maximisation. This system is further rooted in private ownership of the means of production, distribution and exchange, the necessary sale of labour power by a permanent wage-earning class (whose social composition does, nevertheless, change over time), and patterned norms and values. From the point of view of the capitalist such norms and values would centrally embrace the free play of market forces, acquisitiveness, largely unfettered individualism and entrepreneurialism, competition, and equality and freedom in the market-place.[6]

This definition of industrial capitalism, is of course, extremely abstract in character. As such, it constitutes a useful analytical tool which is, nevertheless, a highly and deliberately oversimplified representation of historically specific, diverse and concrete capitalist societies. A major task confronting us in Part One is to explore and tease out the relationships, or 'levels of correspondence', between the 'abstract' and the 'concrete'. We must be simultaneously beware of falsely reducing or collapsing the one level into the other.[7]

It is also explicit in the definition offered that industrial capitalism is not solely an economic system. As noted above, embodied within capitalism are cultural and ideological norms and expectations (the beneficent effects of unrestrained markets, the socially beneficial and largely unintended effects of the pursuit of self-interest) and legal values (individual equality in the market-place, opposition to 'coercive' collective organisations of workers and so on).

In a related yet more specific way, capitalism and capitalist transformation are not confined to the area of manufacturing industry. We will demonstrate in the course of this section that capitalist structures and practices expressed themselves in and transformed the home, the countryside and other centres of economic activity as well as in manufacturing workshops and factories.

The reader's attention will thus be drawn to the simultaneously complex and patterned ways in which interactions took place between the 'abstract' and the 'concrete', and between the various parts of the capitalist system. The latter is seen as a complex, structured whole in which the economic tasks of getting a living and seeking individual and familial security occupied the major part of labouring people's lives, and exerted correspondingly heavy pressures upon other aspects of thought and behaviour.[8]

In moving from a relatively high level of abstraction to a more concrete examination of the key features of late eighteenth- and early nineteenth-century capitalist transformation, five points merit special emphasis.

First, in response to the stimuli of expanded markets, rapid population growth, greatly improved means of transportation, and sufficient supplies of capital, entrepreneurship, land and labour, the full-blown commodity production of industrial capitalism developed a quickened and irresistible momentum. And in its successful drive to economic dominance industrial capitalism confronted and transformed the patterns of consciousness and social relations associated with the petty commodity form of capitalist development.

Second, the triumph of industrial capitalism marked the ascendancy of industrial over commercial and landed forms of capital, and had important effects upon the character of popular protest. In order to elucidate these points, it is important to distinguish commercial or merchant from industrial capitalism. During the seventeenth and eighteenth centuries the greatest accumulations of capital arose from trade and agriculture rather than from manufacturing.[9] In Britain there were close interconnections between landed and merchant capital. The ruling élite was dominated by landowners, and the vast expansion of overseas trade during the eighteenth century provided a major spur towards economic and social transformation. In the United States the fortunes of both the plantation South and the urban North were heavily dependent upon commercial prosperity and buoyant internal and external demand. Up to 1815 and beyond, 'the chief business of the cities was commerce, and their leading citizens were merchants'.[10]

The functions of the merchant capitalist differed in important respects from those of the industrial capitalist. The central concern of the merchant rested with the exchange and distribution of finished goods and raw materials. Some merchants also acted as commission agents or factors for others, and performed, especially during the eighteenth century, numerous banking and insurance functions. By way of contrast, the industrial capitalist's primary concern lay with exchange relations within *production*: especially with the transformation of the workers' labour power into a commodity (the latter being exchanged for a wage); the extraction of surplus value from labour power (by means of technological change, efficiency schemes, lengthening the working day and so on); and with the subordination of labour to capital (in terms of control over labour processes, and hierarchies of power and authority). It thus followed that merchant capital was, as noted by David Montgomery, 'consistent with a variety of labor systems' (such as wage-labour, yeoman farming and plantation slavery) while the essence of industrial capital was, 'to transform productive processes themselves, make wage-labor the norm, and extract accumulation primarily from production'.[11]

The different roles performed by merchant and industrial capitalists and the chronology of relations between the two groups provide important guides to the nature and changing character of popular protest. During the late eighteenth century and early part of the nineteenth century popular protest movements were often concerned with exploitation in *exchange*: with the exploitation of the 'producing classes' (workers, small masters and other petty producers) by 'parasitical' and 'unscrupulous' merchant middlemen, by bankers, speculators and other 'monopolists'. This exchange-based critique, widely articulated in both Britain and the United States, closely corresponded to the central role of merchant capital in economic life. As illustrated above all by the putting-out system, in which merchant middlemen played a central role, most transformations in relations of production came from the influence of capital upon exchange, distribution and the provision of credit rather than mainly from the directly transformative actions of employers within production. In such ways an exchange-centred economic critique was allied to the wider critique of 'Old Corruption' (placemen, sinecurists, tax-eaters and all manner of 'aristocratic' parasites).[12]

The ideology of popular radicalism was not, however, static. The first half of the nineteenth century witnessed not only accelerated and indirect merchant influence upon production, but also the mushrooming of industrial capitalist employers (some of them former merchants) and the direct transformation of relations of production. During the course of the nineteenth century industrial capital achieved economic, political and cultural hegemony. And the ideology of popular protest increasingly came to oppose not only aristocratic parasites, merchant middlemen and bankers, but also 'dishonourable' industrial capitalists intent upon transforming production according to their own dictates.

Our second point of emphasis revolves, therefore, around the assumption that changes in economic structure and relationships exerted powerful influences upon popular ideologies. The notion of powerful influence must not, however, be read as synonymous with the notions of historical law or sufficient cause. Changes in popular ideas did not arise solely from economic developments. And there was no necessary transition from one stage of consciousness to another (from, for example, the notion of exploited producers to exploited working class). Similarly, ideologies, as we will observe, were in practice far less neat, coherent and consistent than so far implied. Noel Thompson, for example, has convincingly demonstrated that the predominantly exchange-based economic critique of the British 'Smithian socialists' (Bray, Gray, Thompson and Hodgskin) also contained within it a belief in the necessarily antagonistic relations between labour and capital under a system of profit-based capitalist *production*.[13] Nevertheless, when all necessary refinements and qualifications have been made, the validity of the argument in favour of strong economic determinations and pressures remains.

We emphasise, third, that while a hard and observable fact of life, capitalist transformation did not occur in smoothly linear and even ways. Much of the recent economic history of eighteenth- and early nineteenth-century Britain has been at pains to insist that growth and change were far more gradual, unspectacular and chequered than the conventional label of 'industrial revolution' would suggest.[14] We have been correctly reminded that there was no necessary progression from one stage of economic development to another, and that industrial capitalism grew in varied and uneven ways. Workshop-based production ('manufacture') did not necessarily give way to factory-based production ('machinofacture'). The latter, complete with steam-powered factories, mechanisation and proletarianised workers, did not typify the economies of Britain and the United States in 1850;[15] and outwork, especially for women, continued to be a prominent feature of nineteenth-century economic life rather than a dwindling and archaic labour system. Industrial production on both sides of the Atlantic continued well into the nineteenth century to be heavily dependent upon the manual skills and customary know-how of the artisan or (largely non-factory-based) skilled worker. And the 'free', waged-labour of capitalist production continued to coexist alongside various forms of dependency, most prominently slavery, and unpaid housework performed by women.

Once again, however, qualifications must not be allowed to obscure the validity of the original thesis. It would appear to be the case that in their haste to debunk the notion of 'discontinuity' (as applied to politics, ideology and culture as well as economics), too many historians have greatly underestimated the extent of change, of accelerated capitalist development.[16] During the nineteenth century industrial capitalists achieved hegemony in Britain and the United States, and the wage labour–capital relationship became characteristic of production. By the middle decades of the century large wage-earning classes had become established facts of life. In 1867 Dudley Baxter estimated that more than three-quarters (77 per cent) of the 24.1 million inhabitants of Great Britain belonged to the 'manual labour class'.[17] In the United States the promises of the frontier and upward social mobility, and the persistence of the family farm in northern agriculture could not disguise, by the 1850s, the creation of a large and seemingly permanent wage-earning class. By 1860 almost 60 per cent of the American labour force was employed in some way rather than being economically independent. Ten years later wage earners, recruited in the northern states predominantly from the ranks of German, Irish and other northern European immigrants and in the South from ex-slaves and immigrants, represented more than 50 per cent of those gainfully employed.[18]

We must also remind ourselves that while factory production was not typical of production as a whole by 1850, capitalist transformation was not confined to the walls of the factory. As we will observe below, labouring people working on the land, at home and in workshops were all being affected, however unevenly, by the spread of capitalist structures and practices.

In sum, the period from 1750 to 1850 was one of accelerated capitalist growth. Such growth proceeded in uneven and combined ways, and marked the decisive transition from petty commodity production to the hegemonic position of unrestrained commodity production.

Fourth, capitalist development had a profoundly disturbing effect upon the 'customary' habits and values characteristic of large sections of the labouring populations of Britain and the United States. Strongly rooted in market-based petty commodity production and, to a much lesser extent, in subsistence and semi-subsistence production, the customary attachments of 'free' and 'unfree' labouring people and petty producers expressed themselves in a variety of ways. Of great importance were the following expressions: limited involvement in, and limited approval for, the unrestrained markets of full-blown commodity production; the 'right', particularly in times of hardship and dearth, to regulate markets in order to restore traditionally 'just' or customary prices and methods of marketing (as seen in the 'moral economy' of eighteenth-century English food rioters) and demands for the 'fair' payment of labour and 'honest' or 'honourable' levels of profit for masters and merchants. Of equal significance was emphasis upon the inherently social, as opposed to purely individualistic, nature of economic activity, and corresponding emphases upon mutual rights and obligations and the absolute good of the whole trade or community (versus 'selfish' sectional interests). We should also draw attention to customary attachments to relatively fixed needs, habits and expectations rather than to the ceaseless pursuit of ever-expanding wants and expectations (as seen in general commitments to household 'sufficiency' or 'competency', and in slave communities to the 'right to subsistence', rather than to unlimited and chronic enslavements or entitlements to profit- and income-maximisation), and to strong desires and endeavours (among artisans, labourers and slaves) to exert independence and controls over life and labour (over the duration and tempo of work, the distribution of tasks, the balance between work and leisure and so on). The new political economy of industrial capitalism, complete with its 'common-sense' of deregulated markets, unending accumulation and income/commodity and profit maximisation (rooted in the psychological and social imperatives of money–commodity–money for the capitalist; and commodity–money–commodity or, as pressures upon capital accumulation began to ease, commodity–money–commodity for the worker), the *complete* transformation of labour power into commodity status, and the necessary subordination of labour to capital, posed an obvious and grave threat to practitioners of 'custom'.[19]

Concrete historical practice placed qualifications and important modifications upon the highly abstract picture drawn in the previous paragraph. As we will observe in due course, 'custom' assumed a variety of expressions and influences in different historical contexts, over time and within different modes of production. For example, price controls and paternalist models of food marketing adhered to by English food rioters and more general regulations upon free-market behaviour (restrictions upon commerce, the pursuit of individual gain and agreements entered into by formally free and consenting parties within production and exchange) were more pronounced in eighteenth-century Britain (a country with long and deep paternalist roots) than in the United States (where paternalist traditions and influences were less strong). Price controls and other formal methods of economic regulation were not unknown in the United States, and had operated with particular force during the War of Independence (five of the state constitutions produced between 1776 and 1780 'directly legitimated embargoes on commerce in time of economic crisis'). But in the post-revolutionary period free-market capitalism advanced with giant strides, and price-fixing and formal economic regulation in general fell into disuse (the United States Constitution of 1787 denied the states 'any power at all to impair contractual obligations').[20]

Further qualifications and differences abound. Strong commitments to customary regulations and norms within production were possibly more marked among male artisans than non-craft workers, and may, as claimed by Maxine Berg, have held weaker appeal to those women whose priorities lay more with domestic industry and the upkeep of the family than with the concerns of 'the trade'.[21] Mode of production also influenced the extent to which workers could exert choice and control over patterns of work and leisure. The customary 'moral economy' of the Afro-American slave was, at least in a formal sense, far less informed by freedom of choice than were the customs of eighteenth-century English and American artisans or yeomen farmers.[22] Furthermore, elements of both the new free-market political economy and of the older customary patterns of thought and behaviour were probably intermingled in daily practice to a much greater extent than a highly abstract model of 'custom' versus unregulated market would suggest.[23] And the existence of custom did not preclude conflicts both within and between communities and trades. Unduly harmonious and idealised views of 'customary' eighteenth-century labouring communities are to be eschewed.

Alive to the dangers of loose, decontextualised and uniform usage, we will nevertheless demonstrate in Part One the continued utility and fruitfulness of a resort to 'custom'. As we will observe below, the appeal to custom provided, in the face of the depredations of capital, a most powerful point of mobilisation and legitimation to all manner of plebeian and 'producerist' protesters, ranging from yeomen farmers and industrial wage earners in America to artisans, outworkers and early factory workers in Britain.

This brings us to our final observation in this section of Part One. Despite the uneven effects of capitalist development and considerable variations in the responses of labouring people, there is no doubt that large numbers of artisans and others gave an acutely hostile reception to the burgeoning industrial capitalist order between 1750 and 1850. Hostility and resistance were most marked among those groups hit hardest by the new 'dishonourable' practices of the free market, and to whom the tenets of 'custom' were most dear. While disruptive of customary patterns of work and consciousness, capitalist transformation was simultaneously instrumental in forging common grievances, points of struggle and articulated interests among all manner of labouring people. This dialectical process, of contradiction, synthesis and new departures and initiatives, lay at the heart of working-class formation.[24] Class did not, however, emerge solely from economic changes. Political, ideological and cultural determinations were also present in the construction of labour movements and class consciousness. As such, these influences merit full attention.[25]

The rest of Part One is organised in accordance with the general emphases and assumptions outlined above. We will first explore the combined and uneven process of industrial capitalist development, and then proceed to a brief investigation of the non-economic underpinnings of labour's emergence.

CHAPTER ONE

The Process of Capitalist Transformation

NATIONAL DIFFERENCES: SOCIETY AND ECONOMY

During the late eighteenth and early nineteenth centuries there existed many important differences between Britain and the United States. Britain was formally dominated and ruled at the beginning of the nineteenth century by a small, tightly integrated landed élite which combined beliefs in God-given social and political inequality with astute capitalist business sense.[26] As a result of their acceptance of the essentials of economic and political change (the Repeal of the Corn Laws and free trade, the First Reform Bill and so on), the landed interests retained many of their formal powers of governance well into the nineteenth century. However, real power and the dominant position in the ruling bloc rested by mid-century with the industrial bourgeoisie. British capitalism possessed a distinctly 'aristocratic' style (as reflected in patterns of leisure and education), but its content was solidly 'bourgeois' (free trade, utilitarianism, religion (especially nonconformity), the patriarchal family, and earnest self-help and respectability), and its power bases increasingly urban in character.[27]

The northern states of the United States lacked feudal or genuinely aristocratic traditions. By the end of the eighteenth century an anti-aristocratic and anti-colonial bourgeoisie exercised hegemony. Defenders of the modern world's first republic, committed to the freedoms of the market-place and the notion of equality of opportunity (and the inequalities rooted in 'character' and 'merit'), the nineteenth-century northern bourgeoisie set itself against the 'Europeanisation' of its 'open' society. And in defence of bourgeois civilisation, it increasingly found itself at odds with the 'aristocratic' values of the southern planters.[28] Nationally hegemonic by the last quarter of the nineteenth century, the bourgeoisie was, however, drawn into periodic conflict with the creation of its own emancipated system, the working class.

Industrialisation in the United States proceeded more slowly than in Britain in the years before the mid 1840s. Despite the facts that the population of the United States had outstripped that of Britain by 1851

(23.3 as opposed to 20.9 million) and economic growth rates during Britain's period of 'industrial revolution' (circa 1780–1830) may well have been slower than traditionally thought, nevertheless Britain was already a heavily industrialised country by the mid nineteenth century. By the early 1850s 43 per cent of Britain's paid labour force was employed in manufacturing, mining and building, as opposed to 20 per cent in the United States.[29] At the same point in time the United States employed 64 per cent of its labour force in agriculture, as against 22 per cent in Britain. And whereas proletarianisation was extremely advanced in terms of British agriculture (the mass of workers being wage-earning labourers), agriculture in the United States was heavily dependent upon family units in the North and West (the *marked* upsurge in tenancy and waged labour in the latter region dated largely from the 1840s and 1850s) and free white and enslaved black families in the South (free blacks constituted about 6 per cent of the total black population in the South in 1860). The central importance of agriculture to the United States placed important constraints upon urbanisation. In 1850 only some 3,500,000 Americans (15 per cent of the total population) lived in places in excess of 2,500 inhabitants, and only 2 million (9 per cent) in places of over 25,000 inhabitants. In Britain only 39 per cent of the population lived in rural areas.[30]

Industrialisation, urbanisation and proletarianisation were thus more marked in Britain than in the United States up to the mid nineteenth century. But we would be wrong to exaggerate the importance of national differences. The labouring populations of the two countries shared a number of common or similar situations, experiences and patterns of thought. And the reader's attention is drawn to four such areas of shared experience.

NATIONAL SIMILARITIES: HOUSEHOLDS, MARKETS AND CUSTOMARY CONSCIOUSNESS

First, in both eighteenth-century Britain and the United States the household constituted the basic unit of production and consumption for the labouring classes. The overriding priority of daily life was to provide a sufficiency for members of the household, and most members of the family were expected to make a contribution towards its upkeep. (This did not, however, suggest either an equal division of labour or more general equality between men and women.)[31] There was no great division between 'home' and 'work', and 'work and 'leisure'. Small workshop production was also very common, especially among male artisans in town and countryside.[32]

Second, life and labour within households and workshops operated within the wider context of (by contemporary standards) relatively advanced markets. In both countries, and especially among the white populations, existence based solely upon an economy of subsistence was extremely rare. In urban and rural Britain (and particularly in England) the degree of market penetration into daily life was reflected in the widespread sale of labour power in order to make a living (wage labour and capitalism in general having enjoyed a long period of development in England from the fourteenth century onwards), and the purchase of bread and other necessities of life. And, according to a highly influential 'liberal' view of American history, the United States had been essentially capitalist from the seventeenth century onwards. The absence of feudal-ism, the scarcity of labour and the abundance of land induced, so we are informed, a marked degree of 'market-embeddedness' among the majority of citizens, an eye for the 'main chance', a thoroughgoing individualism and entrepreneurialism.[33] Similarly, if less influentially, there has been a strand within recent eighteenth-century English histori-ography which argues (in opposition to E.P. Thompson and other advo-cates of the 'moral economy') that the 'imperatives of the market economy' centrally determined the lives of the labouring people.[34]

In both the 'liberal' American and English 'market-imperative' cases, there appear the same emphases and conclusions. These revolve around the sheer profundity of market penetration and free-market conscious-ness and the absence or extremely limited nature of capitalist *transforma-tion* (in the sense that the obstacles to full-blown commodity production are seen as organisational and technological rather than fundamentally structural and cultural in character). There also exists the assumption of a more-or-less fixed human nature (at least among whites), of a maximis-ing, market-orientated kind. And attention is drawn to the allegedly easy and consensual manner in which industrial capitalism 'triumphed' (with a simultaneous tendency to downplay the importance of oppo-sition, conflict and class struggle).

This study challenges such assumptions and conclusions. Central importance is attached to empirical demonstration and historical context, as opposed to a priori assumptions (especially concerning 'human nature') and functionalist methodology (the relatively smooth function-ing of the whole). I suggest that the involvement of eighteenth- and early nineteenth-century workers in the market-place did not necessarily induce 'free-market' consciousness: consciousness must be clearly dem-onstrated rather than simply assumed. As Randall and Charlesworth have observed in relation to the English context, we must not confuse participation in markets with unlimited approval for the unregulated markets of the new political economy.[35] It is also worth noting that markets themselves are *not* (contrary to much current economic and political argument) static, ahistorical structures, but change and operate in different ways over time, and invite conflict as well as consensus among participants. In short, attention to historical context is of crucial importance to any adequate understanding of markets. And it is Randall's contention that eighteenth-century English food rioters and practitioners of the 'industrial moral economy' were not opposed to markets *per se* (markets, indeed capitalist markets, being a necessary part of reality), and sought (unlike the Owenites) not their abolition but, when necessary, their regulation and stabilisation (by means of custom and law) in the interest of the public good.[36] It was *The Market* of the new political economy which sanctioned 'greed' and other forms of anti-social behaviour which met with powerful opposition. Randall's observations concerning the consciousness of Gloucestershire's weavers are pertinent:

> Clearly they did not object to the market as a system of exchange for it was the only such system available. Their opposition was to the growing ideology of 'The Market', increasingly loudly articulated by farmers, dealers and others in 1766, which claimed that only by the unhampered pursuit of individual advantage could the needs of the community be best met. This was an amoral vision of the market as economic arbiter as against the moral imperative of the need for fairness and social and economic responsibility enshrined in the concept of the moral economy.[37]

And underlying the moral economy was, according to Randall, a common value system (rooted in the legitimacy of custom) which, whilst of greater importance in some industries and communities than others, nevertheless enjoyed widespread support.[38]

Randall's conclusions are endorsed by a number of recent studies. In addition there exists a mounting body of evidence to suggest that American workers and petty producers demonstrated significant attachment to custom during the eighteenth and early nineteenth centuries. We will consider the evidence relating to specific groups and occupations in due course. Our immediate task is to present our case in general terms.

US AGRICULTURE: THE NORTH AND WEST

We can usefully begin by considering the case of agriculture in the United States. As Dahnhof and more recent historians have shown,[39] farming households in the pre-1840s northeastern American countryside frequently did *not* embrace the values of full-blown commercialism. Attention in these households was directed primarily to meeting the customary need of a household competency, rather than to the 'gain' of ceaseless profit maximisation in the market-place. Markets were, of course, present; and farming households did market 'surpluses'. But the latter rarely signified an exclusive commitment to cash crops, and market involvement tended to be local and limited. Furthermore, notions of custom and practice, 'fairness' and 'justice', and intimate, non- or semi-commercial relations of exchange and reciprocity greatly outweighed a tendency towards a smooth or complete acceptance of the cash nexus and other practices and values associated with unrestrained commodity production.[40]

Jonathan Prude's description of economic life and thought in the rural Massachusetts townships of Dudley and Oxford in the early nineteenth century exemplifies much of the rural northeastern experience:

> what we find characterizing most of early nineteenth-century Dudley and Oxford are local economies in which market trans-actions were frequent, in which a buoyant consumerism was taking root, but in which, at the same time, a commercial ethos – in the sense of a whole-hearted commitment to profit maximisation – had only a limited constituency. Local yeomen, for all their mounting involvement with buying and selling, still retained many conventions of household production. Nearly always owning the land they cultivated, typically relying for help less on hired workers than on family members and on the custom of receiving (and giving) neighborly assistance during busy seasons, farmers generally ventured into the market not to get rich but simply to acquire the goods and services needed (as they saw it) to preserve their household 'competencies'. Not surprisingly, then, the surpluses they produced did not signify an exclusive commitment to cash crops. Although hardly self-sufficient in any literal sense, yeomen ... sought to raise much, if not all, of the foodstuffs they and their households required.[41]

Agriculture on the western frontier differed in important ways from its counterpart in the North East. The massive stimuli to demand for agricultural products provided by rapid urbanisation and population growth, the transportation revolution of canal and railroad (from the 1820s onwards), the rich soils of the moving frontier, and the improving endeavours of farmers ensured that the transitionary stage from pre-dominantly self-sufficient to market-based agriculture was of shorter duration in the West than in the North East. On the eve of the Civil War commercialisation, individualism, competition, mechanisation, rampant speculation and the concentration of massive tracts of land into the hands of wealthy individuals and railroad companies, and the mush-rooming of tenancy and wage labour were marked features of the frontier areas of Illinois, Indiana, Iowa and Missouri.[42]

The 1850s witnessed particularly rapid development in these states. It was during the 1850s that the Midwest experienced a massive railway boom, a veritable population explosion (more than 2,200,000 people were added to the populations of Illinois, Iowa, Indiana and Missouri during those ten years), a substantial increase in wheat acreage, the extensive introduction of the reaper and widespread large-scale capitalist farming on the prairies. There was also a sharp increase in the number of farm labourers (by 1860 twenty-three out of every hundred people employed in agriculture in Iowa and Illinois were farm labourers), and tenant farmers. Insecurity, wage labour, indebtedness and tenancy rocketed within the farming population in the wake of the depression of 1857. By the 1860s there were some one hundred thousand waged workers on Midwestern farms. It would thus appear that the intimate and partially custom-based world of the northeastern farming household had little place in the West's rush to capitalist farming.

Appearances can, however, be deceptive. We would be well advised not to exaggerate the speed and extent with which capitalist structures and patterns of thought penetrated the West. Up to the revolutionary developments of the 1850s and beyond (and especially the creation of a good railway network to the urban East), shortages of capital, lack of effective demand and transportation, and the underdevelopment of agriculture's productive forces placed important restrictions upon the extent of capitalist transformation. And, as an increasing number of recent studies have demonstrated, the mentalité of significant numbers of western farmers in the ante-bellum period cannot be described as unambiguously capitalist in character. Limited markets, the strongly self-sufficient traditions of many settlers, a keen sense of place and community, non- or semi-cash-based exchange relationships, the sharing of tasks within communities (such as the laying out and construction of roads), and heavy reliance upon traditional techniques of production meant that 'customary' and 'moral' obligations and rights limited 'market-embeddedness' and Turnerian individualism and competition.

John Mack Faragher's study of the open-country settlement of Sugar Creek, central Illinois, nicely illustrates the complexities of farmers' consciousness.[43] Re-settled by Anglo-Celtic pioneers from Virginia, Kentucky and other areas of the upland South during the second decade of the nineteenth century, Sugar Creek had a population of almost 1,200 in 1850 devoted to mixed farming. Sugar Creek was dominated by dispersed family farms (those who failed to become owners tended to move out of the community) which worked both independently and collectively to transform the landscape and create a sense of place, of community. Many tasks, such as road building, cabin raisings, log rollings, haying, husking, butchering, harvesting or threshing were, notes Faragher, 'all traditionally communal affairs'. Exchanges of a customary, largely non-cash-based kind (of labour and tools) were also 'part of the day-to-day operation of agriculture'. Community institutions, such as churches and schools, fostered strong social bonds and common values. And, given limited market opportunities, 'agricultural improvement was not a preeminent goal of the mode of production'. Traditional methods prevailed, there were few agricultural wage workers before the 1850s, and household requirements and sufficiencies remained the key aims of economic activity. In sum, unfettered market consciousness was conspicuous by its weakness.

It is of course true, as noted above, that the 'agricultural revolution' of the 1850s and beyond greatly enhanced commercial farming. But it is by no means self-evident that the outlooks of western farmers, settlers, labourers and tenants became saturated by free-market consciousness. Much more research is urgently required into the mentalité of rural dwellers before a satisfactory answer can be given. But we do know that customary concerns with 'fairness', with the rights of actual settlers to the land, with more equal opportunities for land ownership, with opposition to monopoly control and ownership, with the rights of public access to open prairie, timberland, waterways and roads, and with hostility towards land sharks and a multitude of unscrupulous middlemen, operated with some force in the ante-bellum years, and exploded in the post-bellum decades.[44] It is, at the very least, highly dubious as to whether such tensions and conflicts can simply be attributed to differences between adherents to the same unfettered market values. Rather, more research of the type undertaken by Faragher might equally suggest that 'a dynamic between individual self-interest and collective action... contributed to the active communal life of farmers'; and that at the heart of this dynamic was the stubborn persistence of 'custom' in the face of capitalist 'commonsense'.[45]

THE SOUTH AND SLAVERY

Strong attachments to 'custom' also existed in the very different context of ante-bellum southern agriculture. As Genovese has observed, at the heart of the southern slave system (which in 1860 embraced 4 million slaves and 385,000 slaveowners out of a total population of 12,300,000 in the fifteen slave states) lay a fundamental contradiction.[46] On the one hand there existed central involvement in the capitalist market-place. Plantation owners were dependent upon the world capitalist market for sale of their cotton, tobacco and rice; the development of the slave trade had been an integral part of the growth of merchant capitalism; and within the South there was an internal market in slaves. On the other hand the South possessed a society and a central system of values in many ways antagonistic to those of a capitalist society: property in man versus 'free' waged labour; and a pre-bourgeois 'aristocratic' ruling class which, whilst motivated by profit and having a bourgeois religion, simultaneously adhered to a patriarchal social structure rooted in 'natural' inequality, paternalism, deference, racism, overt class rule and an organic, rather than an individualistic, market-placed view of human relationships. The revolutionary republicanism and acquisitive individualism of the North were thus profoundly at odds with the aristocratic paternalism of the South.

A further contradiction of the southern slave mode of production (which has immediate relevance to the issue of custom) lay in the fact that 'participation in the capitalist market rested upon the solid foundations of subsistence agriculture for the producing unit'.[47] The great majority of slaves, who were employed in agriculture or related occupations, were accustomed to relatively fixed, largely low-level, and subsistence-based needs. Some slaves might, with the permission of the owners, sell produce from the family plot or other commodities. Some (especially urban) slaves received money payments, and profit-sharing schemes were sometimes introduced. But most slaves were not paid, worked extremely long hours, and had as their prime economic goal, family subsistence. Slaves were thus pre-accumulative, on the fringes of the market economy and motivated by customary needs rather than expanding commodity consciousness.[48]

It was the case that free blacks (of whom there were 260,000 in 1860, or 6 per cent of the total black population of the South) in agricultural and particularly industrial and commercial jobs were far more involved in market relationships than slaves. And, as demonstrated by Fields for Maryland (which had the largest population of free blacks in the country by 1810), free black workers were often prepared to take advantage of favourable market conditions in order to enhance their bargaining power *vis-à-vis* employers.[49] But it was equally the case in Maryland and elsewhere in the South that free black people maintained close ties (through work, marriage and friendship) and shared values with black slaves in the face of a largely hostile white world. And part of this shared system of values consisted of commitments to sufficiency and, where possible, independence and control over their lives. As Fields so pertinently remarks in relation to Maryland's freedom:

> Not habituated to that logic of ever-increasing effort to satisfy ever-expanding needs that market society had learned to call 'ambition', they did not seek higher wages with a view toward earning a maximum income. Instead, they used higher wages as a means of shortening the time spent at work on other people's behalf. 'As

soon as the hand earns a little money, he wants to quit', farmers time and again complained.[50]

Given the formidable powers of the owners and overseers over the lives and conditions of slaves, it was often well nigh impossible for the latter to achieve the same degrees of independence and control at work exercised by some free blacks and skilled artisans in the capitalist market-place. Southern slavery was, despite pleas to the contrary, fundamentally rooted in coercion and exploitation. And long and intensive periods of labour, under constant supervision, severely limited opportunities for slave independence. Conversely, we must nevertheless remember that the real, as opposed to formal market powers of many nineteenth-century northern capitalists were, as the defenders of slavery were quick to insist, also frequently coercive and exploitative in character. As convincingly demonstrated by Genovese, Gutman and others,[51] it is, furthermore, wrong to see the slaves as totally passive and the slaveowners as omnipotent. Class struggle was present in southern slavery as well as in northern capitalism. Slaves did forge impressive cultural bondings and defences against the slave system: accommodation *and* resistance were part of the lived experience of slavery. And whilst undoubtedly in control, slaveowners appreciated the importance of providing concessions to those ultimately responsible for the daily viability of the economy, the slaves. In truth a fine balance between coercion and persuasion lay at the heart of slaveowner hegemony.

In a minority of cases opportunities for considerable slave control over patterns of work and leisure did present themselves. For example, John Scott Strickland has described the ways in which the task system of labour operative in both rice and long-staple cotton cultivation in coastal South Carolina in the ante-bellum years provided the slaves with the opportunity to create a 'moral economy . . . a defense of customary social and cultural patterns'.[52] For a century and a half, notes Strickland, Afro-Americans in South Carolina's coastal Low Country had, 'known an intense social and cultural solidarity rooted in large, stable plantation communities, in the intergenerational continuity of slave families, and in the long-established practice of absenteeism on the part of their owners'. In addition the task system of labour differed from the gang system normally used in the production of tobacco, grains and short-staple cotton. Under the latter system hands worked as a unit, performed the same jobs and were under the constant supervision of an overseer or driver. Regimentation and lack of slave initiative and control thus lay at the heart of the gang system. By way of contrast, the task system offered more flexibility and scope for slave independence. Having completed, often by collective means, their allotted tasks at their chosen rate of work (without close supervision), slaves in the Low Country were normally permitted to undertake additional work for cash or in kind. Planters also provided extra ground beyond the slaves' garden plots upon which a variety of crops were grown and sold to whites. Strickland can thus conclude that:

> The experience of task work ... thus helped to fashion a moral economy that prized the virtues of independence, self-determination, and personal achievement, while encouraging collective responsibility for the completion of assignments ... when Northern and Southern whites attempted to establish a free wage-labor system, they encountered a workforce used to exerting considerable leverage over the pace of production.[53]

Such a high degree of leverage was, as noted above, not typical of the southern system of slavery as a whole. And while not simply reactive, slaves throughout the South were denied effective control over the levers of power and authority in the social system. Nevertheless, in their attachments to customary patterns of work and in their attempts to contest total white control over their lives and labour, slaves fashioned their own 'moral' cultures, albeit within a social context very different from the capitalist northern states and Britain. Finally, such customary attachments, allied to the deep desire for ownership or, at the very least, control of land, meant that the freedpeople would provide massive resistance to white attempts to refashion the South along capitalist lines during Reconstruction. Demands for land and control over labour and for continued customary obligations on the part of owners (involving protection and assistance), accompanied by hatred of slavery and opposition to the insecurities and real dependencies of the market-place, showed that ex-slaves welcomed neither a return to the plantation nor the advent of 'free' waged labour.[54]

Afro-Americans were by no means alone in their allegiance to custom and opposition to fully fledged capitalism. Indeed, the largest part of the southern white population, the yeomanry, lived on the fringes of the market economy and, like many of their rural counterparts in the North, were more interested in household sufficiency than in unlimited gain.[55] Habits of mutuality, communal solidarity and non- or semi-cash-based exchanges characterised these ante-bellum yeomen farmers in both the southern Upcountry and sandy land interstices of the Plantation Belt. And, as in the case of ex-slaves, yeomen regarded the advent of unfettered commodity production in the post-bellum South (and the consequent escalation of insecurity, dependence, tenancy, proletarianisation and subjection to the dictates of middlemen and creditors) with great hostility. Massive protest ensued. But a common commitment to custom generally failed to overcome racial divisions between Afro-Americans and white farmers in the South.

RURAL DWELLERS AND URBAN ARTISANS

Unrestrained commodity production and proletarianisation had made deep inroads into the British countryside by the mid eighteenth century. But a large number of the labouring population were not completely proletarianised (gaining part of their material support from non-monetary factors and undertaking a variety of jobs), and an economy of self-reliance and custom intermingled with wage and market dependency.[56] Furthermore, customary values had a tenacious and popular, if defensive, existence. Notions concerning a fair price for bread and other necessities of life, legitimate practices in marketing, milling and baking, the proper rights and responsibilities of magistrates, employers and others in authority, and the rightful access to the use of land (for the grazing of animals, the collection of firewood and so on) – were, as argued by Thompson and Malcolmson, part and parcel of popular culture. And, if grounded in a 'traditional view of social norms and obligations', the tenets of customary thought fuelled rebellion against the principles of Adam Smith. Increasingly, under the pressure of rapid industrialisation, these tenets would also come to constitute an important part of early nineteenth-century workers' class consciousness.

In terms of production carried on in the workshops and households of rural and urban Britain and the United States, we can similarly note that a growing body of research lends support to Randall's concept of an 'industrial moral economy'. We will attend to the full implications of this research in due course. But we can note at this juncture that the work of Wilentz, Prude, Laurie and Ross (for the United States) and Rule, Sykes, Malcolmson, Prothero and Behagg (for England) demonstrates that many late eighteenth- and early nineteenth-century artisans and 'honourable' employers were motivated more by customary needs and practices (the attainment of a 'sufficiency' by means of 'fair' wages, 'just' prices, 'honest' profits and so on) than by profit- and income-maximising imperatives. Such people were, of course, frequently involved in the production of commodities which would be *distributed* and *exchanged* on a global basis. But the market-based motivations and practices taken into production were, at least for the historical subjects under review, not in harmony with the principles of free-market capitalism.[57] Involvement in market-based activity constitutes the starting point, rather than the conclusion, of analysis of norms, values and ways of life.

Notwithstanding several qualifications and variations, customary attachments and practices, anchored within the material context of limited 'petty-commodity' market involvement and approval, thus embraced large sections of the labouring populations of Britain and America. Herein lies our third area of shared experience.

Finally, the dire threats posed to the forces of custom by the expanding and hungry free-market system created our fourth area of common popular interest. It is to an examination of the varied and concrete routes taken by industrial capitalist transformation that we will now move.

THE HOUSEHOLD: FROM DOMESTIC ECONOMY TO OUTWORK

Attention has already been drawn to the central role of the household economy in eighteenth-century Britain and the United States. During this period of capitalist transformation (1750–1850) the household economy lost its key position in economic and social life. Factories and workshops constituted alternative (if also, at times, complementary) places of work, and highlighted for many (especially male) workers the growing divide between work and home, production and consumption.[58] Control over economic life increasingly passed from heads of households and small masters to capitalist middlemen and employers operating within vastly expanded markets. And the relatively fluid, if hardly equal, division of labour within the household economy hardened into a more gender-specific and rigidly hierarchical system (associated with the secondary nature of women's cash-earning activities, the deepened subordination of women within the household and society as a whole, and the rising ideologies of 'separate spheres' and the 'family wage').[59]

Fundamental transformations also occurred within the nature and social relations of paid domestic work. Most significantly, outwork, associated with the 'putting out' system and, later in the nineteenth century the sweatshop, multiplied.[60] Far from being swept aside as an outmoded mode of production by the forward march of 'machinofacture', household labour, in the forms of outworking and subcontracting, greatly expanded and may (at least in the British case) be considered as 'the truly typical organisational forms of the process of industrialisation'.[61] Under the stimuli of widened markets, a massive increase in the labour supply and the general breaking down of customary standards within production (concerning apprenticeship, the level of wages and so on), many of the new capitalist employers were more likely to intensify methods of exploitation within existing units of production rather than to effect wholesale transformations of modes of production.[62] As a consequence, the factory worker stood in a distinct minority in the labour forces of both countries. As E. P. Thompson observed in *The Making of the English Working Class*, the characteristic industrial worker of early nineteenth-century England worked in a small work-shop or at home and not in a mill or a factory. Weavers, knitters, cutlers, shoemakers and the like constituted, down to the 1840s, the largest grouping of workers engaged in manufacture in England. And between 1820 and 1840 weavers were third in the occupational lists, after agricul-tural labourers and domestic servants, and far exceeding any other indus-trial group.[63] In the ante-bellum United States factory work was largely concentrated in textiles (especially in New England and Philadelphia County) and sectors of heavy industry (such as metals and machine tools).[64] Outwork proliferated alongside the workshops and manufactor-ies of New York and Philadelphia, and played a truly crucial role in the industrialisation of New England.[65]

The growth of outwork had a profound and disturbing effect upon two groups within the labouring populations: domestically based male artisans; and married and unmarried women. We will deal with the experiences of these groups in turn.

Male Artisans

In the course of capitalist transformation domestically based male arti-sans (weavers, shoemakers, framework-knitters and the like) who worked alongside their families and enjoyed a considerable degree of autonomy over the performance of their work were transformed into insecure and depressed outworkers. As outworkers, they became increasingly dependent for their livelihoods upon the vagaries of the market and the growing number of 'dishonourable' employers intent upon maximising profits and minimising costs at the expense of custom and practice. Competing in frequently overcrowded labour markets, these erstwhile artisans faced major and persistent difficulties in main-taining their trade-union and other collective defences against the hostile actions of the state and employers.

The transformations outlined in the previous paragraph affected large numbers of workers. It is not, however, intended to provide a compre-hensive survey of such changes, but to illustrate the deleterious effects of the growth of outwork upon two groups of workers who became particularly prominent in labour movements: the shoemakers of New England; and the weavers of England.

Alan Dawley and Paul Faler have ably recaptured the experiences of shoemakers who laboured in Lynn, Massachusetts, the world's largest producer of ladies' shoes and the first centre to adopt the sewing machine and the factory system on a large scale.[66] Up to the middle years of the eighteenth century Lynn was a struggling agricultural village within walking distance of the prosperous mercantile centres of Salem and Boston. Lacking a harbour, Lynn did not share in the commercial development and the rise of industries associated with the carrying trade. However, the absence of natural resources may well have encouraged the early adoption of manufacturing. In any event, masters and merchants took advantage of the vast expansion of markets (especially in the South) and the tariffs imposed upon imported shoes towards the end of the eighteenth century to expand the quantity and improve the quality of shoes made in Lynn. From the early nineteenth century onwards Lynn developed into a major centre of shoemaking with a population which increased from 2,291 in 1790 to 4,515 in 1820, 9,367 in 1840 and to just over 19,000 by 1860.[67]

In origin shoemaking in the United States was an artisan occupation carried on in households and small workshops. Faler informs us that before the 1780s the cordwainer made the entire shoe, cutting out the pieces of leather, sewing them together and attaching the upper part of the shoe to the sole. However, as the demand for shoes increased so there took place a more specialised division of labour. Shoemaking was split into two distinct operations, binding (the stitching together of the pieces that formed the upper part of the shoe), performed primarily by women, often the wives and daughters of the shoemakers, and making (lasting and bottoming), undertaken by male journeymen. In addition, the master devoted a larger part of his time to cutting (keeping the journeymen supplied with cut leather) than making.[68] In Lynn itself, masters and journeymen worked together in 'ten-footers', small wooden out-buildings that stood by the houses, whilst the female binders worked inside the houses. As Dawley observes, all of the elements in the production of shoes – masters, journeymen, ten-footers, tools of the trade (the 'kit' of awls, knives and hammers owned by the journeymen and the master's leather) and real property – were 'fused together in the household'. And the household constituted the essential link between the economy and social structure of the community: 'To be the head of a household was to be an overseer of a small work team, to exercise moral and spiritual authority, and to represent the group as a taxpayer and voter to the community at large'.[69] Furthermore, despite the relative absence of a large local market for custom-made shoes (as existed, for example, in Philadelphia and Cincinnati), Lynn's shoemakers prided themselves upon their artisan status. Craft customs may have been stronger in the workshops of eastern shoemakers (especially concerning apprenticeship regulations), but Lynn's shoemakers congratulated themselves upon their independence and control at work, their lack of deference, their opportunities to become small masters and their attachment to the customs of the trade ('honourable' behaviour, 'just' wages, 'fair' prices and so on).[70] More generally, the revolutionary republican ideology of 'Equal Rights', complete with its emphases upon the labour of the 'producing classes' as the source of all wealth, liberty, independence, virtue, citizenship, mutuality and the irreconcilable conflict between the 'producing classes' and 'corrupt', 'idle' and 'tyrannical' monopolists, speculators and aristocrats, held a strong appeal in Lynn's households.[71]

From the second decade of the nineteenth century onwards processes were at work which fundamentally transformed the household world of the shoemaker. Most significantly, local merchants and shopkeepers took advantage of the increased demand for shoes to expand wholesale production and to concentrate ownership of the raw material and tighter control over the general nature, direction and organisation of the trade (in addition to their longstanding distributive function) into their own hands at the expense of the household masters. Having the capital resources and access to the considerable amounts of credit necessitated by large-scale production (which were often beyond the means of the small masters), the merchants and shopkeepers placed the most important step in the shoemaking process – cutting – directly under their control by hiring skilled cutters to work in the 'central shop' located on their own business premises. They also made room for finishing and packing the product on their premises.

Between the 1830s and the 1850s the success of this mode of operation enabled many to abandon shopkeeping in favour of sole concentration upon wholesale shoe production. They thus became manufacturers who put out work to the binders at home, the journeymen in Lynn's 'ten-footers' and, increasingly, to many outworking families in the New England countryside. And whilst the central shop era gave a few shoemakers (mainly the better-paid cutters) the opportunity to rise to become manufacturers, this experience was uncommon: most of the fathers of the new manufacturers were themselves manufacturers or merchants.[72] There was, furthermore, a decline in household control and an increase in dependency. Men and women in the household continued to make day-to-day decisions about production but, as noted by Dawley, 'the extent of household authority shrank with the rise of the central shop, and the longer production rhythms and larger industrial decisions increasingly fell under the authority of the manufacturers'.[73] In effect, therefore, the household master shoemaker descended into the ranks of the journeymen.

The new central shop manufacturers also bore little resemblance to the 'honest' master content with a sufficiency. Unstinting profit maximisation became the motive force of production and 'dishonour-able' practices mushroomed. Shoeworkers increasingly complained of 'grinding', 'dishonest competition', and the hiring of cheap and ill-trained labour by the new 'capitalist' employers. Wage earners concluded that 'the degradation of free labor was at hand' and that wealth and power were being unfairly concentrated in the hands of a few.[74] Not all 'honourable' employers had disappeared by the strike of 1860 (the biggest strike thus far experienced in the United States) and worker discontent was directed against poor working conditions and wages rather than capitalist ownership *per se*: but the numbers of 'dishonour-able' had greatly multiplied, and were coming to constitute an unwel-come 'European' (i.e. aristocratic and monopolistic) and non-republican system of production and exploitation.[75] Faler points to the growing opulence of the manufacturers and their withdrawal from the productive process:

> The central shop of the larger bosses was not a rented room or a crude, dimly lighted cellar but rather a spacious, three-story manu-factory with carpeted counting rooms and shoe rooms with beauti-fully painted and grained counters and doors. Bosses like Raddin and Newhall no longer spent their waking hours cutting stock and packing shoes. The new manufacturers gave 'a few hasty orders in the morning to their foremen, and then with a splendid turn-out' went off to Nahant, the Ocean House, Lynnfield Hotel, or some other place of fashionable resort. Their attire was not baggy trousers and patched shirt nor were their hands calloused from wielding the cutting knife. Instead they could be seen 'strutting on Exchange in the finest broadcloth and seeking to keep the sun from their delicate hands by the use of fashionable kid gloves.' In short, the Lynn manufacturers had become in wealth and life style much like the aristocrats and capitalists of Salem, who had been the traditional foe of the mechanic.[76]

Lynn's shoemakers believed that the manufacturers' opulence had been achieved largely at their expense. While real wages were slightly higher in the 1850s than in 1830, nevertheless by the eve of the Civil War 'the shoemakers' conditions of employment had deteriorated in almost every respect'.[77] In addition to the longer-term decline in control and independence, the 1850s witnessed an increase in commodity prices, an intensification of competition with outworkers in the countryside, a doubling of Lynn's own population, more exacting demands in terms of work, the virtual disappearance of the weak apprenticeship system and sharp fluctuations in the market which made the economic position of the shoemaker more insecure than in previous decades. In sum, the few economic gains made were 'shortlived and purchased at the cost of longer and more intensive labor'.[78] In such circumstances, 'felt' and accumulated grievances exploded into strike action. And the bonds of mutuality and reciprocity which lay at the heart of the household system were in tatters. Workers and capitalists linked via the cash nexus now characterised social relations of production in Lynn. The advent of factory production into Lynn's shoe industry during the 1860s reinforced rather than created such relationships.

As is well known, the English handloom weavers also endured the transition from domestic artisan to depressed outworker. Without wishing to idealise the situation of the eighteenth-century weaving household (economic hardship and exploitation were not creations of the nineteenth century), we must not underestimate the painful and *felt* decline in the handloom weavers' position. The weavers prided themselves upon their artisan status and their attachment to customary standards concerning wage and apprenticeship levels, prices and general conditions of the trade.[79] Yet, as E. P. Thompson has shown, the years between 1780 and 1830 saw the merging of the three characteristic groups of weavers (the self-employed weaver with the status of superior artisan, working by the piece for a choice of masters; the journeyman weaver, working often at home for a single master; and the farmer or smallholder weaver, working only part-time at the loom) into a group 'whose status was greatly debased', the proletarian outworkers.

Increasingly dependent upon the mill agent or other middlemen and, like Lynn's shoemakers, lacking ultimate control over the trade, the outworking weaver was 'exposed to conditions which were . . . wholly "dishonourable" '.[80] The massive influx of labour into weaving during the 'golden age' of abundant work and wages during the late eighteenth and early nineteenth centuries had catastrophic longer-term effects upon wages, hours of work, apprenticeship and customary standards in general. But, as perceived by the weavers themselves, the roots of their demise were to be found in human greed and exploitation in addition to the impersonal forces of demographic growth and market expansion.

Taking full advantage of the vast pool of (often surplus) labour, and seeing poverty as a necessary spur to industry and personal reformation (complaints against weaver 'extravagance', drunkenness and 'indiscipline' were common amongst employers), the putting-out capitalists exposed the weavers to 'round after round of wage reductions'.[81] And, as is often the pattern in casual and 'dishonourable' labour markets, the early-mid nineteenth-century weaver worked harder to offset wage reductions and competition from other workers. In turn, under- and unemployment followed: and there existed 'a pool of surplus labour, semi-employed, defenceless, and undercutting each other's wages'.

Many weavers responded by challenging, head-on, the rationality of the new political economy. From 1790 onwards the weavers' first demand was for a minimum wage (supported by some of the 'honour-able' employers who were opposed to 'dishonest' competition), but this was rejected by the House of Commons in 1808. Luddism and attempts to enforce apprenticeship restrictions likewise failed in the face of state and employer opposition (the apprenticeship clauses of the Elizabethan Statute of Artificers were repealed in 1814), and in the post-war years and beyond (including Chartism) the weavers were at the forefront of political radicalism.[82]

Living standards fell to starvation levels before the introduction of the powerloom during the 1820s and 1830s. It is true that selected groups of weavers did manage to maintain their artisan status into the 1830s (such as the highly skilled Leeds stuff weavers and the extremely militant Norwich worsted weavers) and that the process of decline was uneven (the West Country weavers having been reduced to outworker status, employed by the great gentlemen clothiers, by the end of the eighteenth century; the weavers in cotton and worsted undergoing degradation from the early nineteenth century onwards; and the York-shire woollen weavers' independence and status experiencing more pro-tracted decline).[83] But there was no doubting the *general* process of decline and mass suffering consequent upon the advent of the 'freedoms' of the unregulated market and the state's commitment to *laissez-faire*. As Thompson observes, 'the great majority of the weavers were living on the edge – and sometimes beyond the edge – of the borders of starvation'. The Select Committee of 1834 reported that it found 'the sufferings of that large and valuable body of men, not only not exagger-ated, but that they have for years continued to an extent and intensity scarcely to be credited or conceived'. And we must not forget that the weavers did constitute a very large body of men, numbering around 800,000 (wholly dependent upon the loom in the United Kingdom) in 1834–5. The last word lies with Thompson:

> It is the enduring myth of freedom in an obsolete ideology that for the Legislature to do nothing, and to allow 'natural' economic forces to inflict harm on a part of the community, constitutes a complete defence. The power-loom provided both the State and the employers with a cast iron alibi. But we might equally well see the story of the weavers as the expression of the highly abnormal situation which existed during the Industrial Revolution. In the weavers' history we have a paradigm case of the operation of a repressive and exploitive system upon a section of workers without trade union defences. Government not only intervened actively against their political organizations and trade unions; it also inflicted upon the weavers the negative dogma of the freedom of capital as intrans-igently as it was to do upon the victims of the Irish famine.[84]

It may be objected that the experiences of English weavers and Amer-

ican shoemakers in Lynn were not 'typical' of working-class experience
as a whole, and that not only were some groups relatively immune from
the processes of deterioration and degradation outlined above, but also
that some workers benefited from the development of industrial capitalism in this period.[85] In reply, a balanced evaluation of standards and
experiences must await the completion of our review of routes of capitalist transformation. It is, however, imperative to note at this point that
the transition to depressed outworker status afflicted not only weavers
and shoemakers but also large numbers of male domestic artisans. And
the transition was generally experienced, in both Britain and the United
States, neither as a painful yet necessary adjustment to the 'realities' of
the modern world, nor as a raising of expectations beyond satisfactions,
but as a profound and 'unnatural' deterioration in status, independence
and living standards.[86] 'Typical' was the Lancashire weavers' sad
'Lament':

> You gentlemen and tradesmen, that ride about at will,
> Look down on these poor people; its enough to make you crill;
> Look down on these poor people, as you ride up and down,
> I think there is a God above will bring your pride quite down.
>> Chorus – You tyrants of England, your race may soon be run,
>> You may be brought into account for what you've sorely
>> done.[87]

Women and Outwork

Many of the thousands of women crucially affected by the mushrooming
of outwork had special cause for lament. Women had played an important role in the household economies of Britain and the United States
during the eighteenth century. They had worked at a variety of paid
cottage crafts (spinning, weaving, lacemaking, gloveknitting, button-
making and the like), made and repaired clothes worn by family members, tended gardens, had been involved, to varying degrees, in the
seasonal demands of agriculture (involvement becoming increasingly
more marked and continuous in the less proletarianised agriculture of
the United States), managed the daily affairs of the household, and had
taken primary responsibility for the care and development of babies and
children.[88]

Despite the magnitude of this contribution, the value placed upon
women's work was increasingly low. Maxine Berg explains this contradiction in terms of women's continued social subordination within the
family. According to Berg, as a result of the growth of domestic industry
women's low-paid cash-earning activities 'became increasingly associated

with household duties'. Paid work and 'housework' were intertwined, and the supplementary nature of women's paid work firmly routinised.[89] Women were defined (and frequently defined themselves) primarily in terms of their families. During the late eighteenth and early nineteenth centuries they were increasingly excluded from artisan organisations and 'skilled' work, and began to be affected by the notions of the 'family wage', 'separate spheres' and 'true womanhood'. Such notions were, of course, modified and, in some cases, flatly contradicted by the overriding practical need to provide financial support to the family: but we cannot doubt their growing influence, especially among the better-paid workers, from the beginning of the nineteenth century in the United States and from the mid 1840s in Britain.[90]

Alice Kessler-Harris has, for example, estimated that only about 10 per cent of American women took paid jobs outside their homes in 1840, rising to 15 per cent in 1860. Among these wage-earning women most were young and relatively poor (free blacks and immigrants, widows and migrants) who worked in domestic service, manufacturing and a variety of other jobs before leaving the labour force after three to five years in order to raise a family. Probably less than 5 per cent of the total of married women in the United States worked outside their homes for wages at mid century.[91]

In Britain the percentages (albeit embracing paid work both inside and outside the home) were higher. By 1851 approximately 39 per cent of women aged fifteen and over and almost 25 per cent of married women worked for wages.[92] But similar processes – the concentration of women into low-waged and low-status sectors of the economy, the 'traditional' nature of much of the work performed (in domestic service, the clothing trades, and household-based trades and crafts); the transference of the sexual division of labour from the family into social production ('which ensured that it was women who moved into the subordinate and auxiliary positions, within it');[93] and the increasing preponderance of unmarried women in the paid labour force (by 1911 only 10 per cent of married women in Britain were in paid employment) – were at work in both countries.[94]

Of particular importance was outwork, which constituted the main provider of paid work for nineteenth-century married women, and which was second only to domestic service as a source of paid employment for all women.[95] The roots of outwork were to be found in the putting-out system and in the internal transformation of the handicraft methods of small workshop production. In terms of the latter, capitalist employers sought to maximise profits by increasing the division of labour, beating down wages and customary standards, and transferring work from better- to lesser-paid workers, and often from craft workshops to the home, garret and sweatshop. As an established source of cheap, abundant, and largely isolated and defenceless labour, female outworkers constituted a ready and attractive workforce.

The specific examples of New York and London usefully illustrate the general processes outlined above. Between 1820 and 1860 New York City became the foremost manufacturing centre of America.[96] The high price of land, the inaccessibility of water power and the difficulties of raising credit to support non-mercantile ventures in a merchant-dominated city ensured that economic development would proceed more by way of subcontracting, outwork, sweating and the proliferation of 'dishonourable' practices within the city's multitudinous small workshops than by way of the factory. 'By 1850', notes Sean Wilentz, 'observers pointed to New York as the London of America, the metropolitan capital of sweatshop work and degraded artisan labor.'[97] Whilst generally excluded from skilled work in New York, women workers were central to the city's outwork system. As such, women stood at the centre rather than on the periphery of industrialisation. Christine Stansell informs us that the master and merchant tailors of New York were the first to hire large numbers of women, and that the clothing trade 'would continue to be the leading employer of female labor in New York throughout the nineteenth century'.[98]

Mixing factory work and home work, and with an assured market in the South for 'slops' and (increasingly) high-quality clothing, garment manufacturers employed large numbers of women, sometimes in direct competition with male tailors. And operating in a seasonal trade and a greatly overstocked labour market (in which competition was often fierce between hard-pressed employers), seamstresses and other outworkers in the clothing trades suffered acutely from underpayment, rate-cutting, alternating bouts of overwork and underemployment (followed by even more furious, and generally fruitless, attempts to maintain wages by long, hard and debilitating labour) and chronic poverty and insecurity.

By 1860, notes Stansell, the outside system had spread from clothing into other women's industries. Three or four dozen of New York's industries employed over 90 per cent of the city's workwomen. In the making of paper boxes, hoopskirts, shirts and collars, millinery, artificial flowers and ladies' cloaks, over 85 per cent of the workers were female. And these were all industries in which wage-cutting, overwork, poverty and casualisation were rife.[99]

A strikingly similar situation prevailed in London. As in New York, some of London's women perpetuated the household tradition of working alongside other members of the family in craft production (in, for example, shoemaking). There also existed limited opportunities for skilled work for women in the exclusively female trades (especially dressmaking and millinery) and in some of London's factory occupations. But, as Sally Alexander has clearly demonstrated, unskilled and casual jobs dominated women's employment. Most women workers in London were domestic servants, washerwomen, needlewomen or involved in some other kind of home work. Given the proliferation of outwork and 'dishonourable' workshops and sweated production and the relative unimportance of the factory in the metropolis, women were once again at the very heart of the process of capitalist transformation. And, as in New York, extremely long hours of work, irregular employment, ill-health and wages often below subsistence level were the lot of the distressed needlewomen, seamstresses, boxmakers and other female outworkers.[100]

The depressed world of outwork did not, of course, constitute the sum total of women's working experience. One might also point out that domestic service (the largest occupation for women) offered girls and young women (many domestic servants were between the ages of fifteen and twenty-five) food and shelter, 'as well as, if she was fortunate, the possibility of saving some money';[101] and that by 1850 the wages of female factory operatives were, relatively speaking, quite good.[102] Conversely, we must remember that the various occupations for women were often not rigidly compartmentalised (in London, for example, young unmarried domestic servants would often later become married washerwomen, cleaners or depressed clothing workers); that low status, poor wages, and lack of independence and authority were *general* characteristics of women's work; and that deference and a general show of submissiveness on the part of women workers were often demanded by male employers.[103]

Finally, we must surely agree with Stansell's contention that not only did outwork meet the needs of industrial capitalism (for cheap labour) and those of the working-class family (for maintenance and care), but also masked women's involvement in wage labour, and 'gave rise to a specific psychology of female subordination in their relations with employers as well as to a particular organization of labor'. As we shall observe in Part Two, the largely isolated or family-based nature of female outwork made it highly unlikely that such workers would, 'develop a sense of collectivity comprised solely of other women, associated through their common self-interest in the labor market'.[104]

THE WORKSHOP: FROM CUSTOM TO CONFLICT

Historians have long debated the effects of capitalist transformation upon the workshop-based artisan.[105] Some scholars have drawn our attention to those craft and skilled workers who remained largely immune from the worst effects of de-skilling and the growth of 'dishonourable' practices, and whose living standards undoubtedly improved. For example, coachmakers, bookbinders, glassblowers, butchers and others involved in the luxury trades or catering to (often local) custom-based markets belonged to a pre-1850 labour élite which in both countries was largely aloof from involvement in radical political and industrial movements.[106] There is, furthermore, no doubt that industrialisation not only undermined craft skills but also created new skilled and 'aristocratic' workers, especially in the metal trades. The growth of industrial capitalism did not, therefore, result in a uniform and undifferentiated decline in worker standards and experiences.

Despite the above strengths, the optimistic case lacks overall conviction, especially when considered in relation to questions of typicality and worker consciousness. We will argue that despite undoubted improvements for a minority of workers and the uneven nature of capitalist transformation up to 1850, the dominant experience for workshop artisans on both sides of the Atlantic was one of mounting insecurity and felt deterioration in status, control, independence and general condition.

As E. P. Thompson has observed,

> The first half of the nineteenth century must be seen as a period of chronic under-employment, in which the skilled trades are like islands threatened on every side by technological innovation and by the inrush of unskilled or juvenile labour.[107]

The process of deterioration was reflected in the leading presence of artisans in popular radical movements, in increased conflict at the workplace, and in the considerable (at times unbearable) strains placed by structural economic change upon the supposedly harmonious interests of the 'productive classes', of which workers and masters/employers were seen as key elements. Class, rooted in antagonistic structures and patterns of consciousness, increasingly challenged the vertical loyalties of 'the trade'. Finally, we will suggest that the process of capitalist development and worker protest were both more marked in Britain than in the United States before 1850.

The experiences of workshop-based artisans in the United States can be illustrated with reference to New York, Cincinnati and Philadelphia. Sean Wilentz has ably reconstructed developments in New York.[108]

Wilentz estimates that approximately two-fifths to one-half of the male workforce in New York in 1815 worked in the trades, either as masters or as journeymen (apprentices are excluded from these figures). The vast majority worked in tiny shops and customary relationships prevailed between journeymen and masters. Apprenticeship 'remained a standard arrangement in 1820', in many trades there still existed a list of 'just' prices, and master craftsmen 'at least claimed that they expected to earn no more than a "competence", an independent estate of simple comforts'. However, between 1825 and 1850 key sectors of New York's economy were 'bastardised' by capitalist development. Rapid population growth and expanded markets provided opportunities for employers in the consumer finishing, construction and printing trades to cast aside customary practices and to seek profit maximisation. Wage-cutting, increased division of labour, sweating, subcontracting, the utilisation of unskilled labour and the undermining of apprenticeship were, as seen in our earlier references to domestically based artisans, part and parcel of the new capitalist rationality. 'Honourable' small masters were pressed into competition against the larger capitalist employers, and were often forced to 'sweat' in order to survive: descent into the ranks of the mass of wage earners awaited many. The new heavy industries (gas production, toolmaking and so on) did stimulate factory development in New York, but, as in the Jeffersonian period, the consumer finishing trades, along with the building trades, remained the most important sectors of the city's ante-bellum manufacturing economy.

By the 1850s these trades had been so devastated by capitalist practices that they 'could barely be called crafts at all'. Manufactories ('machineless factories' of more than twenty workers) and outwork manufactories had become 'the headquarters of the bastard system'. In the former, debased artisans 'completed only a portion of the labor that skilled journeymen used to do on their own'. The outwork manufactories – by 1850 the largest employers in the city – completed only the most skilled jobs on the premises and 'put out' the bulk of semiskilled assembly work to contractors or directly to outworkers. Wilentz estimates that while almost half of New York's craft workers were employed in outwork manufactories, only about 5 per cent were 'inshop' workers; the rest were outworkers.

It is true, notes Wilentz, that not all of the city's workers were adversely affected by economic change. Blacksmithing, butchering, shipbuilding and baking expanded and prospered. Similarly, there continued to exist custom-based shops and some opportunities for occupational advancement within the generally debased crafts of shoemaking, tailoring, furniture-making and sectors of building and printing. But the most important point to note is that such 'aristocratic' sectors were untypical

of New York's working-class community. The growth of class consciousness, argues Wilentz, was intimately related to the deteriorating
situation of the *mass* of New York's craft workers.

Cincinnati, Ohio, furnishes a good example of the combined yet
uneven and protracted nature of capitalist development. The first great
metropolis of the West, nineteenth-century Cincinnati experienced
phenomenal growth. Founded only in 1788 and inhabited by a mere
750 people in 1800, Cincinnati grew to 24,831 residents in 1830 and to
a staggering 161,044 in 1860. By 1860, notes Steven Ross, 'the scope
and value of Cincinnati's industrial production were superseded only
by New York and Philadelphia'. Between the Civil War and 1890 Cincinnati fell to seventh position in the national league table of manufacturing, but 'either led or was among the top five national producers of
carriages, furniture, glycerine, coffins, plug tobacco, whiskey, safes,
clothing, boots and shoes, beer, printed materials, pork and pork by-
products, sawed lumber, harness, and various leather goods'.[109]

Ross skilfully documents the effects of rapid economic growth upon
Cincinnati's workers. Up to the mid 1820s Cincinnati embodied the twin
ideals of revolutionary republicanism and the harmony of the producing
classes. Thus:

> Founded in the wake of the American Revolution, in a transmon-
> taine wilderness free of the entrenched élites and class divisions that
> already characterised older eastern cities, Cincinnati stood out as
> the republican City on a Hill – not a moral settlement, but a
> representation of the harmonious workings of a republican eco-
> nomic, social and political system.

Artisans and artisanal traditions dominated Cincinnati's productive
sector. The 'vast majority' of Cincinnati's artisans worked in small shops,
'engaged in a custom trade with familiar patrons, and preserved traditional patterns of learning and practising the mysteries of the craft'.
Master craftsmen met together to set prices and review standards of the
craft. Wages were usually high and employment steady (reflecting
the high demand for labour). Relations between masters and journeymen
were generally harmonious.

From the mid 1820s onwards cracks appeared in Cincinnati's republican world. Whilst the city's first manufactories supplemented rather than
competed against traditional crafts (serving the expanding commercial-
agrarian sector or developing in the 'new' industries of machine building
and foundries), and whilst real-estate speculation and commercial expansion offered the most lucrative rewards for capital investment, nevertheless the accelerated and expanded rate of economic activity brought
about a fundamental restructuring of some of the city's established
crafts.

As in New York, it was not primarily technological change but rather the altered nature of masters and markets that, 'precipitated the initial transformation of the artisan's world'. New and ambitious capitalist employers, eager to exploit expanding market opportunities, dramatically restructured workshop practices and relationships. In the furniture trades, clothing, shoemaking, cabinetmaking and printing employers utilised a variety of practices (subcontracting, putting out, beating down wages, increasing hours of work, undermining apprenticeship regulations and employing cheap labour) to reduce costs and increase production. The 'dishonourable' sectors of these trades grew, and conflicts based increasingly around class appeared both inside and outside the work-place.

Capitalist industrialisation in pre-1850 Cincinnati did not, however, present a mirror-image of the New York experience. Restructuring at the work-place proceeded most dramatically and profoundly in Cincinnati during the third quarter of the nineteenth century; from the mid 1840s onwards new industries mushroomed, and manufactories both increased their hold on the labour force (from 20.4 per cent in 1850 to 33.2 per cent in 1870) and successfully invaded the world of craft production.[110] Many craft workers reacted with hostility to such developments, but the issue of class had to contend with the formidable powers of ethnic, racial and religious antagonisms in mid-century Cincinnati.

Radicalism was an extremely potent force in 1830s Philadelphia. There, as in New York and Cincinnati, artisans figured prominently in production. According to Bruce Laurie, tradesmen made up nearly half the workforce in early nineteenth-century Philadelphia, even though the latter was still a commercial port selling commodities produced in other locales.[111] Carpenters, bricklayers and other building trades craftsmen accounted for one-fifth of the artisans, followed by tailors and clothing workers (17 to 19 per cent) and leather workers (13 to 15 per cent). Small workshops and close economic and ideological ties between masters and journeymen predominated. However, as noted in our earlier examples, the growth of new capitalist employers and novel and threatening working practices placed strains upon the unity of the 'producing classes'. Although Laurie's account of popular movements during the 1830s and 1840s would suggest that the ideology of antagonistic class interests between workers and employers did not assume the same potency in Philadelphia as in New York ('producerism' being especially tenacious in Philadelphia), nevertheless the proliferation of 'dishonest' practices in shoemaking, clothing and the furniture and building trades produced a growing storm of protest against 'dishonourable' employers.[112] Despite the restriction of Philadelphia's factory development to textiles and heavy industry, and the tenacious persistence of custom-based sectors in various trades, the lives of many former artisans were badly affected by the growth of manufactories at the expense of small craft workshops, and the accompanying increased division of labour, employment of ill-trained workers, the slashing of piece rates, increased hours of work and greater instability of employment. The proud yet depressed workshop artisan had come to suffer from the same 'dishonourable' conditions as the outworker.

The three themes highlighted in the experience of the American workshop artisan – attachment to customary standards and values; the uneven and combined growth of new capitalist practices; and the adverse effects of the latter upon custom and work-place harmony – were also present in Britain. As noted earlier in Part One, the power of the customary 'industrial moral economy' was particularly strong in eighteenth-century Britain; and notions of 'custom and practice', 'honourable' behaviour and the like continued to exert a powerful influence upon artisans and skilled workers well into the nineteenth century.[113] Capitalist transformation had to contend, therefore, with a set of strongly held values which, in practice, proved to be profoundly oppositional in character. Furthermore, so profound was the capitalist transformation of the workshop trades (largely before the advent of 'machinofacture') that the conventional emphasis upon the existence of a large, privileged and generally aloof body of craft and skilled workers does not withstand close empirical investigation in the years before 1850.

The work of Robert Sykes, David Goodway and Clive Behagg nicely illustrates the general points made above. In his investigations into the cotton districts of northwest England, Sykes has clearly shown that there existed only 'a small number of truly "aristocratic" aloof trades' by the 1830s and 1840s. In the cotton districts widespread capitalist restructuring of the artisan trades (by means of increased division of labour, the growing surplus of labour and the encroachments of the 'dishonourable' sweated sector) interacted with the economic problems faced by the factory trades (spinners, calico printers and dressers and dyers), textile outworkers and the more aristocratically inclined engineering workers, to produce extensive inter-trade co-operation and the politics of class during the second quarter of the nineteenth century.[114]

David Goodway's study of London Chartism strongly suggests that not only the lesser-skilled (as argued by Prothero) but also the vast majority of workshop-based trades in the metropolis suffered from the proliferation of capitalist practices.[115] It is true, notes Goodway, that the typical unit of production in London at mid century continued to be the small workshop, but, 'workers in the Chartist period had no doubts that large (or larger) employers, engrossing a disproportionate share of the market had arisen ... nor that a capitalist system was remodelling productive relationships'. The mushrooming of 'dishonourable' practices aroused the anger of London's artisans. A carpenter, for example, complained that the larger 'capitalist' employers in the building trades 'often treat you worse than the dogs that prowl the streets of the metropolis', and explained capitalist behaviour in terms of 'a love of gain, that a few men may amass largely, while the mass of the men of the trade are reduced to a state of slavery, dependent on the caprice of these men for the food that sustains life'. Similar complaints were widespread throughout London's trades. Goodway concludes that the accelerated pace of capitalist development in London during the second quarter of the century, the making of a metropolitan proletariat and the growth of slop production 'moulded the working-class politics and trade unionism of the thirties and forties . . . forging a common consciousness of disparate groups of workers'.[116]

Similarly, Clive Behagg has persuasively argued that structural economic change in Birmingham placed great strains upon the notion of harmonious 'productive classes' during the Chartist period. According to Behagg, competitive production for a mass market altered the nature of Birmingham's economy during the 1830s and 1840s. Whilst the typical unit of production remained the small workshop held in master-artisan hands, factories emerged in most industries and increased the degree of competition within trades. Simultaneously, the small master found himself increasingly dependent upon the market and credit facilities of the merchant or large-scale manufacturer, a relationship which 'continually eroded his traditional independence'. Faced with increased competition and lacking the advantages of economies of scale, the smaller, often erstwhile 'honourable' employers attempted to compensate by turning to 'dishonourable' practices, such as increasing hours of labour and sweating. Worker complaints concerning degradation, proletarianisation and diminished opportunities for upward occupational mobility became widespread during the 1830s. Many artisans became garret masters, and in a period of falling prices and intensified capitalist competition, wages were generally forced down and unemployment and underemployment rose. As a member of Birmingham's Working Men's Memorial Committee observed in 1837:

> When the masters found by these fluctuations in trade, their interests were being sacrificed and they could not maintain their prices they turned upon the men and reduced their wages in the hope of being able, by that means, to meet the competition and carry on . . . wages were reduced to the lowest scale of endurance; and general poverty, distrusts, dislikes and combinations were the consequences.[117]

In such ways did the capitalist remodelling of Birmingham's predominantly workshop-based economy undermine customary relationships and induce conflict. Against the conventional wisdom, Behagg demonstrates that by the late 1830s the notion of the 'productive classes' (so favoured by Thomas Attwood and his middle-class reformers of Birmingham) had become 'a fairly hackneyed formula ... precisely because the class unity it implied was increasingly at odds with workplace reality'.[118]

The experiences of workshop-based artisans and skilled workers in the cotton district, London and Birmingham must be multiplied several times to present an accurate picture of the total British situation. To take the final example of Bristol: David McNulty has shown that most workers in the organised trades in Bristol believed that their position had 'markedly deteriorated by the 1840s.'[119] As in many other places, the intrusion of large-scale capital into marketing arrangements and the growth of surplus labour provided opportunities for 'unfair' employers to undermine customary standards. 'Honourable' areas of work diminished, 'illegal' workers were introduced, working hours increased and general insecurity and poverty intensified. Members of the affected trades sought redress by means of institutionalising the 'customs of the trade'.

At this juncture a cautionary note must be struck. Despite the powerful and general encroachment of capitalist practices into the workshop, it must not be imagined that the advance was totally smooth and even. As we will observe in Part Two, many artisans fought determinedly to preserve their customary standards; and 'honourable' sectors and 'honourable' masters, whilst less in evidence, did not completely disappear. There were, furthermore, regional and other variations and qualifications within the overall pattern of capitalist disruption of the trades. In Kentish London and Edinburgh, for example, continued economic domination lay with craft and skilled workers (in engineering, shipbuilding, building and printing) who were, for the most part, threatened neither by the growth of large 'dishonourable' sectors nor technological de-skilling. Significantly, the politics of class conflict were far less in evidence in Kentish London and Edinburgh than in many other parts of Britain.[120]

In the final analysis, however, qualifications and variations must not be allowed to obscure the massive, concerted and adverse effects of capitalist transformation upon workshop production in Britain in the period up to 1850. As Richard Price has observed of the late eighteenth century and first half of the nineteenth century:

> this was a period when the final assault was made upon the standards and structures of artisan production and it was also the period when the remaining theory and practice of the regulation of market

forces was decisively rejected and undermined. These were the elements that made these years revolutionary in their economic and social implications.[121]

And although common to both countries, the capitalist restructuring of workshop production was more widespread, marked and synchronised in Britain than the United States during the first half of the nineteenth century.

THE FACTORY: THE SHOCK OF THE NEW

As noted earlier, factory employment embraced a minority of workers in both Britain and the United States during the first half of the nine-teenth century. In the latter country, ante-bellum factory work was to be found mainly in textiles and sectors of heavy industry, whilst in the former the majority of those employed in manufacturing in 1851 still did not work in factories. By mid century the factory system was the predominant mode of production only in the manufacture of woollen and cotton cloths in Britain.[122]

Beyond a common minority status (in terms of the overall structure of production) factory industries in Britain and the United States pos-sessed distinctive features. In the first place British factory workers were more numerous and generally concentrated in larger urban centres than their American counterparts. In terms of cotton textiles, for example, there were approximately 331,000 cotton operatives in Britain in 1851 as opposed to roughly 115,000 in the United States.[123] Some American textile operatives did live in large urban areas. By the 1850s Philadelphia County, with a population in excess of 400,000 inhabitants, had become the foremost textile-producing region in the United States. In 1850 Philadelphia's textile sector covered 326 firms and 12,369 jobs. Mills of all sizes were owned by largely immigrant men who had worked in shops and mills themselves and who, individually or in partnerships, produced woollen, cotton and silk goods. Alongside the mills prolifer-ated cottage-based handloom weaving. Indeed, in Philadelphia the eclipse of the handloom weaver by the powerloom took place only after 1850.[124] Outside of Philadelphia County, cotton textile production was heavily concentrated in New England. Lowell, a leading textile centre and the second largest city in Massachusetts, had a total population of 33,000 in 1850, having grown from 2,500 in 1826. Beyond the large and heavily capitalised factories of Lowell, Waltham and other urban areas, the majority of textile mills in New England were small and situated in rural townships of less than 5,000 people.[125] Conversely, Lancashire's cotton industry was concentrated at mid century in relatively large towns, such as Blackburn (total population in 1851 47,000), Preston (70,000), Oldham (53,000), Bolton (61,000) and Stockport (54,000). Manchester, the commercial centre of the cotton districts, had a population of 303,000 in 1851.[126]

Second, in terms of routes of development, patterns of labour recruitment and the sexual division of labour in factories, the American cotton industry displayed greater diversity than its British counterpart. This was seen most clearly in Massachusetts where there developed two distinct patterns of cotton factory organisation during the second and third decades of the nineteenth century, the 'Waltham' system and the 'Rhode Island' or 'family' plan.[127] Concentrated in Waltham itself, Lowell and other urban areas in northern New England and typically owned by absentee merchant proprietors from Boston, the 'Waltham' mills were large, heavily capitalised and from the outset combined water-powered spinning with water-powered weaving.

Catering to the mass American market for cheap, coarse goods, these mills recruited their labour forces primarily from among the single, young native-born women of the surrounding farms. These women were housed together in large, tightly supervised, dormitory-like boardinghouses. The latter were managed by boardinghouse keepers, and the mills supervised by local agents appointed by the proprietors. Close attention was paid in the Waltham factories to the morals and habits of the female workforce: church attendance was mandatory; total abstinence required on company property; and curfews enforced.[128] As Thomas Dublin has observed, economic motives and 'more distinterested considerations' meshed, and 'both contributed to the rise of corporate paternalism'. Hence the particular acuteness of the observations offered by Henry Miles, a Unitarian minister in Lowell in the 1840s:

> The productiveness of these works (the textile factories) depends upon one primary and indispensable condition – the existence of an industrious, sober, orderly, and moral class of operatives. Without this, the mills in Lowell would be worthless. Profits would be absorbed by cases of irregularity, carelessness, and neglect; while the existence of any great moral exposure in Lowell would cut off the supply of help from the virtuous homesteads of the country ... Accordingly, the sagacity of self-interest, as well as more disinterested considerations, has led to the adoption of moral police.[129]

Finally, the corporate owners of the mills paid identical wages, set the same hours of work and established the same regulations for their operatives. In these ways a fixed corporate structure was constructed.

At least up to the mid 1840s, the 'Rhode Island' system was very

different. As Jonathan Prude has observed in relation to the characteristics of this system:

> Clustered mainly in southern New England, these factories were
> typically small, moderately financed, and administered personally
> by at least some of their proprietors. For many years they 'put out'
> certain tasks, including weaving, to outlying handworkers. They
> recruited workers from across the social and economic spectrum,
> both households and domestically unattached individuals, and they
> dispersed their recruits through a range of cottages and larger resi-
> dences.[130]

Concentrated in small rural communities, these 'family' mills were more
common than their more famous 'Waltham' counterparts during the
first half of the nineteenth century. And, encompassing many members
of the family (although families were not allowed to work together, and
management's suspicion of parental authority inside the mills often led
to the exclusion of married women), the factories of southern New
England enforced an extensive sexual division of labour. Building upon
patterns set in England, Samuel Slater's male and female operatives in
Dudley and Oxford, Massachusetts, performed more or less distinct
jobs: boys pieced for the male mule spinners; boys and girls worked
the carding engines and 'doffed' spindles in the spinning room; and
older girls and women ran roving and drawing frames and operated
spinning machines and (from their introduction) powerlooms. Men
monopolised the higher-status and higher-paid jobs (as mule spinners,
machinists, skilled handloom weavers in the woollen villages, and as
dressers, dyers and other kinds of 'finishers').[131] (Despite the numerical
dominance of women and girls in the 'Waltham' system, men invariably
performed the higher-paid and supervisory jobs.)

Workers in the 'Rhode Island' system constituted a more heterogeneous workforce than their counterparts in the 'Waltham' order of
things. In the latter, ties of sisterhood, rural origin and kinship, combined with common working and living conditions engendered a sense
of camaraderie.[132] Among those mainly native-born southern Massachusetts mill workers studied by Prude, common bondings were in short
supply. These workers often arrived in the mill villages as strangers from
widely scattered communities, typically remained only briefly, and their
experiences 'varied tremendously according to age, sex, and income'.[133]
And, although Samuel Slater and like-minded millowners took a close
interest in the personal and collective conduct of their workers within
the workplace, they made 'little effort to control their employees' lives
after quitting time'.[134]

Heterogeneity was also a central characteristic of the cotton textile
workforce in Philadelphia County. The early factories, based mainly

upon spinning and carding, mushroomed in the countryside around
Philadelphia in the late 1820s. Factories recruited heavily among two
groups: native-born male and female migrants (children as well as
adults), largely untrained and constituting a ready supply of cheap
labour; and skilled, and more highly paid, immigrant textile workers,
especially adult males, from Britain (particularly England). Outworking
weavers in Philadelphia were increasingly immigrants from Ireland.
During the 1840s two waves of immigration from Western Europe
increased the proportion of foreign-born Philadelphians from 10 to
nearly 40 per cent of the male labour force. By the end of the decade
workers of all national origins and backgrounds were to be found in
factories; and the Irish domination of handloom weaving in cotton was
complete.[135]

In the foremost counties of cotton textile production in Britain, Lancashire and Cheshire,[136] factory development followed a more uniform
pattern. Despite the particularities and 'colour' of individual towns,
common themes were pronounced. First, as is well known, factory
production began initially in spinning and spread later into weaving
(powerlooms being widely introduced during the 1820s and 1830s).
Second, the development of the factory encroached upon and undermined the domestic system of 'putting out' described earlier. The latter
development (similar to the growth of the factory system in southern
Massachusetts) proved, as we will observe in due course, especially
explosive in the English context: independent weavers, spinners and
others saw the capitalist factory as a threat to their independence, status,
control and living standards, and were particularly prominent in radical
agitation. In many ways the onset and growth of the cotton factory in
England and elsewhere (especially around Glasgow) constituted a key
factor in the development of class feeling and class conflict.

Third, and despite increasing geographical specialisation in Lancashire
during the post-1850 period (into the spinning south and weaving
north), both weaving and spinning operations were typically performed
in the combined firms which accounted for 60.8 per cent of the 1850
labour force employed in the English cotton industry. Fourth, not with-
standing the prominence in Blackburn, Preston, Bolton, Ashton-under-
Lyne, Stalybridge and Stockport of wealthy employer families and large
mills, the representative unit of enterprise in the British cotton industry
was, as noted by Farnie, 'the small rather than the large firm', and the
representative employer was 'a yeoman of industry rather than a captain
of industry'.[137]

Fifth, as in the United States, cotton in Britain was predominantly a
female industry. By 1851 some 15 per cent of Lancashire's adult men
and almost 38 per cent of the adult women in paid employment were

in cotton. The percentage of females employed in cotton throughout the United Kingdom increased steadily during the nineteenth century, from 54.3 per cent in 1835 to 59.6 per cent in 1862 and to 62.3 per cent by 1907. The vast majority of female cotton operatives were, by the end of the third quarter, mainly single and in their teens or early twenties. By 1850 there existed a clear and hierarchical sexual division of labour. Women and girls were generally excluded from the relatively well-paid spinning process itself (the preserve of 'skilled' males), and concentrated their efforts into preparing the loose cotton for the spinners and weaving the spun yarn into cloth. By the end of the century female weavers would constitute almost one-third of all cotton operatives and two-thirds of the total female cotton workforce. The jobs performed by male cotton operatives were usually better paid and of higher status than those carried out by females. But it must also be remembered that weaving was well paid in comparison with the other, generally lowly paid areas of 'women's work'.[138]

As will be evident from the above, the cotton labour force drew heavily upon many members of families. During the early decades of the nineteenth century children's and juvenile labour was especially important: in the early 1830s between one-third and one-half of the labour force in cotton mills was under twenty-one.[139] By mid century it had become illegal to employ children under eight years of age at all and children under thirteen full-time: in 1850 only 5 per cent of the Lancashire cotton labour force was under the age of thirteen.[140]

Before the mass emigration from Ireland during the 1840s, the vast majority of Lancashire and Cheshire's cotton workers had been born and raised within the two counties themselves.[141] By 1851 the population of Lancashire was over 2 million, having almost trebled during the previous fifty years. And, as John Walton notes, this unprecedented growth was, 'particularly marked in the cotton district'. Massive urbanisation was a prominent feature of this growth. Between 1801 and 1851 Manchester more than quadrupled its population to over 300,000, while in 1851 four other towns in the cotton district counted more than 50,000 inhabitants. The Lancashire birth-rate was the highest in England, and the towns and the cotton industry recruited mainly from the surrounding countryside. Liverpool and Manchester had, concludes Walton, much wider catchment areas: but in overall terms migration from beyond Lancashire and Cheshire was of 'limited importance'.[142]

Finally, employer paternalism in the pre-1850 period in Lancashire and Cheshire cotton did not generally match the provisions and regulations in force in the 'Waltham' system. It is true that the ranks of Lancashire's cotton masters included 'active and concerned paternalists', who, 'sought to translate the deferential relationships of the "close" agricultural village into an industrial setting' (a pattern most marked in the outlying factory villages or 'colonies').[143] But, in general terms, we can agree with Dutton and King's claims that up to the early 1850s economic and other constraints prevented the development of employer paternalism 'on anything like the scale advocated by many contemporary observers'; and that, 'working-class "independency" posed a continuous challenge to employer domination, finding expression in a fluctuating but ever-present class warfare which forced the cotton lords into various forms of entirely unpaternal behaviour'.[144] Paternalism was thus limited and class antagonisms both acute and chronic.

This last point leads us into our third and most important area of comparison: the effects of the factory system upon both displaced workers and the new operatives and factory 'trades' in Britain and the United States. There is no doubt that the coming and growth of the factory exerted an unsettling effect in both countries but that, at least in the period up to 1850, the effect was both more disruptive and explosive in Britain than in the United States.

We can best illustrate the validity of this claim by turning once again to the example of the cotton industry. Between the ending of the Napoleonic Wars and the mass climax of Chartism during the late 1830s and early 1840s, the cotton factory districts of Lancashire and Cheshire (in conjunction with the woollen districts of the West Riding of Yorkshire) were strongholds of radicalism and became the cockpits of class and class conflict. Ashton-under-Lyne was possibly the 'most radical and Chartist of all the factory towns',[145] the mass strikes of 1842 centred on southeast Lancashire, and trade unionism, the unstamped agitation, the campaign for factory reform, and the anti-Poor Law agitation all flourished in the factory districts.[146]

A major factor underlying the upsurge in popular radicalism was the emergence and growth of the factory run along capitalist lines. For while the factory may have offered opportunities to some for greater economic independence, and wage levels were certainly higher than in agriculture and the traditional areas of work for women (both of which, of course, provided miserable financial reward), and despite the apologetics offered by contemporaries such as Ure, nevertheless large numbers of working people saw the onset of the capitalist factory as having a profoundly adverse effect upon their lives.[147]

As the most complete form of the capitalist mode of production, the factory was closely associated with a long catalogue of evils and injustices such as the disruption of established communities based upon custom and reciprocity, the break-up of the family economy, the final death-blow to the depressed outworking weavers and other erstwhile domestic artisans, very real threats to the status, independence, security and control of spinners and other 'artisans in the factory', the hostile new work-discipline and authority structures which expected proud and independent workers to 'stand at their command' and the indignities and rigidities of the 'rules of the mill'. The factory also epitomised the enhanced insecurities of daily life, the reification of the worker, the reduction of people to the status of things, instruments of production, items of cost, the purely instrumental and cash-based nature of the new social relationships of production and monotony, and loss of effective control over the patterns and timing of work. Workers condemned the numerous 'tyrannical' and 'hypocritical' actions of the new factory employers (their opposition to worker combinations, their insensitivity to the plight of the operatives and so on) and 'the transparency of the exploitation at the source of their new wealth and power'.[148] And while some of these instances and practices may have been softened in some places at certain times in the period before mid century, nevertheless, the general norm was of a widely perceived, felt and articulated sense of grievance and intensified exploitation.

Critiques of the capitalist factory system were particularly strong in the Chartist movement. Peter Murray McDouall, an active and extremely popular figure in both Lancashire and national Chartism, provided a frontal assault upon the factory system in his *Chartist and Republican Journal* (1841). According to McDouall, the factory system had encroached upon the Pennine hills and valleys with disastrous consequences:

> The noisy prison houses of labour grew on the hill side, and in the valley; gas shone in the magnificent bastilles; bells rung to number the hours of labour; the very fish forsook the polluted streams ...
>
> The palace and the factory, the carriage and the loom sprung up in company. The hand-loom weaver laid aside his necessaries; he now appeared in rags and want ... With him departed the small trader, the small dealer in the markets, the man who was satisfied with little profits and honest ones; with him perished the cheerful fireside of the cottage, the glorious independence of a well paid workman, the glorious freedom of a labourer who worked when he pleased, and as long as he pleased, and as long as he choosed [sic]; with him perished the most noble, the most independent, and the most honest specimen of British labour; and, in the place of the hand-loom weaver arose a new order of things.[149]

In place of the handloom weaver appeared not the free, independent equal worker of the new political economy but the 'wage-slave'. Divorced from ownership of the means of production, totally reliant for an income upon the sale of his or her labour and lacking due protection and reward for labour and security and control over the pace, duration and time of work, the factory operative fully epitomised to McDouall the exploitation endured by the worker under capitalism. The ceaseless pursuit of profit and the total subordination of labour to capital were intrinsic to the factory system. For McDouall the factory capitalist was a narrowly self-interested 'heartless accumulator of gold', a slave to 'avarice and ambition':

> The factory masters were maddened with the prospect of gain; for all now that was wanting to accumulate gold, was the rapid production of goods. What cared they for nature, for life, for infant slaughter; gold, gold, the blood of the infant for gold, was their cry.[150]

McDouall was, of course, by no means alone in his outrage and indictment. For O'Connor 'serfdom' and factory employment were synonymous; and the Anti-Corn-Law League employers were motivated solely by considerations of self and factory, of 'how that living tomb can be worked with cheap labour'.[151] In the view of James Leach, the leading Manchester Chartist, the same League employers were concerned only to 'amass princely fortunes without any regard whatever for the well-being of their ill-used and toil-worn slaves'.[152] And overproduction, unfettered and destructive individualism and competition were seen by these three (and many more) Chartists as essential characteristics of factory production.

By way of qualification, two points should be noted. First, McDouall and others did tend to present an unduly rosy picture of eighteenth-century petty-commodity production; and some factory owners, such as John Fielden, were singled out as 'honourable'. Yet such qualifications should not be allowed to obscure the total picture of sharp shock and deterioration: the destruction (this is not too strong a description) of a whole way of life; McDouall's superb evocation of a profound sense of *loss*; the 'honourable' employer becoming, as a matter of hard perception, a greatly endangered species; and the *mass* support which the Chartist leaders' critique received. It is, of course, the case that the factory created as well as destroyed skills. And in the post-1850 period the engineering factory and workshop would become the 'classical' homes of a skilled élite.[153] During the 1830s and 1840s, however, matters were less straightforward. Not only were the factory trades in spinning, calico printing, dressing and dyeing under threat (from technological change, unemployment, loss of status and, in some cases, falling wages) and strong supporters of Chartism, but sections of the engineering and metal-work sector were also (albeit less heavily) involved in inter-trade and mass political action.[154]

The growth of textile-factory production in the United States was less disruptive and explosive in its effects in the pre-1850 period than was the case in Lancashire and Cheshire. Thus Thomas Dublin's records that whilst women operatives in Lowell were conscious of a group identity, they nevertheless generally accepted the new order of things on the condition that their expectations were met. 'Solidarity', writes Dublin, 'grew up among women, but it was based on shared experience and culture and mutual dependence rather than upon antagonism toward employers'. Both in Lowell's mills and boardinghouses the operatives' lives were largely controlled by managerial regulations, but 'mill employment fulfilled important needs for women, and they were generally willing to accept these regulations'.[155]

Likewise, Prude's study of Oxford and Dudley reveals that there was only one insignificant turnout in the factories before 1840 (in 1827); and, 'exploring the history of these mills throws light on why large-scale confrontations were uncommon among antebellum operatives generally and family mill operatives particularly'.[156] For, in truth, 'there was no significant rise' in political activism among Dudley and Oxford's operatives after 1827, 'no rush to participate in workingmen's conventions or the Ten-Hour Movement during the 1830s and 1840s, and no further strike among any local textile workers until 1858 – and this second turnout was as fruitless as the first'.[157]

In Lowell and the surrounding towns there was a higher degree of labour activism: in 1834 and 1836 the Lowell women struck against effective reductions in living standards; and during the 1840s there was far more continuous and widespread activity in support of the Ten Hour Day campaign.[158] Similarly, there was considerable conflict in the textile trades of Philadelphia during the 1830s and early 1840s. In the handloom weaving centre of Kensington there were frequent strikes and protests against wage reductions; and Philadelphia's weavers were active in the city's General Trades' Union of the mid 1830s.[159] In Manayunk, Philadelphia's main centre of early textile factory production, there existed 'deep antagonism' between operatives and employers, occasioned by long hours and low wages, arbitrary fines, and numerous instances of 'unmanly' and 'un-American' employer 'tyranny'. Protests against 'slavery' in the mills continued into the 1840s, as was clearly illustrated in Pennsylvania's Ten Hour Movement.[160]

Notwithstanding such conflicts and protests, textile operatives in the ante-bellum United States were generally less militant than both their counterparts in Britain and skilled urban workers in the United States. A number of factors contributed to this lower level of militancy. In terms, for example, of the experience of Philadelphia County, Scranton has highlighted the short lengths of time spent in the factories by many operatives; the *simultaneous* expansion of the powerloom and handloom (which greatly reduced the painful process of decline experienced by

British handloom weavers); the relatively low expectations of the rural migrants going into the factories; the positive attractions, in terms of levels of pay and authority, offered to many skilled British immigrants; opportunities to become an employer; the shared cultural and social activities of skilled immigrants from Britain and immigrant employers; and the increasing paternalism practised by employers. Shared values and habits and softened employer practice were, notes Scranton, of particular importance in the change from the turbulent labour relations of Kensington and Manayunk during the 1830s to the placid relations of the 1850s.[161]

In terms of New England textiles, Dublin and Prude suggest that employer paternalism and attempted regulation of workers' lives, the routinisation of the rhythms and structures of the new industrial life, and the influence of Methodist and Baptist disciplinarians contributed to worker accommodation to the factory order. But Prude and Dublin attach central importance to the origins, composition and motivations of the workers themselves.

In Lowell and elsewhere in the 'Waltham' system the (largely unmarried) women operatives had been *attracted* to factory employment. The latter undoubtedly involved hard work. Workers were employed for an average of twelve hours per day, 309 days per year, and there were only three regular holidays – Fast Day in the spring, the Fourth of July and Thanksgiving – to provide breaks to the routines of work.[162] Yet, as Dublin notes, the women were not driven into the mills by 'sheer economic need' (the vast majority belonging to propertied, and far from depressed, farming households). Rather:

> The evidence strongly suggests that most young women themselves decided to work in the mills. They were generally not *sent* to the mills by their parents to supplement low family incomes but went of their own accord for other reasons.[163]

Letters sent home by the female operatives reveal some of these 'other reasons': to earn 'something of my own' (it seems highly probable that the money earned was not sent home: the women themselves decided how to spend their earnings); to earn wages higher than those available in farm work and domestic service; to save money; to buy clothes; to enjoy greater independence than that offered in rural life; and perhaps to meet a future husband. 'These factors made Lowell attractive to rural women', observes Dublin, 'and led them to choose to work in the mills.'[164]

The attractions of mill life are also noted by Prude. While there was no 'average' millworker in Dudley and Oxford (veterans, the poor and the destitute, and a wide assortment of individuals sought work), nevertheless some undoubtedly believed that mill work would provide 'an interesting and profitable interlude'. Thus:

> Comprised principally of individuals rather than families, this relatively prosperous contingent included young adults waiting upon inheritances, property owners and craftsmen seeking funds to enlarge their estates, and ... 'respectable' women who became operatives to sample the independence of their own wage-earning jobs.[165]

Attractions were present in Britain (especially to those suffering from rural pauperisation, and those individuals seeking greater independence),[166] but, in overall terms, were far less marked. In Lancashire and Cheshire the coming of the factory was, as already noted, equated with disruption, and was received with widespread hostility on the part of weavers and others rooted in customary norms and strong 'artisan' traditions. By way of contrast the process of transformation was less painful and protracted in New England. In Lowell, for example, the simultaneous and instantaneous creation and integration of water-powered spinning and weaving processes meant that there was *no* transition from putting-out to factory work. Furthermore, Lowell's female workforce was drawn from a narrow section of the population and, whilst 'daughters of freemen', lacked the artisan traditions and memories of many of their British counterparts. In terms of the 'Rhode Island' system, it is true that many outworking weavers were supplanted by mechanised production during the 1830s and 1840s. But, again, the transition was less painful, massive and protracted than in Britain. Dublin reminds us that putting-out work in New England had far less deep and established roots than in much of Europe; and we must remember that handloom weavers in New England were both less numerous and (in all probability) more isolated than their British counterparts.[167] On a more general level, the factory population of southern Massachusetts was, as already observed, a markedly heterogeneous force – far more so than was the case in Lancashire and Cheshire.

This brings us to a crucial final consideration: operative transiency. Already noted in reference to rural immigrants entering Philadelphia's factories, transiency was a particularly prominent feature of American workers' behaviour. Jonathan Prude has estimated that a 'remarkable' level of movement characterised the Slater and Merino factory employees of Dudley and Oxford. Except for the 1816–20 depression, when operatives clung to their jobs, 'at least 45 per cent of the East Village average annual work force evidently chose to leave'. Samplings from the Merino records yielded even higher returns: 116.4 per cent in 1823, and 108 per cent in 1830. Operatives not only worked for short periods in the factories, but had also travelled, for the most part, long distances in search of factory work: on leaving the factory these same workers moved beyond neighbouring communities.[168] Prude interprets this high level of transiency as indicative of Yankee workers' strong sense of autonomy ('operatives never accepted the moral necessity of remaining in a manufactory longer than they wished'), as among the more private reactions to industrialisation, and, along with other sources of diversity, as a factor which was not conducive to a strong sense of worker solidarity.[169] The latter did, as noted, manifest itself among Lowell's female operatives, but expressed itself only rarely (during the 1830s) in antagonism towards employers. And the very fact that the vast majority of Lowell's female operatives 'entered and left the mills frequently, working for repeated short stretches in the years before marriage' did not lend itself to extensive conflict in the work-place.[170]

There was, of course, considerable geographical mobility within the cotton districts of Lancashire and Cheshire. But our (admittedly limited) evidence tells us that by mid century (and apart from mass Irish immigration in the post-Famine years) much of this mobility was over very short distances (often within a particular area within a specific town),[171] that there was a growing sense of community or 'place', that the labour force was relatively homogeneous, and that many families could expect to have a permanent future in the cotton industry. In such a context, and despite Patrick Joyce's claim to the contrary, there existed a strong sense of class 'selfhood'.[172]

We must finally remember that lower levels of militancy among textile workers in the United States were not synonymous, at least during the 1830s and 1840s, with total passivity. Attention has already been drawn to labour activism and conflict in Lowell and Philadelphia, and the widespread Ten-Hour campaigns. And Prude makes the important point that, despite the paucity of organised conflict between employers and workers, industrialisation in Dudley and Oxford was marked by 'significant tension'. There developed a 'complex choreography of friction and accommodation', an early construction of 'the rules of the game for being industrial employers and employees'.[173] In response to employee transiency and mounting examples of discontent (as reflected in absenteeism, arson, sabotage and stealing), Dudley and Oxford's employers were compelled to 'give' as well as 'take'. As a result there developed a 'kind of balance': many operatives were 'coming to accept the industrial order but simultaneously modifying the regimen with their own requirements'.[174] Prude concludes that there emerged in Dudley and Oxford a very real sense of class, a perceived division of the world of work into workers and employers with separate, and often conflicting, yet generally negotiable goals.[175]

Notwithstanding variations of experience between Britain and the United States, the advent of the factory did symbolise the assertion of the new political economy over older, more customary practices and beliefs. To many, the factory marked the triumph of the 'dishonourable' over the 'honourable', the victory of a new way of life, a new system and a new class. Despite its minority presence in the years before 1850, the factory did, therefore, play a prominent role in the combined process of capitalist transformation.

AGRICULTURE: MARKETS, CUSTOM AND PROTEST

Attention has already been paid in Part One to the widespread appeal of 'custom' and limited approval for full-blown commercialism among those labouring in a variety of agricultural contexts in Britain and the United States up to the mid nineteenth century. It is the task of this section to highlight key aspects of agriculture so far untouched and to assess the extent to which the encroachment of the free market upon customary practices resulted in conflict and protest.

Given our earlier attention to the central characteristics of American agriculture, we can immediately proceed to a discussion of conflict and social protest in the ante-bellum period. An extremely influential viewpoint within American agricultural historiography is that class-based grievances and protests among sectors of the agricultural labour force have been exaggerated. It is, for example, now widely stated and accepted that the growth of tenancy and wage labour on the Mid-western frontier occasioned little resistance. Thus, according to Faragher:

> there is no evidence in the documentary record that antebellum tenants or renters saw themselves as a class. As Allan Bogue has written, some frontier tenants in fact managed to acquire their own property, and most of them probably believed the myth of free land and the opportunity of ownership in the West.[176]

Similar arguments have been put forward in relation to the consciousness of farm labourers. Thus Gates writes:

> Because most of these farm labourers were only waiting for a chance to move up into the tenant or owner class, they did not acquire the class consciousness of the farm-labor population abroad, did little or nothing to make their views known, and had no organization to present their claims upon government.[177]

And Swierenga and Winters have argued that earlier scholars often 'overstressed presumed class conflicts' on the Midwestern frontier.

'Given certain sets of social and economic conditions' claims Swierenga, 'debtors and creditors, renters and landlords, land buyers and land sellers all benefited from their financial dealings and relationships.'[178]

The thesis offered is thus that the majority of members of frontier-based agricultural communities were united in their commitments to speculation and profit maximisation. Conflicts and struggles took place, it is suggested, not fundamentally around class-based issues and conflicting conceptions of economic justice but around unequal access to profitable investments on the part of similarly motivated or 'market-embedded' individuals.

The notions of freely consenting individuals and spontaneously emerging common values have extremely limited usage in relation to the slave South. But a belief in total ideological slaveholder hegemony in the South has enjoyed greater longevity and popularity. As presented in its starkest form by Elkins, the argument in favour of slaveholder omnipotence claims that the 'total' system of slavery produced a broken, fragmented and totally submissive slave population, lacking any effective human agency and the will to challenge the system. We are thus given the slave stereotype of Sambo – 'docile but irresponsible, loyal but lazy, humble but deceitful'.[179]

While containing elements of truth, and undoubtedly interesting and provocative in character, arguments in favour of common agricultural values and totally submissive slaves do not carry overall conviction. In the first place, much more research into Western agriculture is required before convincing generalisations concerning mentalité can be made. Second, as noted earlier, there does, however, exist a growing literature on the consciousness and behaviour of farmers and others in American agriculture which clearly indicates the presence and tenacity of customary 'moral' values and norms.[180] Third, as a number of historians have demonstrated, nineteenth-century American agriculture witnessed profound and persistent tensions between community-based norms and expectations and those of the unfettered capitalist market-place. Such tensions revealed themselves in the Northeast and West in a variety of ways: in defence of the public right to fish streams and to protect the passage of migratory fish against the private right of the factory owner to dam streams to secure water power for the mill; in the profit-maximising activities of capitalists in the midst of villages and townships attuned more to customary, community-based standards; in arguments between rural townships and factories concerning relative shares of the tax burden to support public facilities; in opposition to the extensive enclosures of pastures and woodlands which impinged on customary common rights to pasture and water; and in arguments concerning 'fair' versus 'economic' rents and charges.[181] The crucial and enduring question was whether capitalist millowners, speculators, wealthy farmers, bankers and other 'monopolists' were to be allowed to exercise their considerable powers at the expense of the republican liberties and ideals of 'the People'.

Fourth, it is important to record that large numbers of those working in agriculture turned to various forms of resistance and protest, including organised protest, which fit uneasily within a model of smoothly functioning common values. There had been established during the eighteenth century a strong homestead ethic. As expressed in back country popular rebellions between 1740 and 1799, the homestead ethic included three main beliefs: the right to 'have and hold' a family farm; the right 'to enjoy a homestead unencumbered by a ruinous economic burden'; and the right 'peacefully to occupy the homestead without fear of violence to person and property'.[182] In defence of these beliefs, back country people in Pennsylvania, Vermont, North and South Carolina, Massachusetts, New York and New Jersey opposed both internal and external back country establishment figures – especially political and economic grandees – 'who sought to dominate the back country to the disadvantage of the settlers'.

The characteristic commitment of back country protesters to the widespread ownership of land and their hostility to land speculators and corrupt and greedy judges, officials and attorneys were carried over into many nineteenth-century forms of rural unrest. The late 1830s and early–mid 1840s witnessed 'the most widespread and sustained agrarian struggle of the early nineteenth century', the 'Anti-Rent Wars' which broke out among tenant farmers on the Hudson valley estates of upstate New York. Chafing against the collection of unpaid rents at a time of great financial hardship, the tenant farmers of the Hudson valley organised against the extremely wealthy Van Rensselaer landlord family. Articulating the language of republican egalitarianism, the protesting tenants demanded 'fair' rents, common access to the mineral, timber and water resources of Van Rensselaer's land, and full entitlement to the 'fruits of their labour'.[183]

By 1846 the Anti-Rent movement was torn by bitter factional disputes, but the cause of agrarian radicalism was by no means defunct. In 1844, for example, George Henry Evans and other New York City radicals organised an Agrarian League which became officially known as the National Reform Association. Inspired by a vision of the United States in which 'economic as well as political power would be widely and democratically distributed through the society', the Association demanded three 'transitional measures': homestead exemption (the security of the family farm against foreclosure for debt); the recognition of squatters' rights and a federal homestead law granting land to the landless; and land limitation that 'would prevent the accumulation of land (and property in general) in such amounts as would dispossess others in the society'.[184] Some members of the National Reform Association became active in the Anti-Rent Wars; others (indeed a majority) increasingly busied themselves in the wider politics of 'Free Soil'; and some carried their schemes for land reform to Iowa and other frontier areas.

Significantly, Agrarianism did not, however, 'simply migrate to the state (of Iowa) with eastern radicals'. As Lause has observed, the very settlement of the Midwest posed fundamental questions concerning land speculation and the legitimacy of claims by homesteaders and squatters, and, in all probability, provoked far more popular unrest than the conventional wisdom would have us believe.[185] The Brotherhood of the Union, an organisation committed to radical agrarian reform, 'rather quickly penetrated Iowa'; frontier farmers defended their claims to the land they squatted on and improved by means of claim clubs; and voiced their demands for pre-emption (the right of squatters who had improved the land to first refusal when the land came up for sale), and a free homestead measure which would halt the sale of public lands and provide free grants to actual settlers. Agrarian radicalism was especially pronounced in the years between 1857 and 1860 when declining farm prices and President Buchanan's land policy of ordering the sale of vast tracts of frontier land claimed by settlers forced a massive mortgage debt upon the farmers, and turned them decisively away from the Democratic Party. It is also worth noting that wage earners in midwestern farms increasingly engaged in strikes and sabotage and were the target of anti-tramp legislation.[186] Thus, although less profound and sustained than during the post-bellum period, and less marked than among ante-bellum urban artisans and others, rural protest was far from absent in the countryside of the pre-1860s northern and western states.

Finally, attention should be drawn to the far from quiescent South, particularly during the 1850s. We have earlier noted that the slaves survived the traumas of an inhuman system to fashion their own cultural bondings and means of survival: the Sambo image is wide of the mark. But resistance was also a feature of slave life. It is true that slave revolts were relatively infrequent during the nineteenth century (occurring in 1800, 1811, 1822 and 1831). But the low incidence of outright physical revolt was far more a reflection of the slaves' realistic assessment of the existing balance of power and class forces, of the slim hopes of success, and of the truly awful consequences of failure, rather than of slave docility or hopelessness. Genovese's views are instructive:

> The development of paternalism in the Old South – that is, the

development of a sense of reciprocal rights and duties between masters and slaves – implied considerable living space within which the slaves could create stable families, develop a rich spiritual community, and attain a measure of physical comfort. As they came to view revolt, under the specific conditions of life in the Old South, as suicidal, they centred their efforts on forms of resistance appropriate to their survival as people even as slaves.

In no sense did that decision imply acceptance of slavery. The Spirituals and much other evidence attest to the slaves' deep longing for freedom. Nor did it guarantee peaceful relations with their masters and with whites generally. Both violent and nonviolent resistance to injustice marked every day of the slave regime ... But, resistance and violence in daily affairs usually represented the settling of personal or local scores rather than a collective attempt to overthrow an overwhelming white power.[187]

The slaves' attachment to 'nonrevolutionary self-assertion' revealed itself in a pattern of 'day-to-day resistance'. As Oakes has observed:

> Slaves engaged in a variety of acts designed to ease their burdens and frustrate the masters' wills. They broke tools, feigned illness, deliberately malingered, 'stole' food, and manipulated the tensions between master and overseer. When pressed, the slaves took up more active forms of resistance: they became 'saucy', ran away, struck the overseer or even the master, and on rare occasions committed arson or joined in organized rebellions.[188]

In general the slaves had relatively few southern allies in their resistance to slavery. Despite the existence, notes Genovese, of some black–white relations of 'mutual sympathy', the vast majority of the poor white population in the South was hostile, sometimes aggressively so, towards slaves and free blacks, and generally supported a slaveowner hegemony.[189] At the same time we would, however, be wrong to view the white social structure of the ante-bellum South as totally secure and unified. The 1850s, in particular, saw deepening class antagonisms among whites, and the growth of 'Free Soil' sentiments among sections of the immigrant white workforce in the South. While duly noting intra-class conflict (among immigrant, native-born and black workers), Berlin and Gutman also detected evidence of free southern worker opposition both to blacks and to the privileged and 'aristocratic' institution of slavery:

> But, if free workers were pulled in all directions, their allegiance to the slave regime was never firm. Men and women who had fled the landlord-dominated societies of Western Europe were hardly predisposed to sympathize with the planter class ... Some foreign-born workers had been schooled in antislavery beliefs in Europe, including British artisans who had observed or participated in the abolitionist debates, and many others had learned to wield the phrase 'wage slavery' to their advantage. The defenders of slavery, who sometimes argued that all work should be done by slaves and

even that all workers should be slaves, alienated free workers by undervaluing their labor and, at times, slandering their persons.[190]

The defenders of slavery were, of course, also extremely anxious about, and hostile towards, the existence of a free black population in the South. Barbara Fields, for example, has ably documented the fundamentally subversive nature of free black labour (in its formal market-place equality with capital, and its ability to exercise choice and make demands) for slavery in Maryland; and the attempts of white slaveowners and their political supporters to impose all manner of economic controls and restrictions (in addition to their exclusion from rights of civil and political citizenship) upon free blacks. Behind such restrictions lay the fears that free blacks 'constantly busied themselves with inciting slaves to revolt' and fomented escapes.[191] Finally, as we shall observe in Chapters 2 and 3 of Volume Two, the abolition of slavery and the post-bellum capitalist reconstruction of the South triggered radical demands among the freedpeople and, increasingly, white yeomen farmers. The upshot was deep and persistent social conflict and unrest.

Attention has already been drawn to the different chronology and social characteristics of agricultural development in Britain. By 1750 full-blown commodity production, proletarianisation, and tensions between customary values and those of the unrestrained market mechanism were in marked evidence. During the following century four major developments took place.

There was, first, a decline in the relative importance of agriculture within the national economy (by 1851 manufacturing and mining accounted for 42.9 per cent of the labour force, as compared to 21.7 per cent for agriculture, forestry and fishing) combined with an absolute increase in the numbers employed in agriculture. In 1851 agriculture continued to form the largest single occupational category with more than two million workers).[192]

Second, there was an acceleration in the growth of wage labour. John Rule, for example, has shown that in the south and in East Anglia the proletarianisation of the farm labourer had proceeded a long way by 1750 and that, 'thereafter its momentum quickened to become substantially complete by 1830'.[193] Only in certain districts, such as Cumbria and the Lincolnshire fens, had owner-cultivators 'survived on any scale',[194] and in Wales no large class of agricultural labourers emerged (Wales remaining 'overwhelmingly a country of small family farms, though one of peasant-tenants rather than peasant-owners'.)[195] However, and despite a tendency among historians to underestimate the tenacity of 'peasant' farming, we must note the overall intensification of agrarian capitalism and its penetration into many of the bastions of small-scale farming in England; and, more brutally, the forcible 'clearance' of the mass of subsistence peasants from the Highlands of Scotland.[196] By 1850 Britain possessed a massive proletariat, both industrial and agricultural in character.

Third, proletarianisation in British agriculture was accompanied by profound material deprivation and widespread pauperisation. By and large farm labourers' increasing dependence upon the market – for jobs, housing (with the decline of living-in), clothing, fuel and food (enclosure 'consolidated this dependency')[197] – brought precious few, if any, material or mental rewards. Some historians have claimed that labour shortages during the war years (from 1793 to 1815) led to increases in real wages, but this claim is hotly contested by Roger Wells (the overall price trend was inflationary, labour shortages localised and ephemeral and real wages declined, 'despite any tendency money wages had to increase')[198] There is, however, broader agreement that conditions were extremely bad during the period from 1815 to 1835, dominated as it was by agricultural depression. Wells' observations are apposite:

> Regional disparities must not obscure major common factors; demobilisation, aggravated by relentless demographic growth, swamped cornland labour markets, and facilitated the cost-cutting exercise vital to all farmers irrespective of district. Wages and piece-rates were forced down; seasonal unemployment soared and perennial unemployment boomed.[199]

In addition, the Speenhamland system of allowances in aid of wages lent itself to wage cutting (farmers deliberately paid low wages and so shifted the burden of 'making up' wages on to the Poor Law), helped to create a poverty trap in the countryside (lowly real wages were the norm, and attempts to raise them above the imposed ceiling were fiercely opposed and ruthlessly suppressed), engendered a spirit of despair and hopelessness among many labourers, and directly contributed to the spiralling poor-rate burden of the 1820s. Many vestries accordingly attempted to reduce poor relief expenditure, and, in so doing, turned poor-law administration into 'a battleground for class warfare'. The introduction of machinery constituted, especially in the context of generally overcrowded labour markets, a further factor in the overall discrediting of the paternalist model, and helped to trigger the East Anglian Riots of 1816 and 1822 and the Swing Riots of 1830–1. Finally, the gradual return of agrarian prosperity between 1835 and 1850 did not, according to the most recent account, extend to farmworkers: chronic under- and unemployment, overstocked labour markets and poverty continued to dominate daily life. Only in the tighter labour market conditions of the 1850s did conditions generally improve.[200]

The fourth development concerns the nature and extent of farmworkers' protest. We will address ourselves to this issue in more detail in
Part Two, but a few general observations are in order at this point.
Most significantly, impressions of a uniformly cowed, deferential, or
broken agricultural proletariat must, especially in the light of much
recent research, be either heavily qualified or flatly refuted. It is certainly
true that enclosure did not, 'galvanise prolonged overt resistance outside
a few untypical locations', and that, if opposition to the erosion of
customary rights was more tenacious, yet, 'the effects of both were
essentially too diffused to generate sustained protest movements'.[201] By
the end of the Napoleonic Wars the food riot, as specific expression
of the 'moral economy', was very much in decline. And there is no
doubt that a mixture of repression (especially against attempted
combination), paternalistic concession and the tight control exercised by
the Old Poor Law over the labourers' lives (grumblers, idlers, drinkers
and 'troublemakers' could suffer unfair discrimination in the distribution
of relief) constituted a formidable obstacle to the expression of overt
and sustained rural protest. Conversely, the researches of Dunbabin,
Wells, Peacock, Charlesworth, Reed, Archer and Reay have clearly demonstrated that isolation and repression did not eliminate rural protest.
Covert protest, expressed in arson, crime and the 'anonymous tradition'
was a strong and persistent feature of early nineteenth-century rural
life. And at times, as seen most spectacularly in East Anglia in 1816,
Swing, and in the spread of political and trade-union radicalism into the
country areas during the 1830s, covert resistance could give way to
more openly assertive forms of action. Increasingly, a 'consumerist'
concern with prices was giving way to a more 'producerist' concentration upon demands for work at increased wages.[202]

Whether the above instances of agrarian protest signalled a 'developing proletarian consciousness feeding an overt collective response'[203] is
a matter of considerable debate. But the very existence and extent of
such protest reveals the severe weaknesses of an idealised paternalist-
deferential model of the British countryside, and, in a wider context,
suggests that capitalist agricultural expansion before 1850 was more
conflict-ridden in Britain than was the case in the United States.

THE PROCESS OF CAPITALIST TRANSFORMATION:
SUMMARY

We are now in a position to summarise our major claims and conclusions
concerning the process of capitalist transformation. We have suggested
that there was a widespread commitment among labouring people in

eighteenth- and early nineteenth-century Britain and the United States to 'customary' values and habits, as reflected in the notions of 'sufficiency' or 'competency', 'just price', 'fair wage', 'honest profit' and 'honourable master', and in the ties of reciprocity and mutuality. It is true that 'custom' assumed diverse forms, was stronger in some regions and industries than in others, and may have enjoyed longer and more profound appeal among male, urban- and workshop-based artisans than among rural outworking families or, increasingly, British agricultural labourers. Notwithstanding such variations and qualifications, we have nevertheless suggested that the tenets of custom, rooted in but not exclusively confined to petty-commodity production, enjoyed strong 'community consensus' on both sides of the Atlantic.[204]

We have further argued that, whilst not hermetically sealed against contact with the market (indeed, workers' daily lives necessarily involved market-based activities), and whilst not seeking to abolish the market mechanism *per se*, practitioners of the 'customary economy' were, nevertheless, fundamentally opposed to 'The Market' of ceaseless profit maximisation, unfettered individualism and competition, total deregulation and purely cash-based relationships. The overriding aim was to control and regulate the market (by custom and law) in order to afford labour its due protection (in relation to both consumption and production), to safeguard the social and economic fabric of the community, and to prevent the development of 'dishonest' employers and 'dishonourable' free-market practices.

Our third contention is that between 1750 and 1850 the 'customary economy' was challenged, and in many instances defeated, by the accelerated charge of full-blown commodity production. Industrial capitalist transformation was an uneven and combined process which spread into the home, the workshop, the countryside, the town and the factory. And whilst 'machinofacture' was the characteristic mode of production in neither Britain nor the United States by 1850, yet working practices, attitudes and relationships were radically changed by the onrush of capitalist practices. It is true that capitalist industrialisation created new skills and economic opportunities, and that some craft and skilled workers remained largely immune from the spread of 'dishonourable' and de-skilling processes: but a far greater number of workers experienced and articulated an intensification of exploitation within existing units of production, and saw industrial capitalism as an unnatural and unwelcome system (rooted in the 'dishonourable') which adversely affected their lives. We have noted that capitalist transformation in the pre-1850 period was more widespread and pronounced in Britain than in the United States.

Fourth, the 'triumph' of industrial capitalism was far from smooth.

Opposition to the new practices and values was widespread in both countries, especially on the part of the staunchest defenders of custom. And it was in large measure out of such opposition that popular radical movements were born.

Fifth, it is, however, important to add that, in itself, capitalist transformation, as a broad, sweeping process, constituted a necessary rather than a sufficient explanation of the upsurge in nineteenth-century radical protest. As we will observe, by no means all those people undergoing proletarianisation turned to radicalism. For example, women workers and many agricultural labourers were not centrally involved in working-class movements. To understand patterns of involvement and non-involvement, resistance and resignation, revolutionary, reformist, and accommodative responses we must venture beyond the 'economic' to consider politics, culture and ideology. It is to a brief identification of key political, cultural and ideological influences upon labour's birth and development that we must finally turn. The intention is to be deliberately brief and general – more detailed treatment of these influences will be made in Part Two.

POLITICS, IDEOLOGY AND CULTURE: CLASS AND CITIZENSHIP.

As E. P. Thompson has demonstrated, processes of class making and un-making are rooted in politics, culture (ways of being, speaking and thinking, especially in relation to daily life) and ideology (formal, structured views of the world, intimately related to social position and subjectivity yet presented as objective, natural and, often, commonsensical) as well as in economic structures, processes and events. As we have observed, the very process of capitalist transformation carried within it notions of consciousness and expectations of behaviour which both embraced and extended beyond purely economic ideas and actions.

In terms of the development of class among British workers during the first half of the nineteenth century, cultural, political and ideological influences were of great importance. Middle-class beliefs in their own cultural and moral superiority were everywhere in evidence.[205] Culture became a site for the development of class conflict, control and consciousness.[206] Many middle-class people viewed workers with a mixture of fear and disgust. The latter were seen as animalistic, 'without souls, minds or culture', 'fierce', 'rough', 'undisciplined', intemperate and improvident, easily led astray into 'wrongheaded' ideas, and given to riot and subversion. As Storch has written:

Everywhere one looks in the contemporary literature of description
of the working classes at liberty or at play, and of their habits and
customs, it is nearly impossible to take leave of a universe of
discourse which reflected a profound sense of fear and disgust,
coupled with muffled – and not so muffled – intimations of social
catastrophe.[207]

Middle-class attempts to transform – by means of a battery of cultural
and ideological institutions and practices – the personalities of
workers, and to channel them into acceptance of acquisitive individualism, the 'truths' and 'laws' of political economy, and 'natural' subordination to their 'betters', met with strong resistance. Nurtured on the
principles of the 'Free-born Englishman', often self-taught, and
invariably proud and independent-minded, Chartist and other radical
workers sought to fashion their own destinies. Genuine offers of friendship were not to be scorned. But obsequious and deferential behaviour
on the part of workers and the patronising condescension which often
characterised the attitudes of the middle class met with Chartist con-
tempt. The Chartist leaders were also quick to expose the hypocrisy of
sections of the middle class (the latter's stated commitments to freedom
and independence being combined with simultaneous treatment of
workers as 'slaves' and dependants), and sought to build an alternative
'movement culture' (rooted in democratic practice, personal dignity,
and personal and collective independence) and an alternative political
economy (based upon due protection and reward for the interests of
labour).[208] Class increasingly informed a whole culture, an entire way
of life. And when we set cultural and ideological class conflicts alongside
political estrangement (exclusion from the franchise, widespread criticisms of 'Old Corruption', and the perceived hostility of the state
towards the popular interest) then we can begin to make greater sense
of the process of class.

In the United States culture, ideology and politics lent themselves, at
least up to the mid–late 1820s, far more to popular attachment to the
notion of citizenship than to class. White adult male workers generally
saw themselves as staunch protectors, rather than foes, of the social and
political order. Artisans, in particular, had played an important part in
the anti-colonial, anti-monarchical and anti-aristocratic struggle against
Britain, were strongly committed to the values of the new Republic
('independence', 'virtue', 'commonwealth', 'citizenship' and 'equal
rights'), possessed the vote (if white and adult male), and defined themselves and other 'producers' as the backbone of the nation.[209]

Capitalist transformation in the United States increasingly brought
about divisions within the work-place, yet politics, as a seemingly demo-

cratic and pluralistic process, offered unity and consensus on the basis of common citizenship. Thus Ross:

> Because the United States experienced its political revolution before its industrial revolution, wage earners saw themselves as holding two identities: *workers* who operated in a highly stratified economic sphere and *citizens* who participated in what they believed was an egalitarian political sphere. Their conviction that government served as a neutral arbiter between labor and capital and would act to correct the inequities of economic life led many workers to reject class-oriented workingmen's parties in favor of pursuing their aims within mainstream organizations.[210]

Yet, as Ross himself goes on to suggest, matters were not static: the 'gift of the suffrage' and a liberal-pluralist conception of the state did not ensure the perpetual triumph of citizenship over class. Ross's work on Cincinnati and, most prominently, Wilentz's study of New York demonstrate that as capitalist practices undermined the customary world of the workshop, so artisans and employers increasingly developed and articulated class-based (rather than consensual) versions of revolutionary republicanism. Employers and financiers were defined as 'corrupt' and 'unrepublican', intent upon imposing a 'sinister new system' that would, 'turn freeborn Americans into 'vassals', 'the willing tools of others'.[211] In turn, capitalist employers exhorted workers to turn their backs upon collectivist panaceas and to devote greater energy to the morally uplifting and materially rewarding activities of self-help and temperance.[212] In such ways did class ideologies and cultures increasingly impose themselves upon American politics.

A final general observation concerning the evanescent nature of the various popular attempts to establish *independent* labour politics may be offered. Between the late 1820s and the 1850s many American workers turned, in a variety of locations, to experiments in independent working-class politics in order to counteract the 'unrepublican' actions of the capitalists and their allies in the established parties and the various levels of the state machinery. The frequency with which American workers.turned to independent politics is often overlooked by those intent upon demonstrations of American 'exceptionalism'. Yet it is not only the frequency, but also the short-lived character of third-party politics which constitute a marked feature of the second quarter of the nineteenth century, indeed the century as a whole. The key question is why did American workers turn so often and yet ultimately so unsuccessfully (in terms of the creation of permanent organisations) to independent politics? This question will be pursued in some detail throughout the remainder of the study. At this point it is sufficient to alert the reader both to its central importance and to the extreme difficulty of providing an adequate general answer. On the one hand the very frequency of worker attempts to create independent political parties would suggest that class identity was a far more potent factor in nineteenth-century American politics than the conventional wisdom would admit. On the other hand, the very failure of such attempts may suggest that class was less profound and durable than Wilentz has claimed. In fact the only satisfactory way in which to approach such issues is to confront the historical evidence in all its complexity. It is, therefore, to an examination of the character and aims of popular protest and working-class movements in the early to mid nineteenth century that we must proceed in Part Two.

Class and Fragmentation: Popular and Working-Class Movements before the 1860s

SYNOPSIS

Modern radicalism, the child of capitalist transformation and democratic revolution in France and America, grew apace during the early nineteenth century. Increasingly class-based in character, radicalism expressed itself in a profusion of popular and working-class movements between the late 1820s and the early 1860s. Part Two addresses itself to an examination of the character and aims of these movements.

The period from the 1820s to the 1860s merits detailed attention for a variety of reasons. First, it was during the second quarter of the nineteenth century that popular protest, developing since the late eighteenth century, reached maturity on both sides of the Atlantic. Second, heated historical debate continues to surround the character of protests and movements during the second quarter. Did specifically working-class forms of consciousness and protest develop, or would other characterisations (populist, producerist, sectional) constitute more accurate descriptions? Long familiar to students of British labour history, especially since the publication, in 1963, of E. P. Thompson's *The Making of the English Working Class*, debates concerning class, class consciousness and 'producerism' have recently revived, indeed flourished, in relation to the labour history of the United States. Of major importance in the latter context has been the appearance of Sean Wilentz's *Chants Democratic: New York City and the Rise of the American Working Class 1788–1850*, published in 1984, and a number of articles concerning class and American 'exceptionalism' in the pages of *International Labor and Working Class History*. It is Wilentz's bold and challenging view that 'more than a decade before the Civil War, the working-class presence was established in the American metropolis', and that this metropolitan working class developed a form of consciousness which was not 'exceptional' (that is, distinctly capitalist or producerist in character), but comparable to the patterns of thought and behaviour displayed by British and continental European workers. Wilentz's further challenge – that the entire notion of American workers' 'exceptionalism' be scrapped – has brought matters to a head.[1]

The third factor shaping my chronological focus resides in the marked break in patterns of popular and working-class protest, internal class structure and (in some instances) external class relations which took place in both countries during the 1840s. As we will see, the notion of 'discontinuity', in terms of the mid nineteenth-century British labour movement, has been long and hotly debated by historians. In terms of the United States, discontinuity is far less contentious in the sense that the depression between 1837 and 1842 dealt a terrible blow to the fortunes of trade unions and other institutions of workers developed during the 1830s. The argument put forward here is that, despite continued labour movement activity, advances and, to a lesser extent, class-based actions, the years between the mid 1840s and the early 1860s witnessed the decline of class-based ties and the emergence of far more fragmented labouring populations in Britain and the United States. In addition, the third quarter of the nineteenth century saw the adoption of more limited or 'reformist' goals on the part of the British labour movement, in part a response to a greater accommodation of organised labour's presence by those in positions of power and authority.

In accordance with the analytical and chronological priorities outlined above, Part Two is organised around the themes of 'class' and 'fragmentation'. The first part of the section will investigate the chronology, socio-geographical spread, and general character and aims of popular radical and specifically working-class movements from the 1820s to the early–mid 1840s. The second part will undertake a similar task in relation to the years from the mid 1840s to the early 1860s. It should also be noted that the chronologies and characteristics of workers' movements in the two countries during the period under review were similar but far from identical. The historian can, for example, ill afford to neglect the greater importance of race and racism to the structure and limitations of American labour movements, or the earlier and, arguably, more profound imprint of class upon British labour. Similarly, whilst the Civil War marked a major watershed in American history, the 'reformism' of mid-Victorian British labour persisted well beyond the 1860s. The reader will be fully alerted to such similarities and differences during the course of our investigation.

CHAPTER 2

The Presence of Class: Radicalism from the 1820s to the 1840s

THE CHRONOLOGY, NATURE AND AIMS OF PROTEST: THE UNITED STATES

In relation to the United States, we can usefully identify four main currents in the history of labour radicalism during the second quarter of the century: support for independent political action (seen most dramatically in the Working Men's Parties of the late 1820s and early 1830s, but also present in the Equal Rights agitation of the mid 1830s, the Anti-Rent Wars of the mid 1840s, and in some urban ares in the early 1840s); the massive and impressive movement in favour of inter-trade co-operation and widened labour solidarity, as reflected in the city-wide confederations of unions (the General Trades' Union movement) and industrial conflict of the mid 1830s; the activities of labour radicals within the Jacksonian Democratic Party and, to a lesser extent, within the Whig Party; and the devastating effects of the depression from 1837 to 1842 upon labour radicalism. We will deal with these themes in turn.

Independent Politics

The late 1820s and the 1830s witnessed the rise and decline of the Working Men's Parties and the first modern labour movement in the United States.[2] During the late 1820s economic depression, declining living standards, the adverse effects of capitalist transformation upon artisans and others, dissatisfaction with the existing political parties, the increasingly unfulfilled promise of social mobility, and the retreat of republican values and institutions before the 'un-American' advance of 'monopoly', 'aristocracy' and 'tyranny' provoked the politics of class. As Bruce Laurie has written:

> Journeymen and factory hands skeptical of free laborism's faith in broadened opportunity assembled alternatives to the mechanics' institutes, masters' societies, and even mainstream parties. They organized unions on a widening front that drew together in confed-

erations as well as third parties with ambitious manifestos. Politic-
ized labor stood against imprisonment for debt, mandatory militia
duty, burdensome taxation, and the use of prison labor, and for
mechanics' lien laws and expanded public school systems. Leaders
inveighed against 'class legislation' in all its varieties, from seemingly
innocuous lotteries to the chartering of financial institutions and
manufacturing companies.[3]

Labour's turn to independent action (the result of a perceived identity
of interests among labouring people and opposition to other social
groups) was neither necessary nor untroubled. At the political level, for
example, the notion of citizenship, of active participation in a shared
republican heritage, was hardly compatible with separate and antagonistic class interests. And, as we will observe in more detail later, Democrats and Whigs, with their respective appeals to 'equal rights for all,
and special privileges for none' and nativism, temperance and evangelical
morality, and their shared 'free laborist' beliefs in upward social mobility
as the just reward for character, industry and merit and the beneficent
effects of the forces of supply and demand, did their utmost to thwart
the politics of class.

By the mid–late 1840s the politics of independent, class-based labour
radicalism had indeed become subordinate to the partisan allegiances of
Democrats and Whigs. But in the late 1820s and early–mid 1830s matters
were far less settled. The second-party system of mass parties, partisan
presses and 'machines' was in its infancy, the raw successor to the
political world of patricians, patronage and factions. The developing
mass organisations of Whigs and Democrats did attempt to appeal to
the enfranchised white male artisan population. But, although both
parties succeeded in gaining votes from the working class during the
1830s, neither 'succeeded in winning the allegiance of the labour movement'. As Amy Bridges has observed, independence and a distinctive
political culture characterised large and important sections of the Jacksonian working class.[4]

Workingmen's Parties

This political independence was most clearly seen in the rise of the
Workingmen's Parties. 'The awakening began in Philadelphia', notes
Philip Foner,

> where, in the summer of 1828, the first labor party in America was
> formed. This movement spread westward to Pittsburgh, Lancaster,
> Carlisle, Harrisburg, Cincinnati, and other cities in Pennsylvania
> and Ohio. It went south to Delaware where in 1830 the workers
> elected thirteen out of eighteen of the officers of the borough of
> Wilmington; and north to New York City, Newark, Trenton,

Albany, Buffalo, Syracuse, Troy, Utica, Boston, Providence, Port-
land, Maine, and Burlington, Vermont. All told, independent
workers' political parties were organized in 61 cities and towns
during the years 1828 to 1834.[5]

Leadership and support were drawn mainly from the ranks of the
labouring population, and especially from proud, independent and
embattled artisans. In Philadelphia, the 'cradle of the nation's labor
movement', the resolution calling for the organisation of the Working
Men's Party was drafted by William Heighton and endorsed at a January
1828 meeting of the Mechanics Union of Trade Associations. Born in
Northamptonshire in 1800, Heighton arrived in Philadelphia as a youth
and became a cordwainer. Immersed in the traditions of rationalism and
autodidacticism, so marked among working-class radical leaders on both
sides of the Atlantic, Heighton eloquently articulated and popularised
the labour theory of value among Philadelphia's workers. Thus Laurie:

> No Philadelphian read such economists [Locke, Smith and Ricardo]
> with a more critical eye than William Heighton ... during his rela-
> tively brief stay in the city, he distinguished himself as its most
> influential working-class activist and intellectual. He digested the
> classical thinkers and their critics ... and emerged as the American
> analogue of contemporary radical intellectuals in England. Like his
> English comrades writing in the 1820s, he shifted the emphasis of
> radical discourse from the purely political to a balance of the polit-
> ical and the economic.[6]

Heighton's fellow radical leaders in 1830s Philadelphia included the
cordwainers Solomon Demars, John Caney, William English and Israel
Young; the carpenters Thomas Wise and William Thompson; and the
handloom weaver John Ferral. Support for the Working Men's Party of
Philadelphia was rooted in the city's artisan-based trade unions
(including those in 'honourable' pursuits and those in the depressed
trades). And despite an immigrant presence, largely from Britain and
Ireland, most Philadelphian radicals appear to have been native-born
Americans.[7]

Artisans were conspicuous in most urban-based parties. In New York
City, as in Philadelphia and New England, agitation concerning the
length of the working day led many artisans into independent politics.
In New York City journeymen mechanics dominated the Committee of
Fifty (set up to safeguard the principle of the ten-hour day) which in
the summer of 1829 resolved to run a ticket of journeymen and poor
small masters in the upcoming elections for state senate and assembly.[8]
Leading personalities in New York's radical movement were Frances
Wright, the Scots-born 'Priestess of Beelzebub', freethinker, admirer of
Thomas Paine, advocate of women's rights, and educational reformer,

Robert Dale Owen, son of Robert Owen, Wright's co-editor on the *Free Enquirer*, and likewise a believer that inequality of education, rather than wealth or property, constituted the root cause of poverty, and, above all, Thomas Skidmore. It was the self-taught machinist, Skidmore, author of the 1829 tract *The Rights of Man to Property!* and advocate of the lawful seizure and expropriation and equal redistribution of all existing property, who was a leading figure on the Committee of Fifty and a persuasive exponent of the view that the key to radical economic and social change lay in the capture of political power by an independent people.[9]

Skilled artisans were also prominent in New England. Defeated in their attempts, in 1825 and 1830, to secure the ten-hour day by economic means, Boston's construction workers turned to independent politics in 1830. 'As in New York and Pennsylvania', notes Laurie, 'the Boston movement radiated outward from city to country, dotting village and small-town New England with Working Men's parties that coalesced into a statewide organization for the 1831 elections'.[10]

In large measure the product of artisan radicalism, the Working Men's Parties nevertheless attempted to exert a wider appeal. Farmers, labourers in general, small masters and 'honourable' employers all fell within the targeted group of the 'producing classes'. Indeed, so wide was the definition of the term 'working man', that any man performing a *useful* occupation, mental or physical, was welcomed into the fold. There were, however, limits. Wives and womenfolk were seen as guardians of hearth and home rather than active public and political beings. Like women, blacks did not possess the obvious asset of the vote and were, in any case, not welcomed on account of the colour of their skin. And bankers, speculators and some Tammany Hall bosses were doctrinally excluded from the movement along with 'dishonourable' (and mainly larger) employers.[11]

A wide range of issues underpinned the radicalism of the Working Men. At the most fundamental level radical workers perceived a growing concentration of power, income and wealth in fewer and fewer 'unproductive' hands, a concentration which was threatening the very existence of *their* Republic based on equal rights, personal and collective independence, and social responsibility. The radicals were not socialists. They had no objections to profit and private property in themselves; and they did not advocate collective ownership of the means of production. But, as noted in Part One, the moral industrial economy of radical artisans and their faith in equal rights constituted the basis of a damning indictment of the emerging capitalist order. The increased dependence and misery of many artisans, the 'tyranny' of employers and others, the perceived 'slavery' of wage labour, the excessive accumulation on the part of individuals and corporate entities and their attempts to hijack and direct the democratic instruments of law and government to their own selfish ends, and the profoundly anti-social and destructive effects of unbridled individualism, competition and acquisitiveness upon republican citizens – such grievances lay at the heart of worker unrest.[12]

Many radicals located the roots of the Republic's ills in the field of politics – in the domination of politics by the wealthy and the passage of 'monopolistic' or 'aristocratic' legislation, especially charters of incorporation, 'which empowered a privileged few to engross markets', and banking charters, 'which gave legal life to the most hateful of all enterprise'.[13] Radical workers championed a pluralist, as opposed to sectionalist, view of the state and government. As Bridges writes:

> Workingmen argued that, contravening the principles of equal rights and equal protection, government had been acting to benefit some citizens at the expense of others. The result was a decline in the material condition of workingmen, in their political status, and even in their moral fiber. Rather than being so one-sided, government should regulate relations between classes so that the weak would be protected and the strong not given legal privilege to reinforce their economic advantage.[14]

The Working Men's Parties sought due balance, equity for all citizens and protection by means of greater injections of democracy and fairness into the political and legal systems. Chartered public monopolies would be abolished and a cheaper legal system and more equitable tax laws introduced. The elimination of property qualifications for office-holding, the election of all important public officials and the compensation of jurors, witnesses and city council members would facilitate the participation of workingmen in the political process. In a related way the Working Men's demand for the establishment of a system of public education for the children of workers as well as the rich was designed to promote the classical republican virtue of full, active citizenship; ignorance and dependence being seen as the natural companions of 'aristocratic' or 'monopoly' rule. Finally, the very creation and presence of independent workers' parties constituted an important step towards workers regaining 'a proper standing in the community, and representation in the councils of state'.[15] The Committee of Fifty in New York City observed in its report that, 'we have nothing to hope from the aristocratic orders of society', including the deceiving political parties, and invited those 'who live by their own labor, AND NONE OTHER' to meet to select candidates for the state senate and assembly.[16]

Radical workers attributed exploitation and misery not only to defective political arrangements but also to economic wrongs. There were two key aspects to the economic critique offered. First, Heighton and others argued, in line with the labour theory of value, that capitalism subverted the 'natural order of things' by rewarding not the producers of wealth, manual workers, small masters and farmers, but the 'capitalists' or 'accumulators', merchants, bankers, landlords, speculators, lawyers and the like, who exchanged, distributed and lived off, but did not produce, wealth. Thus, 'those who made the goods and commodities and who were entitled by right to the 'full product of their labor' existed on the edge of subsistence, while those who produced nothing lived in affluence'.[17]

In the unreformed Britain of the pre-1832 Reform Bill the critique outlined in the previous paragraph was directed as much at the representatives of 'Old Corruption' (parasitical elements within the machinery of government and the state, 'taxeaters' and so on) as at merchants, bankers, speculators, landlords and other perceived exploiters within the realms of distribution and exchange. But in the American republic, where 'aristocratic' political influences were far less marked, popular radicals directed their central fire at 'accumulators' in exchange and distribution. Banks and bankers, in particular, met with the fiercest opposition from the Working Men. Banks symbolised 'monopoly' power, wealth and exploitation. As Bridges has observed:

> Of all the inequitable practices grouped under the heading of monopoly and privilege banking was the most pernicious. The attack on banks contained all the elements of workingmen's world view: the importance of governmental 'even-handedness', the evil of failing to produce wealth, and the importance of good character for the future of the republic. Allowed to continue, the paper-money system authorized by the state would create a city of speculators and paupers and a nation of princes and slaves. Banks were pernicious because they did not produce wealth, but only arranged a transfer of the community's wealth to themselves by collecting interest on loans (denounced as unchristian 'usury'), discounting paper, and issuing depreciated or even worthless notes. Banks were a threat to republican liberty because through a heavy national debt they might 'succeed in making us slaves, by grinding us down with taxes'.[18]

In response to such evils workers demanded the abolition of bank notes and the payment of wages in specie (to avoid fluctuations in the value of bank notes). Some of the Working Men's Parties demanded the outright repeal of bank charters, whilst others sought legislation to limit the powers of financial institutions. And a few, as noted by Foner, wanted government control over banking and currency in an effort to ensure financial stability and to safeguard against private monopoly. The climax to general anti-bank agitation was, of course, to come in 1832 when Andrew Jackson vetoed the bill to recharter the 'aristocratic' Bank of the United States.[19]

The second aspect of the economic critique presented by the Working Men lay in the identification of exploitation not only in exchange and distribution but also in the sphere of production. To be sure, a production-based critique was in its infancy during the late 1820s and early 1830s, and was generally overshadowed by the conventional radical critique rooted in the key notion of the 'producing classes'. The latter emphasised the harmony of interests between masters and wage earners within production, and employed the language of 'honest' or 'honourable' 'mechanics', 'producers' or 'workingmen' arrayed against a 'non-productive' 'aristocracy of privilege and corruption'.[20] Yet, as Wilentz has argued, this 'traditional' language of producerism was being applied to a context changed by capitalist development: in the process language often acquired new *meanings* and *motives*.[21] For example, radicals increasingly drew a distinction between honest masters, abiding by the customs of the trade, and dishonest capitalist employers committed, as we observed in Part One, to the new political economy of ceaseless profit maximisation and the treatment of labour power as a mere commodity.

The distinction between honourable masters and dishonourable employers was, as Laurie notes, implicit in Heighton's philosophy:

> Manufacturers who no longer worked with their hands relinquished any claim to producer status, but master craftsmen were excusable and qualified as producers for two reasons: they still performed manual labor and were forced to reckon with 'accumulators more powerful than themselves', who lent capital and extended credit at usurious rates.[22]

Other radicals noted that in some sectors of the economy, especially those transformed by industrial capitalism, small masters were fast diminishing, to be replaced by capitalists consciously 'buying cheap and selling dear'. The Committee of Fifty in New York City was 'united in a belief that rich entrepreneurs were destroying the Republic', alongside more traditional foes.[23] And escalating demands for the right to organise at work, for a legal limit to the working day, and for more co-operative and harmonious means of carrying on production were symptomatic of a growing perception of antagonistic interests between workers and employers.

To posit the growth of a conflict-based mode of thought, rooted in production, is not, however, to lay claim to the development of 'pure' proletarian consciousness. As noted earlier, producerist continuities were very strong. Uneven capitalist development, continued opportunities for upward occupational mobility, the politics of citizenship, and all manner of cultural and racial factors would continue to replenish harmonious ties between some workers and some employers throughout the century. But it is necessary to note important changes occurring beneath and alongside continuities, especially in view of the emphasis in much of the recent historiography of 1830s and 1840s labour upon unchanging consciousness.[24] The Working Men's Parties did not identify exploitative capitalist entrepreneurs as constituting the *dominant* force within production, but they did recognise and were alarmed by their growing presence. Wilentz's comments in relation to New York City nicely capture the intricacies of the situation:

> In its way, the drama of 1829 made clearer than ever before that the ongoing social and ideological conflicts in the trades had begun to resolve into abiding conflicts of class. Of course, the Working Men's movement... was never composed entirely of embittered wage earners... The Free Enquirers and Skidmore, no proletarian socialists, remained proponents of the broad Ricardian distinctions between producer and nonproducer, and not of that between wage earner and employer... But to assess the movement in essentialist terms obscures the most important fact – that 1829 brought an unprecedented social and political convulsion, led by an artisan committee that, whatever its disagreements, was united in a belief that rich entrepreneurs were destroying the Republic. Throughout, there were signs of new departures, of a joining of anticapitalist social radicalism with the incipient class consciousness of the earlier trade unions.[25]

And, as we will see later, the birth of New York City's General Trades' Union in 1833 was to greatly intensify the consciousness of conflict within production and to severely test the harmonious emphases of producerism and shared interpretations of 'republicanism'.

The ideas of the Working Men were both customary and forward-looking in character. As suggested in previous paragraphs, artisans and others set out both to restore republican values, relations and institutions, and to fashion a more democratic, radical and equitable future. The aim was not to overthrow the political-economic order, but to achieve due recognition and support and protection for the interests of labour within a more humane society based upon balance and fairness. 'Our object... strikes at a *fundamental principle* in the distribution of wealth', declared the Working Man's Manual, 'that *labour* shall share with *capital*, in the profits of trade, in a more equitable ratio'.[26] The non-revolutionary pursuit of balance and fairness did not, however, act as a necessary guarantee of stability, harmony and moderation. 'Fairness', 'balance' and 'justice' were very much relative and socially related (that is, ideological) concepts, the pursuit of which could, and did in the 1830s, promote conflict and class more so than harmony and consensus.

Posing a sharp critique of the status quo, the Working Men's Parties did not, however, enjoy long life. As Laurie observes, despite many initial successes the Working Men were 'a meteor in the political sky':

> In Philadelphia they polled well in 1828 and even better in 1829, tripling their initial vote to over 30 percent of the total. They had achieved a balance of power in 1829, but were a spent force by 1831. New York City 'Workies' made an auspicious entry in the 1829 race by capturing a third of the vote for the state assembly and coming within a dozen ballots of sending Skidmore to Albany. No sooner had the cheering stopped than factional discord sundered the fledgling party ... the 1830 race saw three pretenders to the Working Men's colors, each stronger in conviction than popularity. The 1832 race ... ended the role of the Working Men. Luther's New England Association, which entered the Massachusetts gubernatorial contests in 1833 and 1834, never collected more than 5 percent of the vote statewide and did best in rural towns.[27]

In Dudley, Oxford and Webster, for example, the Working Men's Party polled a remarkable 21.4 per cent of the aggregate vote in 1834, and generally fared well among yeomen farmers and artisans, but this support soon faded away.[28] In radical Lynn a slate of Working Men's candidates for town office achieved no success in 1836. And many rural and small-town organisations were, 'labor parties in name only, shadowy groups hastily patched together on the eve of elections and in disarray after a single campaign'.[29]

Poor organisation, internal divisions, the disruptive activities of opportunistic interlopers, adverse propaganda and the increasingly successful co-optive strategies of the Democrats (especially) and the Whigs led to the rapid decline of the Working Men's Parties. In New York City, for example, there was a clear distinction between the Working Men's movement, dominated by militant journeymen, and the Working Men's Party, born in December 1829, 'out of a marriage of convenience between the nonagrarian radicals and a group of craft entrepreneurs friendly to Henry Clay'.[30] The party was, in fact, less an extension of the Working Men's movement than, 'an invention of the Owenites and Cookites, one that assumed the name of the Working Men in a political coup that stunned and isolated Skidmore and effectively killed off what had been a radical political insurgency'. Such splits and faction-fighting, combined with the growth of a more effective appeal on the part of Democrats and Whigs to workers precluded, in New York City, 'the rise of anything like the Working Men's movement for twenty years'. In Philadelphia and elsewhere the Working Men were branded 'infidels' and 'Jacobins'. Blacklisting of radicals by employers constituted a real threat. And Philadelphia's Democrats pursued an increasingly successful co-optive strategy which climaxed in the 'Bank War' of 1832, but which had its origins in attempts to undermine the appeal of the Working Men. 'In the late 1820s', notes Laurie,' city Democrats appropriated the language of radicalism and advocated debtor relief, militia reform, and other measures borrowed from the Working Men's platforms'.[31] Finally, in many rural and small-town areas labour parties were, in effect, captured or originally headed by, 'opportunists in search of constituencies, or entrepreneurs playing at politics or using Working Men's podiums to launch political careers'.[32]

The Equal Rights Agitation

The demise of the Working Men dealt a severe, if not fatal blow to the cause of independent radical politics. In the mid 1830s a series of adverse legal decisions, culminating in the guilty verdict recorded against members of the Union Society of Journeymen Tailors in New York in 1836 (on charges of 'conspiracy to injure trade, riot, assault, battery')[33] sparked off a movement in favour of independent political action. The meeting called in New York City to protest against the conspiracy verdict attracted almost 30,000 people, including leading figures in the labour movement and a strong working-class presence. Judge Edwards' decision was declared 'manifestly partial and unjust', part of, 'a concerted plan of the aristocracy to take from them that Liberty which was bequeathed to them'. And since there was a 'close alliance between the leaders of the two great political parties of this state, to crush the labouring men', it was resolved to call a convention in order to discuss the possible formation of 'a separate and distinct party around which the laboring classes and their friends can rally with confidence'.[34] True to its official non-partisan political stance, the General Trades' Union of New York was not formally represented at the ensuing convention. But leading figures in the labour movement did play a prominent role. They were joined by activists from the Locofoco Party, the latter composed of Radical, anti-banking Democrats who had broken with Tammany Hall in 1835. The convention voted to form a new party and chose the name Equal Rights Party. The latter spread beyond New York, ran tickets and candidates in a number of elections, and compelled the regular Democrats and the Whigs to pay greater heed to the needs of workers and small masters. However, the depression of 1837 and the mounting concessions granted by the established parties ensured that the Equal Rights insurgency did not effectively survive the decade.[35]

Despite its undoubted appeal, the Equal Rights movement should not be interpreted as a re-creation of the Working Men's Parties. The former lacked the depth of working-class support enjoyed by the latter. In 1836 workers in New York and elsewhere did display their displeasure at the anti-labour activities of the courts and the political parties by embracing the notion of political independence. But, as was to prove so often the case in the history of nineteenth-century American labour, independent labour politics were characterised by both their frequent adoption and their equally shortlived existence. As we will observe on many occasions in the course of this study, the American political system, if not its major employers, proved to be far more adept at defusing radical, independent insurgencies than its counterpart in Britain. In the United States the votes of the working men constituted important means to the attainment of power: potential competitors, especially if radical and 'subversive', were to be defeated. Hence by 1837, as in the early 1830s, the processes of co-optation and concession had been brought into play. As Bridges has observed in relation to New York, labour's radical spokesmen of the 1830s increasingly achieved personal success and power as labour's spokesmen *within* the Democratic Party (an experience which was duplicated throughout the country); and, 'Tammany rhetoric had a considerably more radical ring to if after the Locofoco revolt'. Thus Radical Democrats, 'spoke of conspiracies and the political ascendancy of the rich, and workingmen agreed that this was a pernicious situation'.[36] More concretely, Martin Van Buren, as president, proposed in 1837 to establish a treasury system independent of the banking interests, and in 1840 introduced the ten-hour day for federal employees on public works.

Two further factors contributed to the evanescent character of independent radical politics during the mid 1830s. First, workers' outrage at the conspiracy verdict recorded against the tailors was considerably softened by the acquittal of journeymen cordwainers in upstate Hudson (on conspiracy charges) only days after the mass protest meeting in New York City. The Hudson verdict offered renewed hope in the 'honest' and 'equitable' structures of the Republic. Second, and despite genuine labour activist involvement, the Equal Rights movement was dominated by Locofocos. And the Locofocos were, in effect, radical Democrats temporarily preaching the virtues of independence. Their brief insurgency of 1835 and 1836 was quickly followed by a return to Tammany Hall. The upshot, as observed by Wilentz, was that 'the union journeymen remained without their party of labor'.[37]

Attempts to form a party of labour were conspicuous by their scarcity during the early–mid 1840s. But the reader's attention can usefully be drawn to two experiments in independent politics: at Cincinnati in the early 1840s; and among the Anti-Rent campaigners of upstate New York in the middle years of the decade.

Cincinnati: Independent Labour

Deteriorations in living standards, conditions at work and in their independence pushed Cincinnati's artisans in the direction of independent politics.[38] Reliance upon trade unions and strikes had constituted the most common means for remedying economic and social grievances during the 1830s. But the depression of the late 1830s and early 1840s undermined the effectiveness of industrial action, and a number of artisans and masters sought salvation in politics. In the autumn of 1841 the Working Men's Association resolved to offset 'the seizure and corruption of the legislature by nonproducers and corrupt politicians', and 'reinstitute justice' by creating a party which would 'unite the roles and needs of producer and citizen'. The deepening economic crisis, physical assaults against the banks (as seen in the Bank Riots of January 1842), the seeming indifference of the established parties to the workers' plight and government corruption, led to widespread support for Cincinnati's Working Men's Party in the early months of 1842.

The party performed well in April's municipal elections, electing a dozen of its candidates to office. But, as in so many other cases, success at the polls contained the seeds of decline. Above all, the established parties were stung into action. Ross's verdict is apposite:

> Setting a pattern that would haunt third-party efforts for the rest of the century, Democrats and Whigs quickly moved to co-opt the WMP's more moderate leaders and programs into their own organizations ... victorious WMP's candidates such as Mark Taylor and David Snellbaker, both former officers in the defunct Coopers' Union and the General Trades Union, were quickly enticed into leaving the workers' party and the union movement in favor of political careers with one of the major parties. Whigs and Democrats, playing upon the rhetoric workers had used to defend their party and earlier unions, insisted that no further permanent political action need be taken by workers. The producing classes had received their measure of justice; any further actions by the WMP would inflame rather than ameliorate conflict. By the spring of 1843, as flush economic times returned and other party leaders followed the path of Snellbaker and Taylor – both of whom went on to become mayors in the 1850s – the WMP was but a memory.[39]

The Anti-Rent Movement

In the very different context of rural upstate New York the failure of the existing parties to effectively support the 'fair rents' campaign of the tenant farmers, the perceived corruption of mainstream politicians, the close personal and financial ties between many politicians and landlords, and defeat of the anti-rent legislative agenda of 1844 led many of the anti-renters to adopt a strategy of independent politics. During 1844 and 1845 the anti-renters, often with National Reformers to the fore, nominated their own slates in town elections. And in county, state and national elections they adopted a non-partisan approach, offering support to those candidates of the major parties most sympathetic to their cause. As noted by Huston, the anti-renters widely adopted the language of radical republicanism:

> In their more euphoric moments, the anti-renters claimed that their independent political efforts would purify politics and save the republic. By electing patriotic men who were responsive to their constituents, they believed that they could end the plague of office-seeking and the political influence of 'aristocrats', restore the reign of equality before the law, and usher in a new age of prosperity, freedom and 'equal chances'.[40]

The results of the anti-renters' independent political strategy were mixed. At a local level impressive achievements were recorded. Huston informs us that in the manor towns of the six counties the Democrats and Whigs were 'swept from power, their organizations thrown into complete disarray'. However, support within the state legislature was insufficiently large to enact any of their demands before 1846. In effect the leadership and ultimate fate of the anti-rent movement increasingly passed into the hands of Whigs and Democrats. Thomas Devyr's revolt against Whig and Democratic control in 1845 and his attempt to steer a more independent political course met with defeat. Devyr and his supporters subsequently left the movement to form the Free Soil Party, a coalition of Anti-Renters, National Reformers and Abolitionists.

By the 1840s exercises in independent politics were rare. And by mid century the independent politics of class were increasingly subordinate to the politics of Democratic and Whig partisanship rooted in ethnicity, race and free labour.

Trade unionism and the General Trades' Union Movement

·During the late eighteenth century and early nineteenth century American artisans in a number of northern urban areas demonstrated 'a new collective identity'. This growing identity of interests was increasingly reflected in the formation of journeymen's societies, in perceived conflicts of interest between employers and workers and in quickened industrial conflict.[41] As we have seen, many artisans in the late 1820s turned to politics in order to remedy their economic and social ills. But, disillusioned by the failures and faction-fighting of third party politics, artisans and others transferred their allegiances, from 1833 onwards, to non-partisan trade unionism. Up to the 1837 depression trade unionism, and especially the General Trades' Unions of the workers, dominated the emerging labour movement and constituted 'a central, transforming event in the history of American class relations'.[42]

Rapid price inflation and worsening living standards, combined with the mushrooming of 'dishonourable' practices on the part of employers, formed the backcloth to the upsurge in trade unionism. In 1833 journeymen in New York and Baltimore rallied to provide financial and moral support to striking hatters and carpenters. Following the extremely bitter carpenters' strike for higher wages, nine trades organised, in 1833, the General Trades' Union of the City of New York. 'Over the next four years', notes Wilentz,' the GTU led a series of offensives that saw New York wage earners organize over fifty unions and nearly forty strikes'.[43] Similar confederations of workers developed in Philadelphia, Boston, Baltimore, Washington, Louisville, Cincinnati and other trans-Allegheny cities. 'By the end of 1834', records Laurie, 'over a dozen urban centres had general unions'.[44]

The years between 1835 and 1837 witnessed a massive increase in trade-union membership in general, a further rise in the fortunes of the General Trades' Unions, and, especially in 1835 and 1836, 'an explosion of strikes that would not be duplicated until the labor turbulence on the railroads in 1877'.[45] By 1835 the largest federation of workers, the General Trades' Union of Philadelphia, had fifty-three locals. The federation in New York, the second largest, encompassed nine trades in 1833: a year later a further twenty trades had organised and 11,500 men had joined the New York unions and those in Brooklyn – 'somewhere between 20 and 30 per cent of Manhattan's entire white male workforce, skilled and unskilled combined'. By 1836 it was estimated that in excess of two-thirds of workingmen in New York City had joined unions. Observing that the proportion of American workers in trade unions was probably never much more than 15 per cent before 1900, Wilentz can thus conclude that, 'the percentage of New York craft workers who enrolled in the unions in the 1830s was among the highest at any time in the nineteenth century'.[46]

Beyond New York and Philadelphia substantial, if less spectacular, gains were recorded. 'Following the lead of workers in Philadelphia, Baltimore, New York, Washington and Boston', writes Ross, 'fourteen trade unions representing over 700 journeymen' founded Cincinnati's first General Trades' Union in 1836. With artisans to the fore, Cincinnati's General Trades' Union, 'pledged to struggle as loyal "citizens of the republic" to restore the artisan to his rightful position and to prevent the "murderous course that has been pursued towards the working classes in other countries" from happening in the United States'. The

GTU organised a city-wide strike fund to support 'honourable artisans attempting to resist the incursions of corrupt masters', and sent officers to the National Trades Union convention in Philadelphia in 1836.[47] Buffalo and other frontier towns, along with New England, also witnessed considerable trade union growth. And Laurie estimates that in overall terms between one-fifth and one-third of urban journeymen belonged to the unions of the 1830s, 'the highest [fraction] in antebellum history'.[48]

The strike wave of the mid 1830s both embraced and extended beyond members of the General Trades' Unions. The demand for the ten-hour day, a central factor in the rise of the Working Men, lay at the heart of worker militancy. Ten-hour feeling was particularly intense in Boston where two unsuccessful strikes in favour of the reduced working day had been undertaken by construction workers in 1825 and 1830. In 1835 the Boston journeymen, backed by the city's General Trades' Union, once again took up the ten-hour demand. Seth Luther's 'Ten Hour Circular', arguing that the ten-hour day was vital to the independence and other prerequisites of republican citizenship, had an electrifying effect upon workers not only in Boston but also in the West and the length of the northeastern seaboard. Most famous was the Philadelphia general strike of May and June 1835. 'It began inauspiciously in late May', writes Laurie:

> when the coal heavers on the Schuylkill docks left their jobs in protest against long hours. Parading through the city on June 3, they caught the eye of cordwainers peering through workshop windows. The cordwainers threw down their awls and rushed to join the procession, shouting 'We are all day laborers'. The mushrooming line of march attracted carpenters and other tradesmen in quick succession and precipitated spontaneous rallies of artisans throughout the city. Smiths, leather dressers, plumbers, painters, and cigar makers among others voted to standout by the end of the week. The republic's first general strike was on; and general it was.[49]

Laurie estimates that possibly as many as 20,000 of Philadelphia's workers, including textile operatives and outworkers, participated in walkouts. All were successful, although the city's millhands had to be temporarily content with the achievement of an eleven-hour day. Beyond Philadelphia journeymen enjoyed similar successes in their ten-hour struggles. Ironically workers in Boston, initiators of the movement, experienced defeat.

Women, Industrial Conflict and the Constituency of Trade Unionism

The general strike movement involved women as well as men. In Philadelphia, Paterson and New England women textile workers were prominent. Such action was part of a broader movement of female militancy. 'By 1834', notes Stansell:

> 'Lynn women shoe binders, Baltimore seamstresses and Lowell factory girls had all organized; Philadelphia shoe binders and women and child cotton spinners would soon do so. New York workingwomen – umbrella makers, seamstresses, shoe binders, and bookbinders – were especially prominent in the activity.'[50]

On some occasions – the 1835 strike of female bookbinders in New York City, the women shoebinders strike in Lynn in 1833–4, and among Philadelphia's textile and shoe-binding workers in 1834 and 1836 – male trade unionists actively co-operated with striking women. On the occasion of the 1836 Philadelphia shoe binders' dispute strong bonds of mutuality were in evidence: women shoe binders 'turned out to join striking men and the men pledged to "flourish or sink" with their sisters'. But such support and co-operation were infrequent. Organised women did tend to receive help from men in those trades in which (such as shoemaking) there existed a strong tradition of family-based work, a clear division of labour which protected men from female competition, and in which women performed subsidiary and less well-paid tasks. However, in those occupations in which the threat of open competition was present men generally reacted with hostility to women.

Christine Stansell does not, however, view the 'old language of sexual antagonism' as characteristic of the males of the General Trades' Unions.[51] The increasingly class-based militancy of the mid 1830s involved, as in Britain, a widening of workers' horizons, the retreat of narrowly exclusive and 'aristocratic' sentiments, and the adoption of more generous, inclusive practices. But the latter, especially in relation to trade unionism, did have their limits.

Such limits can clearly be perceived in relation to gender. Stansell has described the attitudes and behaviour of the males who monopolised the trade-union movement as 'radical paternalist' in character, as the exercise of 'benign authority' on the part of 'republican patriarch(s)'. These male trade unionists valued rather than scorned women's labour: but it was labour to be performed within the household. The practice of the 'family wage' and the retreat of married women into the home would, in the eyes of these men, spare women the indignities of waged labour and restore 'natural' male–female relationships by enabling wives to practice 'virtuous maternity' and men to 'resume their places as their natural protectors'. Stansell thus observes that the republic of the General Trades' Unions was, in essence, a republic of men in which women would figure as home-makers and caring supporters rather than as independent equals practising mutual support and dependency. In sum, prevented by 'the natural weakness of their sex' from truly independent and 'manly' action, women were to be exhorted to abandon the rough-and-tumble world of 'work' to men. Most pointedly, neither individual craft unions nor the confederations of the General Trades' Unions admitted women to membership.

Stansell's conclusions are most apt:

> Certainly the unionists' pronouncements left behind, in most respects, the old language of open sexual antagonism. To assume responsibility for women's economic situation was also to repudiate a frank hostility toward women – shared with men of other classes – in favor of a respect rooted in a common working-class experience. In place of the derision for women as nags and bawds, the N[ational] T[rades'] U[nion] voiced an attitude of care and an unprecedented acknowledgement of the importance of women's domestic labor. Rather than stressing the intrusion of wage-earning women into a male collectivity of craft, the journeymen redrew the boundaries of class to include women, recognizing women's exploitation at the hands of their employers and emphasizing the interdependence of the sexes. The assumption of benevolence at least allowed the men to posit one role for women in the labor movement – as members of an auxiliary of equal rights, valued for their role in their households. It blinded them, however, to the alternative possibility: that women might organize themselves along with men.[52]

As we will observe throughout this study, the harsh realities of working-class life often flew in the face of the 'ideal' of female domesticity. Poverty and insecurity compelled women to work for meagre wages. And, as noted in Part One, when employed in collective and mainly sex-segregated ways women often demonstrated a capacity for collective action which owed little or nothing to the protection and guidance of men. In 1834, for example, the female textile operatives of Lowell went on strike against a reduction in wages. Two years later management's decision to raise the price of room and board in company boardinghouses triggered off a second Lowell strike.

The latter action formed part of a more general strike wave in 1836. The general strikes of 1835 had greatly increased the appeal of trade unionism. 'Established unions overflowed with new members', writes Laurie, 'poor immigrants as well as some evangelicals, and locals took the first steps toward coordinating activities between cities.'[53] In 1836 there were frequent and widespread strikes for wage advances. In Philadelphia, for example, where the General Trades' Union had grown into the formidable representative of more than fifty unions and over 10,000 wage earners, handloom weavers, tailors, bookbinders and many others undertook strike action and received generous support from other workers. And, as Wilentz declares, 'If 1834 was New York's year of the riots, 1836 was the year of the strikes: ten major turnouts hit the skilled trades, and convulsive strikes took place on the waterfront and building sites'.[54] Employers' societies responded by vowing to 'bust strikes and destroy unions'. And the pro-employer interventions of the police and the courts, especially in New York, served to exacerbate the situation. The crisis continued throughout the autumn and early winter of 1836–7. Memories of the conspiracy verdict passed against the New York tailors in late March were still strong, the General Trades' Unions continued to expand, and industrial conflict refused to disappear. 'There was every indication', writes Wilentz, 'that the crisis of 1836 would lead to renewed and even wider conflict in 1837'. This was not, however, to be the case. The economic depression of the early summer of 1837 was to persist for some five years. And in the process trade unionism and radicalism were to be undermined: workers increasingly turned to personal rather than collective means of survival.

We can now step back from the dramatic chronology of the General Trades' Union and strike upsurge to offer a few observations concerning the character and aims of the union movement. In the first place, we cannot help but be impressed by the vitality, depth of support and organisation of the movement. The General Trades' Unions, confederations of trade unions in specific locations rather than (as in the British case) unions of workers scattered across different industries and occupations, were a testimony to the sound and democratic organisational principles of labour activists. The main body of the General Trades' Unions (all of which were similar in structure) was the convention consisting of delegates elected by member unions on a proportionate basis. Monthly meetings of the convention conducted debate and made policy, elected GTU officers and a finance committee. Officers served for a year or six months. Operating costs were raised by means of monthly dues paid by the represented trades, supplemented by a monthly per capita payment by each journeyman. Emergency levies and voluntary contributions also helped to finance the General Trades' Unions in their central goals to assist unions on strike and to support newspapers, libraries and lyceums along with guest lecturers. By no means immune from internal debate and disagreements, the General Trades' Unions nevertheless offered a sound example of institutional democracy and discipline, 'a modus operandi far more democratic than that of virtually any other reform group or any political party'.[55]

As in the earlier Working Men's movement, the trade-union movement attracted many able and eloquent leaders. Seth Luther, the leading figure in New England, was a textile operative-turned-carpenter. John Commerford, president of New York City's GTU in 1835, was a journeyman cabinetmaker, 'destined to be a leading figure on the New York radical scene for decades to come'. Also prominent in New York was John Windt, rationalist and printer who became a small printing shop owner. And in Philadelphia John Ferral of the weavers, Benjamin Sewell, the tanner, William Thompson, the carpenter, William English, William Gilmore and Samuel Thompson, all shoemakers, and Edward Penniman and Joshua Fletcher of the coachmakers demonstrated impressive organisational abilities and forceful oratorical skills.[56]

Class and Ideology

Such men were, above all, able to mobilise the support of large numbers of workers from varied occupations and cultures. Schooled in earlier trade-union struggles and radical politics, they preached the increasingly popular message that the key to economic and social advancement lay in labour unity, especially around the common fact of wage earning. Artisans, especially those feeling the full effects of the 'bastardisation' of their crafts, were at the forefront of trade unionism. But a most impressive aspect of the General Trades' Union movement lay in the attempts of such artisans to embrace competitors in the labour market in the common cause of trade unionism. In New York City, for example, the bakers 'claimed to have enlisted every journeyman in the city trade'; and unions of the beleaguered tailors, shoemakers, cabinetmakers and saddlers 'embraced pieceworkers and sweated journeymen, heard their complaints, and fought on their behalf'. In Philadelphia and elsewhere, outworking handloom weavers, factory operatives and skilled craftsmen were caught up in the union movement, and offered mutual support and encouragement.[57]

There were important limits to occupational solidarity. We have earlier noted that, despite limited support for women's industrial action, male trade unionists did not allow women into their unions. And, as Laurie observes, labour unity did not extend to black workers ('There is no evidence of radicals endorsing the rights of Blacks, either as workers or as citizens').[58] Despite these major limitations, and the tendency of some of the most privileged and secure trades to remain aloof from the movement (such as the butchers and some of the skilled maritime trades in New York City and elsewhere), the trade union upsurge of the mid 1830s marked a qualitative and massive leap in terms of occupational solidarity.

The most dramatic manifestation of solidarity took place in Philadelphia in 1835 and 1836. Not only was the Quaker City's general strike triggered off by the actions of dock labourers, but in the following year artisans and others cast off their prejudices against the unskilled, rushed to the defence of imprisoned dockers and voted to admit them into the General Trades' Union. 'By embracing the laborers', notes Laurie, 'Philadelphia artisans became the first skilled workmen to join with the unskilled in the same union'. Elsewhere the unskilled were excluded from the General Trades' Unions. But unions generally had greatly expanded beyond bases in 'aristocratic' or sweated trades. And, whilst by no means eliminated, the divisions between male craft workers and the unskilled did narrow in New York City and other places during the course of the workers' revolt.[59]

Greatly enhanced occupational solidarity was accompanied by a marked weakening of cultural divisions. Laurie and Wilentz, for example, have conclusively demonstrated that the trade union explosion of 1835 and 1836 attracted large numbers of new recruits, 'most of whom were strangers to trade unionism', many of whom were recent immigrants, and whose numbers included workers pursuing a variety of life-styles ('traditionalist' and abstemious, secularist and revivalist and so on).[60]

Of fundamental importance was the overshadowing of ethnic divisions and conflicts by a common allegiance to class. Throughout the North and West radical leaders were quick to denounce the divisive intentions of nativists and racists, and were strong supporters of abolition and ethnic harmony. For example, in Philadelphia John Ferral countered the nativist slogans and anti-Catholic insults of Whiggish politicians by convening a meeting of Irish Americans, 'without regard to religion'. Ferral appealed to his audience to 'recall their past experiences in Ireland', where 'aristocracy' exploited religious hatred in order to 'keep the honest and industrious population divided, rendering them ... an easy prey to their enemies'. Significantly, the mixed Irish Catholic and Irish Protestant working-class areas of Philadelphia supplied plentiful recruits to the trade-union movement, resisted ethnic conflict, and 'returned solid Democratic majorities during the thirties'.[61]

Divisions were more in evidence in New York. There were racist and anti-abolitionist riots in the city in 1834 among crowds largely made up of small masters, artisans and journeymen. And whilst anti-Irish Catholic nativism was less pronounced than it would become during the 1840s, nevertheless the mid and late 1830s (especially the post-1837 years) did witness an escalation of ethnic conflict. Conversely, trade-union leaders and the GTU press in New York actively campaigned against nativist attempts to 'glut their vindictiveness against the common people, by arraying the native-born laborer against his fellow being'.

And such campaigning met with a large measure of success. Although native-born journeymen dominated the GTU's hierarchy in New York, large numbers of immigrants of varied beliefs were active and welcome participants in the trade-union cause.[62] For a time at least, intergenerational, economic, ethnic and wider cultural allegiances interacted harmoniously to produce a class awareness which outweighed potential and actual ethnic divisions. This pattern was repeated in all the main centres of General Trades' Union strength.

Many elements were present in the ideology of the General Trades' Unions. There were, first of all, the emphases upon revolutionary republicanism, equity, balance, protection and due reward for labour already discussed in relation to the Working Men's Parties. 'Producerism' was also present. But, as a number of recent historians have observed, the trade-union movement of the mid 1830s stretched and, on an increasing number of occasions, moved beyond producerist arguments, to adopt a more incisive and extensive attack upon employer exploitation in production and to posit a growing and *structured* conflict of interests between workers and employers.

Laurie, for example, has highlighted the autonomous and independent nature of trade unionism, its assumption of a separate (and increasingly antagonistic) set of interests between employers and workers. In the context of the mid 1830s, suggests Laurie, perceptions and practices of conflict did mushroom. And the new worker autonomy 'fostered an upsurge of militancy on the job and then instigated a search for options to capitalist institutions that transcended anything political radicalism had to offer'.[63]

Sean Wilentz has pushed the anti-capitalist theme even further. Wilentz notes that an emphasis upon 'the virtuous producing classes' remained 'an important feature' of the New York trade unionists throughout the 1830s. But, concrete events, and especially the experience of economic conflict, moved workers into anti-capitalist directions. Thus:

> as the union men and the rank and file probed the questions raised by the Bank War and their own strikes, analyses of the peculiar problems of wage earners appeared with increasing regularity in union broadsides, speeches, and public appeals.[64]

In an address to New York's GTU in 1833 John Finch claimed that 'the battle loomed not simply between producers and nonproducers but between masters and men'. According to Finch, 'the *employer* was rapidly running the road to wealth [while] the *employed* was too often the victim of poverty and oppression, bound to the vassalage of inadequate reward for his labor'. Other trade-union leaders maintained that 'the concerted interests of the masters' and not 'an impartial law of supply and demand' prevented wages from rising during periods of high prices and labour scarcity. And, notes Wilentz, to John Commerford, 'the enemy was plainly "capital" – a class of men *including* exploiting masters who with "deep and matured design" so controlled society that they could reward themselves by virtually "filching from labor" '.[65]

The examples of an intensified wage-earning and conflict-orientated consciousness outlined above could be multiplied several times over. Claiming their labour as their *own* property, and asserting their right, as wage earners, to regulate the value of their property, the organised workers of New York City thus, 'turned the most fundamental of entrepreneurial ideas – the very notion of labor as a commodity – on its head and threw it back at their employers'. Thus Wilentz:

> If property was indeed sacred, they reasoned, then their masters were guilty of theft, for their exploitation and plunder of their employees' labor. Under existing property relations, an inalterable antagonism between masters and journeymen was inevitable; everything favorable to the property rights of employers could be expected to be oppressive to the property rights of workers. Faith in a natural, self-adjusting market in labor and products was absurd in a world of selfish competition, a world of capitalist robbery, a world where arrogant masters could be expected 'to *coerce* the independent spirited men who [take] upon themselves the unquestionable right of affixing a value to their own labor'.[66]

Wilentz's conclusions are twofold. First, he claims that the New York workers' 'fusion of anticapitalist "producerism" and the analysis of workshop exploitation' was, 'as profound a critique of early industrial capitalism as any that appeared among the craft workers' movements of Britain and France in the 1830s'. And second, that New York's trade unionists came to see the 'dishonourable' or 'offending' employers less as selfish or corrupt individuals, but rather as an exploiting *class*.[67]

Wilentz's excellent depiction of the consciousness of New York's trade unionists has greatly enriched our understanding of the intellectual history of American workers during the 1830s. But it is debatable as to whether the anti-capitalist consciousness of New York existed with sufficient *depth* throughout the northern and western states to enable us to speak of the widespread *maturation* of anti-capitalist working-class consciousness. We may usefully record a single complicating case. Ross has strongly argued that in 1830s Cincinnati, where the process of capitalist transformation of the work-place was less advanced and extensive than in New York City, workers did embrace trade unionism and some of them did identify employers as enemies. But, generally speaking, Cincinnati's masters were still regarded as 'honourable'. There was a (growing) number of 'dishonourable' employers, but they did not, at least in the 1830s, constitute, in the eyes of Cincinnati's workers, a dominant class or system. Rather they were perceived as wayward individuals or 'bad apples' in a fundamentally sound producerist system of relationships.[68]

We will return in more detail to such questions following our discussion of the ideology of British workers in the 1830s and 1840s. For the moment we can, however, note the undoubted existence and, in all probability, growing influence of non-socialist, class-based ideas among American workers in the 1830s. 'During the 1830s', concludes David Montgomery:

> all groups of Philadelphia workmen – Protestant and Catholic, native and immigrant, superior craftsmen, outworkers, factory operatives and laborers – had been caught up in an awakening of class solidarity as significant as any in American history.[69]

Less intense beyond Philadelphia, that awakening had, nevertheless, embraced the constituencies, ideas and independent spirits of class in countless towns and villages. Between 1833 and 1836 class expressed itself primarily in trade unionism. But during 1836 and 1837 a growing number of workers sought a 'permanent solution' for their grievances in the transforming powers of co-operative production. The latter, a means towards social equality and worker control rather than self-helping capitalist status, was, however, dealt a severe blow by the 1837 depression.[70]

Labour and the Mainstream Parties

In keeping with the independent spirit of the mid 1830s, and to reinforce the common *economic* tie of workers to wage labour, the General Trades' Unions prohibited discussion of the potentially divisive issues of religion and politics. But outside the union hall working-class activists were steeped in politics. As we have already seen, many of them had played important roles in the Working Men's Parties of the late 1820s and early 1830s. At that point in time both the Democrats and Whigs were perceived to be more sympathetic to the claims of bankers, financiers and merchants than to the demands and grievances of workers. Unions and their supporters were denounced as either 'plunderers' (by the Whigs) or 'monopolists' (by the Democrats), intent upon subverting the 'natural' laws of supply and demand and individual freedom of contract. And both Democrats and Whigs rallied to the causes of self-help and mobility ('free labor') as the effective antidote to class and class-based institutions.[71] However, the very rise of the Working Men occasioned quickened accommodation on the part of the mainstream parties to the interests of labour, a process further hastened by Jackson's anti-Bank crusade. Non-partisanship was the political keyword of the General Trades' Unions. But the collapse of the union movement resulted in intensified and more open involvement in mainstream politics on the part of labour's radicals. The Democrats were the main beneficiaries, but in some places the Whigs also inherited Working Men's leaders and supporters.

Political developments in Philadelphia and New York City illustrate the general trends outlined above. Following the failure of the Working Men's Party most of the trade unionists in Philadelphia supported the Democratic Party. The latter moved leftwards in the early 1830s and, despite its heterogeneous constituency and differing appeals at the national level (to Southern planters, to poor native-born and immigrant workers, and to aspiring professionals and merchants), presented itself as the party of the 'common man'. 'Equal rights for all, and special privileges for none', opposition to 'the hydra-headed monster of banking, corporate charters, and easy credit', the denunciation of tariffs and forms of 'class legislation', and support for free public education, the abolition of militia duty and imprisonment for debt, and for less government, cultural pluralism and religious freedom and toleration (as opposed to the prohibitionist and evangelical sentiments of the Whigs) – these were the central appeals of the Democrats to labour activists.[72]

The Democratic Party of the 1830s was not, however, united in relation to such issues. Two factions, radicals and regulars, emerged. And the pro-state banks and easy credit policies of the party regulars, and their lukewarm or hostile attitudes to debtor relief and other issues close to the hearts of working people, ensured that tensions and ruptures (as seen in the Locofoco and Equal Rights movements) would punctuate relations between radical workers and the party. Much depended upon the balance of forces within the Democracy at the local level.

As Laurie has clearly demonstrated, in suburban Philadelphia, birthplace of the workingmen's movement, the balance was increasingly right. Thus:

> radical Democrats of middle-class status eagerly courted working-class voters. They gave their blessing to the ten-hour day, public ownership of granaries and coal yards, and other popular measures, and carved out a niche for radicals in their party. Working-class leaders, in turn, took advantage of the party's openness. Joshua Fletcher, William Thompson, Israel Young, and John Ferral, for instance, headed ward committees and canvassed voters in elections; Young and Ferral ran successfully for borough offices in Moyamensing and Southwark; William English, Edward Penniman, and leaders of local unions entered the state legislature in the late 1830s.[73]

In the era of Philadelphia's General Trades' Union the radical trade-union leaders managed to keep separate their political and trade-union commitments. But, 'divested of their trade-union functions by the panic and depression', the leaders 'pitched into party work' during the late 1830s and throughout the 1840s. Many were rewarded by the attainment of elective and appointed office. But, concludes Laurie, the final irony lay in the fact that, 'while the Democracy drained off the cream of radical working-class leadership, it resisted their ideas'. However influential in some parts of Philadelphia, radical influence was not great within the city's party as a whole. And by the early–mid 1840s the politics of radicalism had been overtaken by the divisions of ethnicity, religion and culture.[74]

New York City also witnessed, especially after the failure of the Equal Rights revolt of 1836, increased attachment of workers to the Democratic cause. As we will see later, by the 1850s the Democratic Party in New York had created a mass base around its language of militant workerism and its appeal to a culturally robust and ethnically diverse, yet increasingly racist constituency. However, as Amy Bridges has usefully reminded us, by no means all working-class radicals of the 1830s were incorporated into the Democratic Party.[75] The Whig Party, committed to free will, upward social mobility on the basis of character and determination, temperance, evangelical religion, the 'American system' of protective tariffs, internal improvements and sound banking, and to the mutually harmonious interests of workers and employers, also attracted, if less strongly than the Democrats, the support of former Working Men and trade-union radicals in New York City. It was, above all, Whig emphasis upon the mutualism of the trade, as opposed to the Democrats increasingly strident 'workerism', which found favour among the more 'aristocratic' and less threatened trades (such as butchering and carpentry). Beyond New York the Whigs' insistence upon the mutually beneficial effects of a high tariff upon the interests of workers and employers exerted, alongside the ethnocultural issues of sobriety and self-help, considerable popular appeal.[76]

The Depression, 1837–42

Scattered references have already been made to the massively debilitating effects of the depression, beginning in 1837, upon 1830s labour radicalism. It is now time to pull together those references. By June 1837 the American economy, dangerously fuelled by the speculative mania of the mid 1830s, had collapsed. Unemployment mushroomed, wages plummeted and the trade-union movement was effectively destroyed. A few union militants did attempt to regroup in the late 1830s, and in

Philadelphia and elsewhere bitter, if scattered, strikes continued into the early 1840s. But trade unionism generally failed to survive the five-year depression. More generally, radicalism, as a potent force within the working class, lost its erstwhile importance. By the early 1840s most American workers sought salvation not in the field of collective radicalism but through the personal channels of religion and temperance. And the massive expansion of immigration, especially from Ireland and Germany, in the post-depression years, provided a context in which the politics of ethnic conflict and nativism increasingly operated at the expense of the more class-based practices of the 1830s. In sum, and whilst not positing any *necessary* conflict between, on the one hand, ethnicity and religion and, on the other, class, there is no doubt that fragmentation was the main feature of American working-class life during the 1840s and 1850s. Democrats and Whigs consolidated their hold upon working-class voters and supporters at the expense of independent politics: class was forced into retreat.

We will return to the theme of fragmentation in the second half of Part Two. The purposes of the next section are to identify the main characteristics of working-class movements in Britain during the second quarter of the century, and to evaluate the respective experiences and movements of workers in Britain and the United States up to the mid 1840s. Particular attention will be paid to our key themes of class and exceptionalism.

BRITAIN

According to E. P. Thompson, it is possible, by the end of the 1820s, to 'speak in a new way of the working people's consciousness of their interests and of their predicament as a class'. Various interrelated areas of struggle – around the vote, trade-union recognition and rights, customary controls and practices at work, the battle for a cheap radical press, and around wider cultural concerns with independence, self-respect and citizenship – had forged a consciousness of conflict 'between the loosely defined "industrious classes" on the one hand, and the unreformed House of Commons on the other'. 'From 1830 onwards', continues Thompson, 'a more clearly defined class consciousness, in the customary Marxist sense, was maturing, in which working people were aware of continuing both old and new battles on their own'.[77] Two periods – that between 1829 and 1834 and the Chartist years from the mid–late 1830s (the main Chartist organ, the *Northern Star*, was founded in November 1837; and the People's Charter was published in May 1838) to the late 1840s – were crucial to the overall development and mature expression of this consciousness. It is, accordingly, with the events of these two periods that we must now concern ourselves.

1829–34, Political Crisis, Economic and Social Conflict

In noting the 'special character' of the years between 1829 and 1834, John Rule draws our attention to 'new levels of activity, a new language of class feeling, and the overlapping of forms of activity, all propogated by an extraordinarily vibrant and expanding radical press'.[78] Rule's observations are based upon the escalation of crisis and conflict in a number of areas of life.

Political Agitation

Politically, for example, the Reform Act of June 1832 which extended the franchise to large sections of the middle class (by means of the inclusion in the borough franchise of the £10 householder), was 'preceded by almost two years of intermittent tumult'.[79] The House of Lords' rejection of a second reform bill in October 1831 (the first having been defeated in the spring of 1831) provoked, according to Hunt, 'what were probably the most serious disturbances to occur in nineteenth-century Britain'. Massive demonstrations, rising to above 100,000 in Birmingham and London in the autumn of 1831 and May 1832, took place. And there were serious riots at Nottingham, Derby and Bristol in October 1831, all being indicative, claims E. P. Thompson, 'of a deep disturbance at the foundations of society, which observers anxiously expected to be followed by the uprising of London's East End'.[80] But such an uprising was not to come about. Not averse to threats of violence themselves (although terrified by the potentially radicalising effects of revolution), the middle-class reformers skilfully exploited the threat of working-class insurrection to finally force political concessions from 'Old Corruption'. But it was a close-run affair. Thus Thompson:

> But the well-nigh neolithic obstinacy with which Old Corruption resisted *any* reform led on to a situation in which the nation stepped, swiftly and without premeditation, on to the threshold of revolution.

And:

> In the autumn of 1831 and in the 'days of May' Britain was within an ace of a revolution which, once commenced, might well ... have prefigured, in its rapid radicalization, the revolutions of 1848 and the Paris Commune.

In the event, however, the Bill was passed, and the means found to 'attach numbers to property and good order'.[81]

The campaign for the vote was, of course, far from being a purely middle-class affair. From the 1790s onwards, and proceeding via Peterloo, there had developed a predominantly working-class reform movement. And in the tumultuous build-up to the Reform Act of 1832 artisans and other workers had played an important role. But in return for their support for reform, the working-class campaigners received little or nothing from their erstwhile middle-class reforming allies. Whilst many of the latter had been enfranchised by the Act of 1832, the vast majority of the former had not. 1832 became known among working-class radicals as the 'Great Betrayal'. And this sense of betrayal was deepened by the actions of the new Whig administration. The Irish Coercion Bill of 1833 (called 'perhaps the most repressive Irish measure ever proposed by an English government'), the rejection of the Ten Hour Bill of the same year, the attacks on the trade unions (as seen especially in the conviction of six Dorchester labourers (the 'Tolpuddle Martyrs') in 1834 for forming a branch of a trade union and administering oaths, the 1834 Poor Law Amendment Act, the Municipal Corporations Act of 1835 (which established a system of government in the municipalities which mirrored that at Westminster, and with powers to establish modern police forces), and the Newspaper Act of 1836 (which reduced rather than abolished the stamp duty on newspapers) – all these measures were instrumental in the development of popular hostility towards the Whigs and deep suspicion of the real intentions and actual behaviour of middle-class reformers. As Dorothy Thompson observes, 'After the Reform Bill, working-class radicals expressed feelings of betrayal towards those reformers among the middle classes who had used the rhetoric of liberty and equality, but who accepted the finality of the 1832 settlement.'[82] The defence of property outweighed the claims of manhood suffrage. Yet, ironically, the very dishonesty and hypocrisy of the Whig reformers engendered a spirit of political independence on the part of labouring people, a spirit which was to find full expression in Chartism.

Political radicalism had limited effect in the English countryside. As noted in Part One, the repressive actions of the countryside's rulers combined with mixtures of paternalism, rural isolation, abject poverty and despair, served to restrict the growth and staying power of radical political movements. It would, however, be equally unwise to see rural life as a uniform picture of deferential labourers and kindly squires and parsons. Charlesworth, Peacock, Dunbabin, Wells and others have demonstrated that tensions and conflicts, often of a raw class character, were present.

During the early 1830s the 'Swing Riots' of 1830–1 were 'the most impressive episode in the English farm-labourers' long and doomed struggle against poverty and degradation' and for fair wages and the right to work.[83] Embracing thousands of agricultural labourers, the riots (taking their name from the signature of 'Captain Swing' which appeared in threatening letters) extended over twenty counties in the course of three months. Concentrated mainly in the cereal-growing areas of southern England and East Anglia, the disturbances nevertheless spread into the Midlands and Lincolnshire. The threshing machine, seen as synonymous with unemployment and increased insecurity, constituted the main object of the rioters' hostility, but the firing of ricks, wage demands, and opposition to rents, tithes and Poor Law officials were also conspicuous features of the movement. And Wells has recently noted that 'articulations of radical political sentiments' (as reflected in the political biographies of arrested rioters, and the spread of pro-reform sentiments into the countryside) comprised an important and much neglected aspect of 'Swing'.[84]

Beyond the counties of southern and eastern England rural protest was far less marked. But in Scotland the Highland Clearances continued to forcibly depopulate the countryside, ride roughshod over customary popular rights to land (the 'moral economy' of the clan), and to provoke 'a sullen refusal to co-operate, a passive resistance' and, albeit less frequently, anti-clearance riots.[85] In the rural iron- and coal-working areas of south Wales members of the 'Scotch Cattle' employed a variety of sanctions, both moral and physical force in character, to enforce trade-union organisation and extract concessions from employers during the 1820s and early 1830s. By the end of the latter decade grievances concerning distress, the New Poor Law, tithes, alien (English) landlord domination, and the introduction of toll-gates had sparked the first phase of the 'Rebecca' Riots in Carmarthenshire, Pembrokeshire and Cardinganshire.[86]

Harsh penalties awaited rural rioters and general 'malcontents'. At those moments when (especially in England) the daily practices of paternalism failed to achieve their intended hegemonic results, the full force of the law was invoked as a savage deterrent to further acts of indiscipline and insubordination. (In the 'Celtic fringes' the niceties of a soothing and persuasive paternalism were far less in evidence: physical force, especially in Ireland, constituted a larger part of daily life.) Thus John Rule informs us that by the late summer of 1831 (when more than 1,400 'Swing'-related incidents had been recorded) there had been 2,000 arrests. Subsequently 500 were imprisoned and nineteen executed. The Highland Clearances constituted a stark example of 'the exercise of arbitrary landlord power' involving forcible eviction, loss of livelihood, and, on a number of occasions, the firing of crofters' homes, physical abuse and, more infrequently, arrest and imprisonment. Throughout the British countryside 'troublemakers' could expect few favours from the law, squirearchy or other representatives of the establishment. The transportation to Australia of the 'Tolpuddle Martyrs' was a full measure of the risks involved in radicalism.[87]

Industrial Conflict and General Trades' Unionism

Despite 'Swing' and other forms of rural protest, popular unrest was more characteristically an urban rather than a rural phenomenon between 1829 and 1834. Especially important was the growth of inter-trade solidarity in the years following the Repeal of the Combination Acts in 1824 and 1825 (the new law of 1825 recognised the right of combination and collective bargaining over wages and hours but made unions once again subject to the common law of conspiracy). The defence of customary practices at work in the face of the widespread process of capitalist restructuring detailed in Part One led to the identification of common problems and urgent need for joint action among trades in Lancashire, the Midlands, West Yorkshire, London and elsewhere. At the same time, as seen especially in the case of John Doherty's attempt to organise the spinners throughout Great Britain and Ireland, there were intensified efforts towards national trade unionism. And, as illustrated especially in the attempts of building trades craftsmen to enforce uniform wage rates, regulate apprenticeship, and oppose the wage reductions attendant upon the growth of 'general contracting' within the industry, movements towards the general union of trades within specific industries were extremely important.[88]

Attempts at both national and general unionism usually met with vehement employer opposition and defeat. Doherty's Grand General Union of Operative Cotton Spinners suffered early defeats in strikes at Bolton, Chorley and Ashton. But the strikes at Ashton and Stalybridge in the winter of 1830–1, in which the son of a millowner was shot and in which some 2,000 spinners met with defeat, proved to be the death of the union. The Builders' Union, representing the interests of some 40,000 operatives in the industry, and preaching co-operative production in order to undermine the influence of the general contractors, overreached itself in 1834. The failure of strikes at Manchester and Liverpool in 1833 was followed by a disastrous defeat in London in 1834. All over the country former union members were forced to sign the 'document'. By 1835 general unionism in the building industry was coming to an end, and the 'exclusives', singing the praises of trade unionism of the separate trades, were in the ascendancy.[89]

Attempts at general unionism did, however, extend beyond individual industries. In 1829, for example, 1,000 workers from twenty trades attended the inaugural meeting of Doherty's National Association for the Protection of Labour. Organised to provide funds to support constituent unions in the fight against wage reductions (the defeat of the spinners had demonstrated the futility of action by isolated trades), the Association reached a membership peak in 1830 when it had approximately 60,000 to 70,000 members. Most were recruited from the beleaguered textile trades of Lancashire and Cheshire, but, according to Sykes, the NAPL 'had a major impact on provincial trade unionism, stimulating surges of unionisation in the East Midlands and Potteries especially, and being more important in inspiring inter-trade co-operation in Yorkshire than has previously been acknowledged'. Above all, the NAPL spoke the language of class, was 'indeed constantly presented by its leaders in class terms', had as its ultimate, if unfulfilled object, the unity of 'the entire working class', and rejected middle-class forms of political economy based upon unfettered competition, individualism and profit maximisation. 'There was', concludes Sykes:

> a widespread belief that excessive domestic competition was producing systematic exploitation. 'It is a uniform system; not something uncertain, accidental, temporary and unavoidable; it is what it is most appropriately termed – a "system" and a *grinding* system.'[90]

Some of the textile and other workers involved in the NAPL looked to co-operative production as the ultimate solution to poverty and exploitation. Commitment to the idea of co-operative production did not, however, necessarily signify Owenite influence. As Sykes observes in relation to Lancashire and the NAPL, the influence of Owenism was patchy and limited, and co-operative production schemes were related far more to the employment of unemployed or strike-bound union members than to Owenite ideology.[91]

Owenism was far more influential in terms of the most famous experiment in general unionism, the Grand National Consolidated Trades' Union of 1834, although it is now clear that the influence of Owenite ideas upon the mass of the GNCTU's membership has traditionally been exaggerated. Above all, it is important, as argued by Sykes and Rule, to situate the emergence of the GNCTU within the broader context of quickened industrial unrest.[92]

The years between 1829 and 1831 had, as noted earlier, seen 'a very marked surge of industrial conflict and unionisation'. But the immediate context of the GNCTU's birth was the industrial turbulence of 1833 and 1834. In London both tailors and shoemakers conducted fierce and unsuccessful struggles against 'sweating', and, as shown by Prothero, there were strikes in the metropolis by plasterers and bricklayers, hatters and coopers, and evidence of union activity among gasworkers, washerwomen, bakers, bonnetmakers and other male and female groups traditionally beyond the boundaries of male- and artisan-dominated trade unionism. The Derby lock-out of 1833–4, enforced by anti-union employers in several trades, provided the catalyst to the birth of the GNCTU in February 1834, and the protests against the Tolpuddle decision in April generated further support for the ideas of general unionism and Owenism.

The GNCTU, based primarily upon the London shoemakers and tailors but also reaching out to the smaller trades, represented a further example of inter-trade co-operation. Special emphasis was placed upon mutual support in strikes, provision of sickness and superannuation benefits and the employment of unemployed members. But it is important to note that the GNCTU's influence spread beyond the ranks of artisans, and its ideas beyond trade unionism. As Rule observes, 'undeniably there was some reaching out to the unorganised, including women workers'. Gardeners, coal-whippers, female shoebinders and two general female lodges were among the non-artisan affiliated groups. And the vision of a harmonious co-operative commonwealth, most strongly articulated by Owen himself, lay at the heart of the movement.

Vision was not, however, in tune with reality. Despite the grandiose claims of the Webbs and others, the GNCTU's membership was relatively small, probably in the region of 16,000, of which 11,000 were from London. In addition the defeat of the London tailors' strike in 1834, amidst increasingly acrimonious relations between the striking tailors themselves and those within the GNCTU impatient to construct the socialist commonwealth rather than support immediate and more mundane industrial battles, augured badly for the future of the GNCTU. Indeed, by the end of 1834 the GNCTU was in terminal decline. Henceforth, both examples of inter-trade co-operation and a more exclusive, 'aristocratic' spirit were to be found in the 1830s and 1840s trade-union movement, but by 1835 Owenite influence was insignificant.

Class and Industrial Conflict

From the perspective of class, there were important limits to the industrial agitation of the 1829–23 period. Hunt, for example, has emphasised the minority character of trade unionism during this period. It has been estimated that in the good year of 1834 trade-union membership stood at 1 million or more (less than one worker in five), and that in the bad year of 1842 membership fell to about 100,000 (about 1.5 per cent of the labour force). And unions often lacked durability, failing to withstand attacks from employers and the judiciary.

Second, Musson has highlighted the 'aristocratic', determined yet cautious, and moderate character of trade unionists, their aloofness and frequent hostility towards the unskilled, and their general pursuit of sectional aims. In Musson's opinion, the impulses towards general unionism and Owenism constituted 'ephemeral excitements' which should not be allowed to mask the dominant and enduring characteristics of moderate trade unionism.[93]

Third, many historians have noted the extremely limited general involvement of the unskilled and women in trade unionism. Attention has been drawn to the hostility expressed by many male union members (as seen, for example, in the London tailors' dispute of 1834) towards female presence and competition within the labour market. And Barbara Taylor has astutely observed that the 'feminization' of the declining trades, and the accompanying acute threat to the 'traditional' sexual division of labour ('in which men functioned primarily as bread winners and women primarily as family servicers, integrating household tasks with casual wage-earning activities') provoked growing working-class male support for the equation of 'womanliness' with home-based dependency.[94]

Finally, Prothero and Stedman Jones have suggested that the anger of British artisans and other workers in the 1830s was directed primarily against the unfairness of the political system and exploitation within exchange. It was the corrupt politician and the middleman, rather than the employer in production, who constituted the perceived enemies of 'the People'. And co-operative production was accordingly adopted as the antidote to exchange – rather than production-based exploitation. The notion of the 'producing classes', considered at length in our earlier discussion of the United States, is thus held to be the cornerstone of 1830s popular radicalism on the British side of the Atlantic.[95]

In view of the four limitations listed above, both the Webbs' belief that the years between 1829 and 1834 constituted a 'revolutionary period', and Foster's view that between 1830 and 1834 there occurred a progression from 'trade union' to 'revolutionary' consciousness in Oldham, would appear to lack adequate empirical support.[96] But there is, nevertheless, good reason to support E. P. Thompson's view that 1829 to 1834 was a crucial phase in the development of class consciousness. As Sykes, Rule and various other authors have pointed out, trade-union membership was a poor indication of the depth and extent of involvement in industrial disputes. 'At this time', notes Sykes, 'unions were frequently episodic formalisations of pre-existing informal practices. In key confrontations the numbers taking action were frequently vastly larger than those known to be long-term subscribers to formal trade societies.'[97] In comparison with the pre-1829 years we must emphasise the much greater extent and frequency of industrial conflict and, as noted above, accelerated examples of inter-trade co-operation and the largely unprecedented widening of horizons to include sections of the unskilled and some women in trade unionism.

Images of the wife as 'the Angel in the house' still vied, records Barbara Taylor, with the older ideal – and reality – 'of women as active economic partners in the household and in the labouring community as a whole'.[98] This sense of an active and shared, if hardly equal, partnership was arguably stronger among those who constituted the more broadly based and, often, occupationally less well-off labour movements of Britain than among the more narrowly craft- and artisan-based and patriarchal constituents of protest movements in the United States. We have already noted that female employment which was believed to increase male unemployment was regarded (by both sexes) as 'unnatural' in Britain, and that women's primary attachment to the household had a limiting effect upon trade-union involvement. Yet at a general level British women were active in protest movements. Such involvement was, in many cases, secondary and supportive in nature. Yet in matters pertaining to the household and the community, women were far more centrally involved. We will discuss this matter in some detail in our examination of Chartism. But we must note at this point the active and prominent roles of women in food riots, in opposition to the New Poor Law, in opposition to clearances and enclosures and many more community- and household-based forms of protest. This level of involvement was far less in evidence in the more formal and structured trade-union and political protest movements of 1830s America.[99]

As noted above, general unionism, and especially the GNCTU had a limited but important appeal to sections of the unskilled beyond the ranks of women. To refer to the area of agricultural workers and rural protest, Roger Wells has identified not only the 'unionist mentalities . . . central to Swing', but also the growing industrial conflict in cornland towns between 1830 and 1834 and the involvement of agricultural labourers in the GNCTU.[100]

Finally, and despite the continued importance of the ideology of the 'producing classes', there is little doubt that the escalating conflicts of the early 1830s induced much greater feelings of popular hostility towards employers in production. Noel Thompson, for example, has clearly established the popularity of 'Smithian socialist' ideas which identified capitalist producers and middlemen as necessary exploiters of workers. And the practice of trade unionism was 'infused with a tone of class hostility' which struck at the very roots of the notion of production-based harmony.[101] Thus, not only did the labour movement become less exclusive in this period, but also exhibited sharp oppositional practice to the claims of capital and 'a fierce, class-conscious independence'.

Two factors profoundly influenced the shape and direction of labour movements in the post-GNCTU decade. First, the numerous industrial defeats suffered between 1829 and 1834 induced a growing feeling among radicals that future advancement lay less with trade unionism than with political action. Thus Bronterre O'Brien, Peter Murray McDouall and other Chartists were to win large support for their belief that the power of trade unionism was limited (by the greater powers of capital and the state), and that the real key to 'secure and permanent remedy' for the workers' ills lay in the attainment of the suffrage and the capture of legislative power.[102]

Second, the continued unpopularity of the measures passed by the Whig administration, and the fracturing of alliances between radicals of the middle and working class (common commitments to an extension of the suffrage breaking down in relation to attitudes towards the New Poor Law, trade unionism, and other economic and social matters) between 1836 and 1838, greatly increased the impetus towards the creation of an *independent* popular movement for universal suffrage. Feargus O'Connor, the future leader of the Chartist movement, was especially critical of the Whigs and those radicals, such as Roebuck and O'Connell, who supported the New Poor Law and opposed trade unionism. As Bronterre O'Brien wrote in the wake of the 1834 Act:

> In one respect the New Poor Law has done good. It has helped to open the people's eyes as to who are the real enemies of the working classes. Previously to the passing of the Reform Bill, the middle orders were supposed to have some community of feeling with the labourers. That delusion has passed away. It barely survived the Irish Coercion Bill. It vanished completely with the enactment of the Starvation Law.[103]

Daniel O'Connell's attack upon the Glasgow cotton spinners (found guilty of belonging to an organisation engaged in illegal activities and sentenced to seven years' transportation in January 1838) and trade unionism in general, further antagonised trade unionists and others towards middle-class reformers. And by the time of the publication of the People's Charter, in May 1838, the tenuous alliance between O'Connell, Roebuck and others with the radicals of the working-class movement had been broken.[104] The country was about to witness the growth of the most impressive popular movement of the first half of the nineteenth century, Chartism.

Chartism

The story of the Chartist movement has been told many times, and it is not my purpose to repeat the details. Rather, a brief description of the chronology of Chartism will be followed by an examination of the movement's socio-geographical characteristics, its grievances and aims, and its relations with other groups and classes. We will then be in a position to assess the extent to which Chartism was class based and/or revolutionary. The text will then move to a consideration of comparisons and contrasts between labour movements in the two countries up to the mid 1840s.

Chronology

As formally set out in the Charter of May 1838, the Chartist movement called for universal male adult suffrage, the secret ballot, the abolition of property qualifications for Members of Parliament, the payment of Members, equal electoral districts and annual parliaments.[105] Chartism was, above all, a political movement, seeking to resolve popular grievances by means of parliamentary reform and to inject democratic processes and values into the life of a basically unjust and oligarchic society. As Dorothy Thompson has observed:

> Of the population of Britain in the 1830s, only a very small fraction took an active part in national politics. The electorate in England and Wales was around 653,000 from a population of just over 13 million, and in Ireland 90,000 from 7.8 million. The Reform Act of 1832 had enlarged the electorate by about 50 per cent above the figure in 1830 ... Excluded from the vote were all `women, all people under the age of twenty-one and the majority of men in the country. Even among the enfranchised, a majority never used their votes independently, for the system of open polling ... meant that every kind of pressure could be put on the voters ... Serious choice, and the exercise of influence over the make-up of the House of Commons, remained the privilege of a very small number of people.[106]

The demand for universal manhood suffrage was not new (being part of the radical programme from the mid–late eighteenth century onwards),[107] but what was new in Chartism was the scale and heightened class-based character of the demand for the vote. Indeed, it was the mass-based, national, organised, rational, coherent *and* threatening character of Chartism which gave the authorities most cause for alarm. They were facing not an undisciplined and evanescent form of protest, but a disciplined and well-organised movement, equipped with an alternative cultural, economic, political and social vision, a vibrant press, able leaders, and degrees of sophistication and scale hitherto unmatched in the radical tradition. Thus Dorothy Thompson:

> For the ten years from 1838 to 1848 the authorities in Britain were faced with a popular movement which came nearer to being a mass rebellion than any other movement in modern times. Working people in all parts of the island – in Scotland and Wales as well as in England – demonstrated in favour of a political programme, formed organisations to promote it and in many ways set up a whole alternative culture and life-style in the process. A mass of published material was produced, newspapers, pamphlets, broadsides, placards and books were circulated, sermons were preached, plays and pageants performed, hymns and songs were written and sung. Traditional forms were adopted alongside new forms of organisation and demonstration.[108]

There were a number of key dates and events in the construction, growth and decline of Chartism. As early as 1835 Workingmen's Associations had been formed in Scotland and the north. The following two years saw the formation of the London Working Men's Association (1836), the East London Democratic Association (1837), the revival of the Birmingham Political Union (1837), and the publication of what was to become the leading journalistic organ of Chartism, the *Northern Star* (1837). In addition to the publication of the Charter, 1838 witnessed the merging of various strands of radicalism (anti-Poor Law agitation, the campaign for factory reform and so on) under the broad umbrella of Chartism, the mushrooming of radical associations of one kind or another (in 1838 and 1839 female radical associations both revived in centres of established radicalism and 'sprang up throughout the country in places that had never previously known female associations'),[109] and the calling of mass meetings in the Manchester district, Glasgow, Birmingham and elsewhere to elect delegates to the forthcoming Convention. Indeed, by the end of 1838 many erstwhile middle-class sympathisers had fled the movement, increasingly horrified by talk of 'physical force' and the 'proletarian' visage of Chartism.

Trends towards the construction of a mass movement composed predominantly of labouring people in the manufacturing districts of Britain, middle-class alienation from, indeed hostility towards, Chartism, and the increasingly threatening tone and practice of the movement, were consolidated in 1839. 'Sober' and 'respectable' middle-class men did form a majority of the original delegates to the General Convention of the Industrious Classes which met in February 1839 to supervise the presentation of the Chartist petition to parliament and to consider wider tactics and strategy. But disagreements concerning the precise functions of the convention, and (mainly tactical) conflicts concerning the use of 'physical force' in the likely event of the rejection of the petition by parliament, led to the resignation of some of the middle-class moderates and their replacement by younger and far more confrontationalist-minded delegates. In the event the Convention's *Manifesto*, issued after the rejection of the petition by parliament in July (by 235 votes to 46), did propose the adoption of a series of 'ulterior measures', including an appeal to arms. And the rejection of the petition, allied to the Bull Ring Riots in Birmingham in July (when a posse of London policemen was brought in to break up the regular gatherings of Chartists) and the arrests of growing numbers of Chartists by the authorities, made the question of 'ulterior measures', especially the proposal for a 'sacred month' (in effect a month's general strike throughout the country), most pressing. In addition, Chartists in many districts armed themselves, spoke the language of imminent insurrection and marched in military formation.[110]

A concerted attempt at insurrection did not, however, ensue. On 6 August, just six days before the planned commencement of the 'sacred month', the Convention, largely at the instigation of O'Connor, cancelled the general strike as being premature and doomed to defeat, and instructed localities to introduce a three-day withdrawal of labour. The leadership of the convention thus failed to cross the threshold from violent rhetoric to confrontational action which contained within it the probability of violent clashes between the Chartists and the forces of law and order. O'Connor may well have been right in his assessment of the balance of political and military forces (which weighed heavily in favour of the state). But there is no doubt that 'throughout the country [Chartist] supporters were expecting to be called on to act'. At this point O'Connor's leadership was criticised more heavily than at any other time before the period of 'late' Chartism. The government was, in any event, not slow to act. Dorothy Thompson observes that, 'the three days of the truncated National Holiday ... resulted in more arrests throughout the country than any other period before 1842'. Several hundred Chartists were tried and imprisoned, including most of the well-known local and national leaders. But insurrectionary hopes were not entirely dead. In November 1839 thousands of iron workers and colliers marched across the hills of South Wales to Newport in order to wage an insurrection. Probably intended as the start of a successful regional revolt (which would hopefully provide the inspiration for Chartists in other localities to capture their towns and cities and 'proclaim the Charter as law'),[111] the Newport Rising ended in disaster. At least twenty-two marchers were shot dead by the military and the three main leaders of the march, John Frost, Zephenia Williams and William Jones were placed under arrest (their sentences of death were later commuted to transportation for life). Reports from magistrates of widespread arming and drilling in Yorkshire, Lancashire, Nottingham and the Newcastle district also proliferated throughout the autumn and the early winter months. January 1840 saw abortive risings in Sheffield and Bradford.

Despite its defeats and the imprisonment of its main leaders in 1839, Chartism continued to exercise a massive influence upon working-class communities and radicalism up to the end of 1842. In July 1840 the National Charter Association was formed when delegates at Manchester decided to create a national political party, complete with a national executive and card-carrying membership. The Association therefore constituted an important step in the creation of a more efficient and centralised Chartist organisational structure. And the rapid growth of the Association during 1841 and 1842 (from 80 associations in February 1841 to more than 400, with 50,000 members, in June 1842), O'Connor's successful rebuttal of 'Knowledge Chartism, Christian Chartism and Temperance Chartism' as alternative strategies to primary concern with the suffrage, and the collection of over 3 million signatures (more than twice the number of the 1839 petition) for the second petition of 1842, were all signs of Chartism's robust health. The rebuffs given to the middle-class reformers of the Anti-Corn Law League and those of the Complete Suffrage Union in 1842 were further signs of Chartism's independent and class-conscious nature.[112] Finally, the general strikes of 1842 (embracing 500,000 workers from Staffordshire to Scotland) involved large numbers of Chartists, often in key leadership roles. Notwithstanding the facts that by no means all centres supported the 'political' nature of the strike, and that some Chartists remained equivocal about the relation between the wage question and the Charter, there is now little doubt that there was majority support for the aim of the Lancashire trades to, 'extend the strike nationally and to remain out until the Charter became the law of the land'. The strikes thus represented an unqualified success for those Chartist activists, such as McDouall and Leach, who had campaigned since 1840 for more united action by trade unionists and Chartists.[113]

Both the second petition (rejected in May by 287 votes to 49) and the general strikes ended in failure (the strikes were followed, as in 1839, by mass arrests). But the period between 1837 and 1842 had represented the emergence and growth of a highly influential, indeed hegemonic Chartist movement within the working class. 1842 signified, however, not the consolidation but the highwater mark of Chartism's mass influence. From the end of 1842 onwards the mass politics which had dominated the previous five years 'began to lose its hold within sections of the working class'. The defeats of the petition and of the general strikes led to confusion as to the future directions of the movement, and, for many, disillusionment with the politics of open confrontation and insurrection. In the less harsh economic climate of the mid 1840s some, especially skilled, workers 'turned away from ambitious plans for social reconstruction towards the more limited objective of building up and consolidating the strength of their organisations within the confines of the system'.[114] Increasingly these workers paid more attention to the economic and social means of advancement, by way of trade unionism, Co-operation (the founding of the Rochdale Pioneers Society in 1844 was to constitute a key date in the successful development of mid-Victorian Co-operation), friendly societies and mutual improvement societies, than to political means. This shift in focus did not generally signify a conscious ideological break with Chartism. But it did increasingly mean in the mid-Victorian years that the struggle for the suffrage lost its dominant position within working-class movements. There was a growing separation and specialisation of function, as between political and other forms of action, within what had been a highly united and integrated movement. The period between 1850 and 1870 was to belong to the trade unions, co-operative societies and friendly societies rather than to politics.

But we are running ahead of our story. If far less hegemonic, Chartism in the late 1840s, even the 1850s, cannot be dismissed as insignificant. 1845 saw the launching of the Land Plan, a commitment to the development of smallholdings and allotments and to the removal of surplus labour from the urban areas. In practical terms the Land Plan proved to be a failure (many of the allottees were industrial workers with apparently inadequate knowledge of agriculture). But as Dorothy Thompson observes, far from diverting attention from the political movement, 'it was almost certainly the existence of the Land Company that kept the movement together'.[115]

As a political force, Chartism revived in late 1847 and during the first half of 1848. Indeed, as John Saville has recently demonstrated, whilst not attaining its strength of the 1837–42 period, Chartism in 1848 did achieve considerable if uneven influence. By the mid–late 1840s London had become a strong centre of the movement. And Chartism's successful alliance with the Irish repealers both increased, as noted by Belchem, the overall vitality of the movement and brought the questions of violence and insurrection very much to the fore.[116] In April 1848 the Kennington Common meeting was a prelude to the rejection of the (much weaker) third petition by parliament. The late spring and early summer months saw arming and shadowy but real plans for insurrection, the extent of which have probably been underestimated by many historians. Mass arrests in the summer and autumn of 1848 considerably diminished the strength and appeal of the movement.

During its 'late' period, between 1848 and 1858, Chartism exerted a markedly reduced influence. By 1850, and despite many efforts to revive local Chartist associations, 'languor and apathy' were everywhere apparent. The early 1850s saw the rise to ascendancy of Ernest Jones's anti-middle-class and pro-socialist position, and the decline of O'Connor's health (O'Connor died in 1855). Indeed, albeit with reduced appeal, independent working-class politics were to survive the lean years of the 1850s, especially in the manufacturing districts of Lancashire and Cheshire. But, in general, there was no doubt that Chartism's support dropped away sharply. By 1858, and despite the continuation of the tradition of political independence by the Manhood Suffrage Associations and the Reform League into the 1860s, Chartism was effectively dead. Liberalism was increasingly adopted as the political creed of the majority of labour activists.[117]

Geographical Characteristics

In turning to consider the socio-geographical bases of Chartism's support, we can endorse Asa Briggs' claim that the appeal of early Chartism was strongest in centres of decaying or contracting industry and in the new or expanding single-industry towns.[118] Chartism was present in the big cities – London became the stronghold of the movement in the 1840s, and Leeds, Birmingham, Manchester, Newcastle, Sheffield and Glasgow were undoubtedly important – but was often more militant and stronger in the adjacent industrial areas. As Dorothy Thompson has observed:

> Britain . . . was a nation of growing urban manufacturing districts – districts made up of clusters of communities in which one or two industries were carried on. Many of these districts had grown up during the century preceding Chartism, and had grown up comparatively independent of many forms of traditional authority. They had developed their own traditions for regulating their trades and the behaviour of their inhabitants, and had incorporated these into their own notions of customary standards. The Chartist movement gained its greatest strength in manufacturing districts in which the actual communities were small enough to sustain a unity of purpose, in which communication was quick and easy, and in which the traditional authority of church and state was weak. Such communities could be centres of factory production, mining, or hand trades. It was the size and nature of the community together with the comparative homogeneity of the industrial experience within it which gave strength to the movement, rather than the actual nature of the productive process on which its members were engaged.[119]

The common, if not identical, experiences of capitalist transformation outlined in Part One, and the effects of this transformation upon work, independence, status, the family and community underlay much of the support for Chartism in the manufacturing districts. It was in the textile towns of the West Riding – Bradford, Halifax and Dewsbury – of Lancashire and Cheshire – Ashton, Stalybridge, Oldham, Stockport and Bolton – and of Nottinghamshire and Leicestershire, the mining and ironworking districts of South Wales and northeastern England, and in places like Barnsley or Dundee 'in which a community of locality, of one or two major industries, and of shared leisure and recreational activities made for speed of communication, common concerns in work and in political action', that Chartism took strongest root. The agricultural counties, in which the authority of squire and parson were long established, in which the coercive powers of employers and others were employed to full effect, and in which the defeat of 'Swing' and the transportation of the 'Martyrs' had induced widespread demoralisation, were accordingly weak centres of Chartism.[120]

Social Constituencies: beleaguered workers, women and the non-skilled

As one would expect from the geographical spread of Chartism, it was those workers whose independence, authority and living standards were threatened by the advance of industrial capitalism who formed the backbone of the movement. And, as will be evident from our earlier discussion, such beleaguered workers were to be found in the factories (spinners, calico printers and dyers as well as the rather lower status powerloom weavers), in the older trades (shoemakers, tailors, building trades' workers and so on), in outwork (especially weavers, woolcombers and framework knitters), and, to a lesser extent, in the engineering and metal-working sector.[121] Despite variations of experience, the common problems of economic insecurity, declining status, increased competition in the labour market, dilution of skills, the undercutting of customary standards, and mushrooming 'dishonourable' practices on the part of capitalist employers constituted, as we have already seen, the shared economic context in which these 'new' and 'old', skilled and lesser skilled workers discovered class.

Many of the most secure artisan trades, such as printing, coachmaking and bookbinding, did possess strong trade unions, but usually remained aloof from Chartism and more general involvement in radical movements. But, as once again noted in Part One it would be wrong to exaggerate the size and influence of a cautious and aloof 'labour aristocracy' during the second quarter of the nineteenth century. Rather, as demonstrated by Goodway for London, Sykes for Lancashire and

Cheshire, and Behagg for Birmingham, it was the *general* insecurity of
the trades which propelled them into radical politics.[122]

As much recent research has demonstrated, Chartism's embrace
extended beyond the groups of workers described above. Irish immigrants, whether employed in the older weaving trades, in the building
industry (mainly as labourers), or in the rapidly expanding cotton industry (Irish women were prominent in the cardroom and in weaving),
often defied the proclamations of the Catholic church and the wishes
of Daniel O'Connell in order to participate in Chartism and trade
unionism.[123] Historians may have also traditionally underestimated the
involvement of miners. It is true that miners in the Wigan area were
given more to ethnic and religious conflict than to participation in
radical politics, that some of the leaders of the Miners' Association of
the 1840s were critical of an overt connection with Chartism, and that
when considered as a whole mining did not contribute in large proportion to Chartist members and local leaders. But against this picture
we must set miners' strong involvement in South Wales Chartism, their
presence in Chartism in Scotland and the northeast (especially in the
late 1830s), their important role in the strikes of 1842 in Staffordshire
and elsewhere, their frequent appearance as the 'shock troops' for the
more violent actions, the 'strong political flavour' of the coalfield strikes
of 1842 and 1844, their large representation in the Land Company, and
the active involvement of some of the key leaders of the Miners' Association in Chartism.[124] Historical orthodoxy has, as noted above, a
stronger case in relation to agricultural labourers. But even here Wells
has cited evidence of a Chartist presence which may, in the light of
future research, lead to a serious modification of the accepted wisdom.[125]

The conventional wisdom has also greatly overlooked the active and
widespread participation of women in Chartism. Recently Dorothy
Thompson and others have corrected the gender-based silences of Chartist historiography.[126] Although they did not impart specifically feminist-
based concerns into Chartism, and although their role was mainly supportive (in terms of the concerns of their menfolk and their families),
women did form female radical associations ('well over a hundred' such
associations have been recorded for the early years of Chartism), did
carry their agitation against the Poor Law (complete with its attack on
the family and parental control over their homes and children) into
Chartism, and took out membership cards of the National Charter
Association. Many towns in Lancashire and the West Riding had established records of female radicalism, as seen in the crescendo of mass
meetings leading to the climax of Peterloo. But it appears to be the case
that women also became involved in Chartism in areas where traditions
of independent women's organisation were weak. And although the

amended Charter did not include the original proposal in support of women's suffrage (on the grounds that demands for the latter might retard male suffrage and strengthen the voting power of the propertied élite), Thompson suggests that support for the idea of the vote for unmarried and widowed women 'was always widespread among the Chartists'. Indeed, 'by the early 1840s it seems to have been one of the main reforms which most Chartists expected to follow from the gaining of the Charter'.

None of this is to suggest, however, that men and women enjoyed equal status within Chartism. Attention has already been drawn, with reference to 1830's general unionism, to the tradition of shared and unequal partnership in working-class families. Women and men combined their energies to struggle for collective survival in a hostile world: but they did not struggle as equals. At the heart of Chartism lay the assumption that wives and husbands were one, and that the husband was largely that one. Wives were expected to define themselves through their husbands, and to offer appropriate support and care. As Thompson observes, although Chartist women 'presented banners, made and presented gifts to visiting speakers, and invariably marched in the great processions and demonstrations', they 'seldom spoke on public platforms' and were not conspicuous as leaders. Unmarried women, especially in the cotton towns, enjoyed a greater measure of independence, and there did exist women, who, by force of character, became renowned local radical 'characters'; but the latter were untypical of women as a whole. Primary attention to the home and children was seen as the 'proper' role of women: the Chartists saw women's work outside the home as a burden, particularly for married women.

Despite such inbuilt inequalities of gender, it does nevertheless seem to be the case that class-based loyalties were paramount for Chartist women as well as Chartist men:

> The women at this stage did not see their interests as being in opposition to those of their husbands – or if they did, they did not see any solution to such conflict in political action. Chartist women seem for the most part to have worked together with their husbands, sons and brothers in a joint opposition to oppression perceived as coming from employers and administrators. Those Owenites who attacked marriage and the family met with little response among working women.[127]

In truth early Chartism formed part of a tradition of protest in defence of custom, community and the family against the ravages of capitalist development. And women occupied an important place within this tradition. Generally speaking, the 1840s were to see the growth of more formal, structured and increasingly work-place based kinds of protest in which women, as guardians of the home, were to be further marginalised.

Finally, Chartism received important support from occupational groups straddling the labouring community and the middle class proper, and occasional middle-class backing. Small traders, masters and many shopkeepers were often little removed from workers in terms of life-style and living standards. Shopkeepers were also dependent upon working-class custom for their livelihood. And, as demonstrated by Foster for Oldham, such borderline occupations could share the radical politics of the Chartists.[128] More generally, newsagents, publicans, book-sellers and similarly independent groups were able to provide meeting places and, more infrequently, leadership for local Chartists. Genuinely middle-class Chartists were 'very few in number'. But occasional radical and independent spirits were to be found in the professions.

Chartism was thus a mass protest movement which embraced a wide range of occupations. But at the heart of the movement, and despite the prominence of non-labouring figures at the national level (O'Brien, O'Connor and Jones had all had a legal training) and the occasional sympathy displayed towards the movement by clergymen, surgeons, lawyers and schoolteachers, stood the labouring people. Thompson's observation neatly sums up our case: 'The great mass of the membership ... and the majority of leaders, both national and local, came from among the working members of the trades and crafts of the manufacturing districts.'[129]

Grievances and Aims

Such people took part in the Chartist movement for a number of seemingly diverse yet increasingly interconnected reasons. Anti-Poor Law protestors, trade unionists, supporters of factory reform, those who had long campaigned for the vote, a cheap press and an end to 'Old Corruption', and many more were attracted to the broad embrace of Chartism. The emphasis upon politics as the central means of advancement and emancipation, and the specific concentration upon manhood suffrage, constituted the key unifying appeals. But there were factors beyond the vote which constituted common rallying points. The general hostility of the state to popular demands, the condescension and hostility displayed by the middle class and aristocracy towards the culture of the working people (the latter being widely seen as 'fierce', 'rough', 'undisciplined', 'lacking restraint', intemperate and improvident, easily given to riot and subversion, and requiring the firm cultural imprint of more 'rational' and 'enlightened' beings), poverty, hunger, the perceived oppression and exploitation of employers, and the uneven yet combined effects of capitalist transformation which we have been at pains to describe – all these factors created a sense of common suffering within seeming diversity.

Along with Edward and Dorothy Thompson and others, we are not arguing in favour of a working class *totally united* by common grievances. Differences and divisions, based upon sectionalism, living standards, culture and so on, did not disappear within labouring communities. But during the Chartist years such differences and divisions were generally *overshadowed* by a sense of common grievance which constituted a central component of the process of class maturation. In view of the largely static and methodologically flawed criticisms directed against the class-based nature of nineteenth-century working-class movements in recent years, we would be well advised to note that the case in favour of class is not rooted in the assumption of an immutable and undifferentiated working class.[130]

During the 1830s and 1840s workers turned to a variety of methods and adopted a number of aims in order to rectify their grievances. Trade unionism, Co-operation, temperance and mutual improvement by means of education constituted some of the more important methods. 'Customary' and more forward-looking aims coexisted between and within different movements, as did 'moral' and 'physical-force' and 'moderate' and 'extreme' methods and goals. However, as was the case in relation to grievances, so a broad sense of common purpose informed seemingly disconnected aims and movements.

Of prime importance was the hegemonic position achieved by Chartism within the various working-class movements of the late 1830s and early–mid 1840s. Not only were various forms of protest channelled into Chartism (such as the Poor Law agitation), but also more autonomous forms of action enjoyed generally close ties with Chartism. For example, apart from the small group of aloof 'aristocratic' combinations, most trade unions had (despite the widespread 'no politics' rule) strong informal and formal links with Chartism. This was particularly the case during the early 1840s and the strikes of 1842.[131]

At a more general level we can suggest that Chartism was informed by:

> a common stock of general political, economic, social and cultural
> aspirations which found specific, practical expression in a variety of
> ways, ranging from the Land Plan, to the demand for a 'fair day's
> wages for a fair day's work', to Ernest Jones's socialism.[132]

Whilst not committed to any single 'ism', and whilst not generally socialist in character, Chartism offered both a sharp critique of the status quo and an alternative social vision. I have elsewhere outlined the main features of Chartism's alternative:

> a far more open, democratic and egalitarian society based upon co-operative and human, rather than competitive and cash, values; freedom from monopolists and parasites, and the oppressive and tyrannical actions of capitalist employers and the State; the eradi-cation of glaring inequalities of wealth, power and income; the provision of the material and other preconditions (due protection and reward for labour in the form of wages, hours, conditions of, and control over, work, controls over prices and profits, and greatly improved access to education and other forms of mental culture) essential to the ending of wage-slavery, and to the enjoy-ment of the benefits of a civilised existence befitting genuinely free and independent citizens; the termination of structured inequalit-ies and antagonisms between employers and workers by means of checks upon the size of units of production, the ownership of such units either co-operatively or by small and 'fair' masters, and enhanced opportunities for upward occupational and social mobility; and the humanisation of economic affairs by the organis-ation of production primarily for rational and useful purposes, rather than for mindless and unceasing profit maximisation.[133]

As was the case with American workers during the 1830s, the Chart-ists thus sought due balance, protection and reward for labouring people in a climate in which the interests of capital and 'monopoly' had taken precedence over the interests of 'the People'. The political contexts were different – white adult males held the vote in the United States, and the state machinery was perceived to be less fundamentally antagonistic to the interests of workers than in Britain – but, as will be evident from our earlier discussion of the General Trades' Unions and from the quotation cited in the previous paragraph, there were many ideological similarities. Workers on both sides of the Atlantic were concerned not only with formal political democracy and real liberation from hunger and poverty, but also with 'moral' questions concerning the workers' pride, independence and right to be treated as rational and creative citizens rather than as passive and dutiful machines. The notion of independence lay at the heart of popular radicalism. Independence was allied to the necessary resurrection of human values, of mutuality and trust, at the expense of the unrestricted competition and acquisitive materialism so beloved of orthodox political economy.

Finally, American and British radicals appealed to 'custom' to legit-imise their actions. The notion of the 'Freeborn Englishman' performed the same function as 'revolutionary republicanism'. And both sets of workers defended the customary practices of the 'moral economy' *and* offered suggestions for change which met with the disapproval of the political economists and many of those in positions of authority. A sense of lost rights (of becoming an outsider and a dependent slave) constituted, alongside plans for a better future, a rich source of class consciousness.[134]

Chartism and the Issue of Class

We have already observed that in identifying grievances and pursuing means of improvement American workers encountered a series of obstacles and enemies. 'Monopolistic' bankers and speculators, parasitical and exploitative merchants and capitalist employers, and dishonest and antagonistic politicians and political parties played their full part in the development of class in 1830s America. Similar, and in some cases more marked processes were at work in Britain. The Chartists faced and opposed, as noted earlier, an extremely hostile state, an antagonistic aristocracy and, by and large, an unsympathetic middle class. This was the British crucible of class.

As with 1830s American radicals, the Chartists offered critiques not only of 'Aristocracy'/'Old Corruption' and exploitation within the realms of distribution and exchange, but also of capitalist exploitation within production. Within Chartism 'producerist' ideas were arguably subordinate to class-based ideology. The Chartists did not adopt blanket opposition to the middle class. Rather, O'Connor and others distinguished between, on the one hand, shopkeepers and other borderline occupations and, on the other, capitalist manufacturers. Whereas the latter consciously and systematically exploited workers by 'buying cheap and selling dear', by seeking the complete subordination of labour to capital, and, in more general ways, by subverting the 'honourable' precepts of petty-commodity production, it was in the objective interests of the former to sell goods to a well-paid workforce. As O'Connor declared, 'You must enlighten the shopkeepers and tradesmen of all denominations and fight against the real enemy – the steam Lords.'[135]

The Chartists were, furthermore, prepared to accept offers of help from the reforming sections of the middle class, if genuinely and sincerely offered on the basis of equal co-operation. And in some instances where opposition to a cruel and parasitical landed aristocracy overshadowed conflicts between capitalist manufacturers and workers, as for example in Glasgow, Edinburgh and many other parts of Scotland increasingly populated by victims of the Highland Clearances and landlordism in Ireland, such inter-class political co-operation took place.[136] Likewise, middle-class involvement in Chartism, the relative absence of 'physical-force' characteristics, and a reasonably smooth transition into Liberalism occurred in those urban areas (such as Kentish London and Edinburgh) where 'aristocratic' trades predominated, and in which social divisions between the skilled élite and the rest of the labouring population were greater than any overall conflict between workers and employers. In addition, where there existed, as in Edinburgh, a heterogeneous industrial structure and a local élite rooted in the professions, commerce and finance and largely removed from immediate, daily contact with manual workers, then the appeal of militant, class-based politics was often not strong.[137] And even in some of the Lancashire mill towns, where social differences were far more pronounced, instances of inter-class political co-operation were not totally absent. Taylor's work on Bolton, for example, demonstrates that in 1838, 1841 and in the post-1842 period reforming sections of the middle class were keen to ally themselves with the Chartists in opposition to the dominant local Tory oligarchy. Similarly, Gadian has claimed that the relatively small scale of Oldham's mill structure facilitated, in opposition to Foster's thesis, inter-class harmony.[138]

We would, however, be mistaken to suggest that the characteristic *national* relationship between the Chartists and middle-class reformers was based upon harmony and co-operation. Rather, experience generally suggested that the middle class was not to be trusted, and that the Chartists should pursue an independent and predominantly working-class-based strategy. Such experience manifested itself in politics, in economics and in culture.

A key political feature of national Chartism was its mistrust of mainstream Toryism and Whiggery and its emphasis upon the importance of political *independence*. The Chartists regarded the Tories as the true defenders of reaction, repression, hierarchy, the union of Church and State, and the enemies of democracy and popular liberties, including the demand for the vote. Outside of the West Riding of Yorkshire Tory radicalism, complete with its opposition to the factory system and its defence of the interests of the poor, was weak. In Lancashire, for example, many Conservatives were millowners and, as such, had a vested interest in the continued viability of the factory system. And although Joseph Rayner Stephens spoke the language of Tory radicalism in the Ashton-under-Lyne and Stalybridge areas of southeast Lancashire and northeast Cheshire from the mid–late 1830s onwards, he was not, at least during the 1830s, part of a wider Tory-radical movement, and was in fact regarded with suspicion, indeed hostility, by many local Tories on account of his prior involvement with Liberals and radicals. *Pace* the work of David Walsh on operative Conservatism, Conservatives in the cotton districts of Lancashire and Cheshire failed, as clearly demonstrated by Robert Sykes, to put down strong popular roots during the Chartist era. The Operative Conservative Associations, established from the mid 1830s onwards, generally did not enrol significant numbers of operatives (at least during the late 1830s and early–mid 1840s), were dominated by members of the middle and lower-middle classes, had little or nothing to do with the Tory radicalism of Yorkshire's Richard Oastler, were primarily concerned with the promulgation and defence of the tenets of the Anglican church, were treated as a joke by Chartists and Liberals, and had largely ceased to function by the time the Corn Laws were repealed in 1846. Contrary to the view of Renée Soffer, the mass of 1830s northern working people did not take their political cue from the Tories.[139]

The actions of the post-1832 Whig administrators also did little to endear the principles of Whiggery to most workers. As observed by Dorothy Thompson, 'The Irish Coercion Act, the emasculation of the Factory Act, the attacks on trade unions, all contributed to the disillusion felt by working-class radicals with the Reform Act and the administration which followed it.'[140] The New Poor Law, the establishment of modern police forces, the exclusion of many workers from active participation in the processes of municipal government under the ratepaying franchises set in several places under the provisions of the Municipal Corporations Act of 1835, and the arrests of Chartists, often carried out by Whig authorities, in 1838 and 1839, also helped to produce the Chartist view of the Whigs as deceitful and untrustworthy.

At Stockport, for example, some of those middle-class radicals who had threatened a resort to violence in the tumultuous background to the 1832 Reform Act, advocated and enforced, as magistrates and other figures of authority, the arrest of 'physical-force' Chartists in 1838 and 1839. Stockport's Chartists in turn labelled the Whigs 'a treacherous, deceitful, bad lot', and henceforth transferred their electoral support from the Whigs to the Tories. This action did not signify sudden Chartist support for the principles of Toryism (the Tories being seen as the 'traditional' yet 'open' enemy), but was adopted as a tactical electoral device to register protest at the treachery of the Whig authorities in the town.[141] And at Bolton the Chartists refused to be used as an instrumental battering ram by their middle-class allies against Conservative power. Alarmed by the increased militancy of Bolton's Chartists, middle-class reformers retreated: by 1839 the alliance had broken down. It was resurrected during the 1841 parliamentary election, but was again disrupted by the strikes of 1842. In the more balmy economic climate of the mid 1840s the Anti-Corn Law League did build a strong base in Bolton's working class, and by the late 1840s the movement into Liberalism was pronounced among Bolton's Chartists. But as Taylor notes, even in Bolton, where middle-class involvement in Chartism was exceptionally strong by the standards of southeast Lancashire, the Chartist-Liberal alliance was 'fraught with class tensions and ideological contradictions', especially between 1837 and 1842. Middle-class reformers in Bolton were generally opposed to trade unionism, failed to 'generate significant working-class loyalty via the employment relation', supported early Chartism for essentially instrumental rather than principled reasons, and, along with most Tories, were opposed (at least up to the mid 1840s) to the cause of factory reform. In sum, records Taylor, and especially in 1838 and 1839, 1842 and to a lesser extent 1848, Bolton Chartism was 'essentially ... a working class movement'. Both throughout the rest of the cotton districts of south Lancashire and nationally, the independent character of Chartism was, by 1839, more pronounced than in Bolton.[142]

It is, of course, important to identify different elements and philosophies within the broad arch of Liberalism. Some Liberals were opposed to specific aspects of 1830s 'Whiggery', and were favourable to degrees of political and social reform. Dorothy Thompson thus reminds us that there were 'a certain number of radicals among the middle classes who supported in principle the idea of manhood suffrage'. As Taylor, Sykes, Seed, and Kidd and Roberts have emphasised, Liberalism in Manchester and the Manchester area was far from being totally synonymous with the dogmatic *laissez-faire* views of many members of the 'Manchester School'. At Bolton, Rochdale and elsewhere some Liberal candidates opposed *in toto* or in part the provisions of the New Poor Law and supported the further extension of the suffrage.[143]

Equally, however, we must remember that the views of such reforming Liberals often did not go far enough to satisfy the Chartist demand for universal manhood suffrage (Thompson noting that even those radical middle-class politicians in principled support with manhood suffrage, 'never made common cause with the Chartists for more than a fleeting moment'). In economic and social terms the Liberal emphasis upon the harmonious interests of the 'producing classes' failed to adequately address the divisions between workers and employers within production and Chartist opposition to unfettered individualism and competition.[144] And, in truth, the popular base of early Victorian Liberalism was not impressive. For example, according to Sykes, the Liberals of south Lancashire 'made no real attempt to emulate the Conservatives in creating supporting operative associations in the 1830s'. Beyond their bases in Bolton and Manchester (the latter mainly among Irish workers), the Operative Associations of the Anti-Corn-Law League failed to attract many workers.

As Sykes declares, the failure of both the Conservatives and Liberals to enlist strong organisational support from within the working class in the 1830s 'confirmed the existence of a deep class divide' in the politics of the south Lancashire cotton districts. The Chartists assumed the familiar radical view that, 'the established Whig and Tory parties were both objectionable factions opposed to the interests of the people', and accordingly adopted an 'essentially instrumental and opportunistic approach to the parties and elections'. As Sykes further argues, 'the only real issue was how the party battle could be exploited for radical gains, either by achieving some worthwhile reform, or by promoting the political instability which would weaken the whole political system'. In some contexts (as, for example, at Stockport and Nottingham during the 1841 elections) this strategy of calculative instrumentalism, anchored in political independence, resulted in specific support for Conservative candidates expressing opposition to some of the hated Whig measures of the 1830s. But, certainly in Lancashire and many other parts of England, Scotland and Wales, it mostly amounted to support for Liberals and radicals at election time.

The 1840s did see further national and local attempts on the part of middle-class radical political groups, and efforts on the part of Chartists such as Lovett, to effect closer ties between Chartists and the middle-class reformers. But, generally speaking, such endeavours ended in failure. As in the case of the Leeds Parliamentary Reform Association (1840–1), the degree of franchise reform supported by the middle class often fell short of the Chartist demand for universal manhood suffrage. On other occasions, as exemplified by the Complete Suffrage Union in 1842, even when prepared to accept manhood suffrage, middle-class reformers did not wish to adopt the names Charter and Chartist (complete with their connotations of violence and extremism), and were prepared to work alongside the Chartists only as leaders and tutors rather than as equals. And the hand of friendship offered by some middle-class groups, especially those involved in the Anti-Corn-Law League, was rejected by O'Connor and others on the grounds that workers were to become the pawns of the middle class, effectively diverted from their true goal, the attainment of the Charter.[145] It is not surprising, therefore, that solid political reasons underlay the staunchly independent character of mainstream Chartism throughout the 1840s and that political independence was synonymous with strong class feeling.

Economic experiences also generally lent themselves to an independent, class-conscious perspective. As noted earlier, O'Connor and many other Chartists were extremely critical of what were perceived to be the evils of the capitalist system and its main practitioners, capitalist manufacturers. Overproduction, long hours of work and low wages, unemployment and poverty in the midst of plenty, excessive competition, greed and conscious exploitation, ceaseless profit maximisation, reification, de-skilling and attacks on the workers' collective organis-

ations, independence, authority and control – these were, as demonstrated in Part One, some of the features of industrial capitalist
development attacked by Chartists and others.

It is true that not all employers were criticised, that the Chartists did
not develop a theory of exploitation in production based upon the
extraction of surplus value by employers from workers, and that, whilst
opposed to wage-slavery, the Chartists did not 'seek to expropriate
the expropriators, smash the State and establish a system of common
ownership'.[146] But the 'failure' of the Chartists to formulate a mature
Marxist theory and strategy (some aspects of which Marx himself had
not developed by the mid–late 1840s) should not blind us to the fact
that Chartists such as McDouall, O'Connor and Leach did articulate
a very sharp, non-socialist-based critique of capitalist exploitation in
production. According to many Chartists in the factory districts and
in centres of workshop production, *experience demonstrated* that
'honourable' employers were fast dwindling in the face of rapid and
unwelcome capitalist advancement. And the latter was seen by McDouall
and others as constituting a *system*, a mode of production which contained within it the element of underlying structural dynamic (ceaseless
profit maximisation) and the notion of conscious agency (the overriding
desire of the capitalist to subjugate labour to capital's will). Thus there
existed within Chartism an economic as well as a political language of
class oppression and class conflict.

Class also saturated both the patterns and commonsense of everyday
life, of culture. As Dorothy Thompson has observed, the middle classes
'certainly believed themselves to be superior in every way to the
classes above and below them in morality, knowledge and understanding'. And, 'Class domination was not confined to the work-place. All
aspects of social life – dwelling-places, shops, drinking-places, recreational and instructional institutions, churches and chapel seating –
were segregated on class lines.'[147] And attempts on the part of the middle
class to control and transform workers' cultural lives, to 'channel them
into the paths of acquisitiveness, individualism, competition, self-help,
and "natural" acceptance of a state of subordination and dependency',
met with fierce resistance. Chartists responded by creating an alternative
'movement culture' with premiums upon workers' independence, control and freedom from 'the patronising and unwelcome attentions of
both bourgeois and aristocrat'.[148] In such ways were class and independence nurtured within culture.

Thus, in terms of our criteria of constituency, conflict/hostility and
independence, Chartism was an intensely class-conscious movement.
Two recent lines of criticism – the claim that all manner of divisions
permeated the working class, and the belief that Chartism was a tra-

ditional non-class-based movement – do not carry much conviction. As noted earlier, the first line of criticism, presented by Musson, Glen, Ward, Hunt and others suffers from three extremely damaging weaknesses: the false attribution to the Thompsons and other advocates of class consciousness of an undifferentiated view of the working class, of total unity; an exaggeration of the size and influence of a 'labour aristocracy' within the pre-1850 working class; and a serious underestimation of the constituency of class-based loyalties and ties in the Chartist period.[149]

The second, and most recent line of criticism is associated with Gareth Stedman Jones. Stedman Jones has characterised Chartism as a 'traditional' radical movement of a non-class-based kind in that Chartism offered a political rather than an economic (i.e. production-based) theory of exploitation and oppression. For Stedman Jones 'producerist' economic harmony characterised Chartist thought. But, despite its popularity, Stedman Jones' view of Chartism is also fatally flawed. In employing an absolute, narrow and 'true' standard of class (class consciousness equals revolutionary Marxism/socialism) and in judging the Chartists to have failed this touchstone of class, Stedman Jones effectively ignores the powerful presence within Chartism of the class- and production-yet non-socialist-based language referred to above. Actually, existing consciousness is devalued in favour of an ideal standard of what ought to be the case. Stedman Jones also greatly underestimates the extent to which, as noted earlier, class feelings and actions emerged *within* politics and culture in the Chartist period. In effect, Stedman Jones employs a formalistic, static and generally unsatisfactory approach to the study of words and ideas. There is precious little sense within his argument of the ways in which words and ideas can acquire, and often do acquire, new meanings in changed contexts. Rather, we are given the false impression that radicalism, as a stock of ideas, carried largely autonomous and fixed meanings between the mid–late eighteenth century and 1850. Changed meanings and contexts are belittled, and language and political ideas are improperly torn apart from any material influences. The end result is an unconvincing idealism.[150]

Chartism and Revolution

If we have established the class-based character of Chartism, we must still address two final questions concerning the content of class consciousness. To what extent did revolutionary intentions and actions inform the movement? And to what degree did there exist during the late 1830s and throughout the 1840s a potentially revolutionary situation in mainland Britain? We will take the questions in reverse order.

As John Saville has recently demonstrated in his study *1848: The British State and the Chartist Movement* (1987), there did not exist in the turbulent years of 1839, 1842 and 1848 a potentially revolutionary situation. There were no serious divisions within the upper echelons of British society or within the armed forces. Rather Britain had a self-confident ruling élite, a state machinery composed of skilful and determined men who did not hesitate to employ necessary force to defeat the radical opposition, and, by and large, massive allegiance on the part of propertied groups to existing institutions. 1848 demonstrated, in particular, that the state machinery (taken to include the government, military, police, magistracy and judiciary) was much better prepared to suppress radical activity than had been the case in 1839, and that for the mass of both the petit and full bourgeoisie the defence of property overrode commitments to liberty and equality. In addition, divisions within Chartism in 1839 and 1848, and the leadership's lack of a coherent strategy, meant that a united and well-organised national revolutionary force did not exist.[151]

To argue against the existence of a revolutionary situation is not, however, to underestimate the extent and depth of insurrectionary feeling and, in some instances, insurrectionary activity. The reader's attention has already been drawn to extensive arming and drilling in the autumn and early winter months of 1839. As Dorothy Thompson has observed:

> There can be little doubt that many of the strongest Chartist districts were considering projects for some kind of rising – Napier as commander of the north was aware of it, Harney recalled the 'concensus [sic] of opinion that force would have to be resorted to to obtain justice and the acknowledgement of rights', and the reports from magistrates of arming and drilling in Yorkshire, Lancashire, Nottingham and the Newcastle district were too widespread and consistent to be merely the imaginings of worried and frightened men.[152]

The year 1842 witnessed 'the nearest thing to a general strike that the century saw', the mixing of political and economic demands on the part of large numbers of strikers, and more arrests and sentences for offences concerned with 'speaking, agitating, rioting and demonstrating' than in any other single year during the nineteenth century. The inadequate and limp term 'Plug Plot Riot' does scant justice to the complexity and fullness of the events of 1842. Finally, there undoubtedly existed renewed schemes for insurrection in 1848, albeit on a lesser scale than in 1839.

That large numbers of people were prepared to entertain thoughts and acts of armed insurrection against the existing system is a matter for serious consideration. Given the considerable risks to livelihood, family and life itself, people do not lightly turn to acts of physical revolt. It was a measure of their deepseated grievances, bitterness and profound sense of alienation (of being despised outsiders) that so many respectable and reasonable Chartists were moved to consider acts of violence. Daily class-based and other experiences were instrumental in inducing such anger and alienation.

At the same time, however, there is little evidence that insurrectionary feelings and actions ever amounted to concerted and consistent plans for a national revolution. An underground movement did develop in 1839. And as Jones and Wilks have demonstrated, the Chartists of South Wales anticipated that their rising would spark off uprisings in other parts of Britain. In 1848 it would also appear to be the case that the Chartists of the Manchester district hoped that their local actions would ignite discontent elsewhere. But, as Thompson notes of 1839, 'none of the evidence necessarily adds up to the positive existence of a coordinated plan'.[153] In relation to the Manchester district in 1848, and despite the Ashton 'rising', there is plentiful evidence of organisational weakness and planning blunders of the most elementary kind.[154] Both divisions within the Chartist leadership, especially doubts as to whether to translate the language of popular constitutionalism into revolutionary action, and the skilful, cool, often restrained and calculated responses of the state in 1839, 1842/3 and 1848 did much to prevent the development of a coherent and co-ordinated revolutionary strategy.

Those Chartists who undertook insurrectionary activities did so more for democratic and economic regulatory than for revolutionary socialist reasons. Despite Wilks' claim that the Newport insurgents sought 'seizure of control over the means of production from the ironmasters and coalowners', there is more evidence to support Jones' view of Newport as a regional revolt undertaken to secure 'a better return for labour' and 'the political rights which were denied them'.[155] Similarly, Foster's belief in the existence of revolutionary, and presumably socialist, consciousness in Oldham is greatly weakened by the slight influence of 'physical-force' methods in Oldham in 1839 and a more general lack of evidence concerning revolutionary socialist influence among Oldham's workers.[156] We may argue that many Chartists *were* prepared to risk life and limb, but that such courage was motivated less by socialist concerns than by outrage at the general unfairness and hostility of the established system and by demands for political democracy, decent living standards, and due protection and reward for labour.

PROTEST MOVEMENTS IN BRITAIN AND THE UNITED STATES, 1820s–1840s: AN ASSESSMENT

We are now in a position to pull together and evaluate the chronological threads of working-class and popular protest in Britain and the United States between the 1820s and the 1840s. Evaluation is offered in terms of our three yardsticks of class: constituency; hostility; and independence.

From the perspective of constituency, there is no doubt that popular movements on both sides of the Atlantic became more broadly based in these years. At the heart of protest stood our endangered artisans, outworkers and others who were in grave danger of becoming fully proletarianised by capitalist development. But we have demonstrated that a broad spectrum of occupations from predominantly labouring populations, and situated in a variety of geographical contexts, adopted radicalism in order to improve their material and other circumstances. And in the course of identifying grievances and points of struggle, such people, often from different backgrounds and cultures ('rough' and 'respectable' in Britain, 'traditional' and 'revivalist' in the United States) began to act together in class-based ways.

Such a conclusion must, however, be qualified in three important ways. First, in Britain the socio-geographical constituency of popular radicalism was both deeper and more varied than its counterpart in the United States. In the latter country the generally slower and more uneven pace of capitalist transformation, the existence of the slave South and the pervasive effects of racism throughout the states, the possession of the vote by adult males, the more flexible political system and the importance of political citizenship, the extremely high rates of geographical mobility and labour turnover, the comparatively good opportunities for advancement and decent living standards, the extremely powerful appeals of personalised evangelical religion, and the ideologies of free labour, self-help and patriarchy may all have limited the constituency of radicalism. Diminished opportunities in the 'land of opportunity' obviously fuelled popular protest in 1830s America. But it was still the land of opportunity, freedom and political democracy. By way of contrast Britain was profoundly undemocratic and hierarchical. The widespread and accelerated nature of capitalist transformation in Britain, allied to the hostility of the state and a system of cultural apartheid, were more productive of widespread radicalism.

Thus, as we have seen, 1830s protest in the United States was largely northern and urban-based, and was dominated by white skilled and craft males. Textile operatives, women and other non-craft groups were involved, but largely in peripheral and shortlived ways. The central emphasis upon trade unionism and, to a lesser extent, politics as the main organisational forms in the 1830s further diminished the influences of women and others who were more prominent in less structured and more informal, community-based forms of protest. There were stirrings of discontent in northern and western agriculture and in rural manufacturing communities in New England; and the Anti-Rent Wars in Upper New York State were both bitter and protracted. However, mass rural discontent was a feature of the 1850s and post-Civil War decades. In the southern states there were slave revolts in Louisiana in 1811 and in Virginia, under Nat Turner, in 1831, to which might be added the conspiracies of Gabriel Prosser in Virginia in 1800 and of Denmark Vesey in South Carolina in 1822. But, as Genovese notes, southern slaves did not adopt insurrectionary means either frequently enough or in such large numbers to forge a revolutionary tradition.[157]

Furthermore, radicalism was extremely weak in the South, and ties of sympathy and support between the races minimal, at least before the 1850s. As Laurie has observed, 'In the South slavery and pervasive racism subsumed class divisions within the ruling race.' In the border states white journeymen sometimes unionised or waged industrial conflict. But in the Deep South 'unionism was as weak as slavery was strong'. White masters and journeymen joined forces throughout the South to restrict slavery to the plantation and household. Above all, black slavery conferred status and superiority upon objectively impoverished southern white workers. Thus Laurie:

> Most realized that slavery was both a labor system, which protected them from objectionable work, and a caste system, which kept the races separate, locked the blacks in their place, and fostered a semblance of social equality among whites. Slavery attentuated the glaring social distinctions within the master race and created the illusion of 'white egalitarianism'.[158]

We have observed that in Britain radical movements were also weaker in rural than in urban areas, and that craft and skilled workers were prominent. But 1830s and 1840s British radicalism did embrace a wider and more varied cross section of the labouring population. In particular, factory operatives, outworkers and even labourers were more strongly represented than in the United States. Given the greater variety of movements in Britain (and especially those of a community-based kind), the long tradition of household labour, sheer economic necessity, the wider spectrum of radicalised occupations, and, in real terms, the lesser importance of the domestic 'ideal', women were also more strongly represented in Britain, whether as members of female Chartist associations, members of protesting crowds or as strikers in the events of 1842. Even rural workers were more attracted to radicalism than once thought. And, despite geographical variations, Chartism, trade unionism, friendly societies and, increasingly, co-operative societies made a national impact. In sum, in terms of constituency, class was arguably more profound in Britain.

Similarly, in terms of our criterion of hostility – especially the expression of anti-capitalist behaviour and ideas – both countries experienced class. But, despite suggestions to the contrary,[159] anti-capitalist consciousness was more marked in Britain. We have observed that industrial conflicts escalated in both countries and that capitalist employers came to be seen as conscious exploiters of workers alongside bankers, merchants and aristocrats'. But the more uneven pace of capitalist transformation in the United States and the greater popularity of free labourist and self-help ideas, combined increasingly with ethnic and other cultural loyalties between employers and workers (especially after 1837), served to limit the spread of anti-capitalist ideas and to keep afloat and (in the 1840s) to strengthen the appeal of 'producerist' harmony in production. We have seen that 'producerism' was by no means defunct in 1830s and 1840s Britain. But economic and social strains and conflicts, cultural divisions, and ideological and political conflicts mushroomed, to ensure that class-based anti-capitalist ideas and practices became an integral part of radical vocabularies.

As reflected in their trade unions, in Chartism, in the Workingmen's Parties and in a host of cultural ways, workers on both sides of the Atlantic also embraced our third criterion of class, independence. But our final qualification is that independent radicalism was more in evidence in Britain. As we have seen, the flexibility of the American political system, the possession of the vote, and the co-optive strategies of the two main parties set important limits to independent class-based actions. In Britain working-class alienation from the entire system and from the established parties, and workers' willingness to entertain insurrectionary strategies were far more pronounced than in the United States. The Conservatives and Whigs may have invited support from workers on certain issues and occasions, but this was mainly tokenism. Unlike the Democrats they did not welcome genuine working-class participation in and, in some instances, control of party affairs. And we have clearly seen that political and other attempts to build inter-class alliances generally failed to overcome class-based divisions in 1830s and early–mid 1840s Britain. As seen above all in Chartism, independence and class pride were perhaps the dominant characteristics of British labour by the early 1840s.

We can thus both endorse Bridges' conclusion that British and American workers displayed (despite their different political contexts) many similar grievances and aims, and add that class was stronger in Britain. It is also worth noting that British workers' movements were generally more durable. As we will shortly observe, the 1837–42 depression had a weakening effect upon labour movements in both countries. But, allied to the rapidly changing social and ethnic composition of its working class, the United States experienced a depression which had a far more debilitating effect upon the labour movement than was the case in Britain. Furthermore, the 1840s and 1850s saw the emergence in both countries of more narrowly based labour movements than had been the case during the 1830s, a greater willingness on the part of labour to accommodate itself to the seeming permanence of industrial capitalism, and more fragmented working classes. It is to an examination of these developments that we must now turn.

CHAPTER THREE

Fragmentation: Labour Movements from the 1840s to the 1860s

The 1837–42 depression greatly weakened workers' capacities to organise successfully at the work-place. Despite continued industrial conflict, trade-union membership in Britain had fallen to under 100,000 during the slump of 1842 (as contrasted with a membership figure of 1 million during the good year of 1834). Massive unemployment in the United States during the late 1830s saw a precipitous decline in the influence of both trade unionism and radicalism. Initially radical denunciations of the actions of financiers and speculators drew immense crowds. But, notes Laurie, under the influence of extended unemployment which set in in 1838, 'rally grounds emptied, general unions disintegrated, and the few unions that did survive turned into friendly societies dispensing funds to jobless members. The labor movement died with a whimper'.[160]

THE UNITED STATES; TEMPERANCE, RELIGIOUS REVIVALISM AND ETHNIC AND RACIAL CONFLICT

By the early 1840s large numbers of American workers had turned from the collective solutions offered by labour radicals to the more individualistic responses to distress presented by temperance and religious revivalism. Chiliasm, born of despair, was everywhere apparent. In New York City's Bowery, observes Wilentz, 'chiliastic sects sprang up along with new congregations of distinctly lower-class Methodists and Baptists, in what soon became the greatest plebeian Protestant revival in the city's history'.[161] In Philadelphia and in countless other places in the North the Second Great Awakening also assumed a distinctly proletarian character:

> Obscure ministers in storefront churches and urban missions funded by lay groups looked past the traditional middle-class following of the Protestant church to urban journeymen. Not even the seamiest neighborhoods deterred these eager divines. Bibles in hand and often accompanied by plebeian churchwomen in black broadcloth, they preached the gospel on street corners and pursued converts in

workshops, garrets, and even tippling houses, braving the insults of drinkers half amused and half outraged. Revivals that droned on for days at a time enraptured workmen down on their luck and a step away from the soup kitchen. Ministers convinced penniless workmen that Christ brought on hard times as retribution for worldly sin, but held out better days and salvation for those who would mend their ways. *Church membership skyrocketed.*[162] (my italics)

Temperance sentiments also flourished, reaching a much wider popular constituency than their mainly middle-class appeal of the 1820s and early 1830s. Most dramatic was the rise of the Washington Temperance Society, founded in 1840 by six Baltimore artisans describing themselves as 'reformed drunkards'. Ministering sympathetically to the hardened drinker, and possessing a 'down-to-earth egalitarianism', the Washingtonians preached a simple message: 'alcohol made hard times worse and had to be avoided completely'. Within two years the Washingtonians 'became the rage of working-class America': official estimates counted 200,000 members in 1841 and 3 million two years later. By the mid 1840s the Washingtonians' mass influence was in decline, but temperance sentiments continued to influence large numbers of (especially Protestant and native-born) workers.[163]

Commitments to temperance, sobriety, self-help and religion are, of course, not necessarily incompatible with labour solidarity and articulations of class. Many Chartists and 1830s American labour radicals practised temperance (as being compatible with self-respect, independent thought and sound commonsense) whilst denouncing the hypocrisy of those middle-class advocates of temperance who ignored the structural roots of poverty and insecurity. Similarly some Chartists, especially in Scotland and Wales, preached radical Christianity; and, as we will see, workers in 1840s New England criticised the excessive competition and long hours of work of capitalism partly from the standpoint of Christian emphases upon community and brotherhood.[164]

In the specific context of the 1837–42 depression temperance and evangelical sentiments did, nevertheless, mushroom at the expense of radicalism and class solidarity. Proponents and followers of temperance and revivalism not only rejected collective radicalism in favour of personal salvation but also adopted 'community of interest' ideals which cut across classes. Thus the Washingtonians embraced a relatively wide spectrum of occupational groups within their leadership and directed their appeal to all drunkards, irrespective of social status and religion.[165] The revivalists' 'community of interest' was more narrowly defined, being confined to Protestants, practitioners of total abstinence and, apart from some Protestant immigrants, the native born. Indeed, as Laurie has suggested, 'nativist tendencies inhered in the temperance and evangelical crusade from the very beginning'.[166]

In the early to mid 1840s such nativist tendencies became of paramount significance. The mid 1830s had witnessed the intensification of nativist feelings. In New York, for example, the Native American Democratic Association had directed its fire against the alleged threat to republican institutions provided by the Papacy, and some New York workers blamed immigrants, especially Irish Catholics, for the bastardisation of the crafts. But this nativist movement had quickly fallen apart, the victim of internal divisions and the power of class feeling among New York's workers.[167] By the early–mid 1840s matters had radically changed in New York and elsewhere in the North. As a result of the depression, poverty and the scramble for work greatly increased. Immigrants, again especially Irish Catholics, were increasingly seen as a source of cheap labour and the destroyers of 'custom'. In addition, revivalist and temperance zealots intensified their campaigns against the Irish Catholics' attachment to drink and to a Papacy allegedly intent upon universal domination. Yankee individualism, independence, sobriety and democracy were, it was claimed, gravely threatened by the dependency, backwardness, bawdy inebriation and roughness, superstition and dictatorship allegedly integral to Roman Catholicism. American republicanism thus assumed a threatened, narrow and ugly nativist form; and this *before* the onset of massive immigration from Ireland in the post-Famine years.[168]

The immediate spark to nativist outbursts in the storm centre of Philadelphia in 1844 lay in the usage of the King James Bible in schools.[169] Catholics recognised the Douay Bible as their scripture and, not yet having constructed its own schools, the Catholic church in Philadelphia requested, in the person of Bishop Francis Patrick Kenrick, that Catholic children be excused from the King James Bible reading sessions and allowed to conduct separate services in school with their own bible. The School Board partially agreed to the request, excusing from bible reading those children 'whose parents are conscientiously opposed thereto', but refusing to sanction the use of the Douay Bible. However, many of Philadelphia's evangelicals adopted a less considered approach. They interpreted Kenrick's request as 'further confirmation of a Catholic conspiracy to infiltrate the schools and then deliver the republic into the hands of the diabolical pope'. In the autumn of 1842 representatives from almost every Protestant church and sect in Philadelphia formed the American Protestant Association which during the next eighteen months engaged in widespread and inflammatory anti-Catholic propaganda and helped revitalise a strong anti-immigrant movement led by themselves and the American Republican Associations. The latter, which were political bodies, sought to deny the vote to immigrants for twenty-one years after their arrival in the United States and to ban them from public office.

Matters came to a head between March and May in 1844. At the March elections the American Republicans, chanting 'Save the Bible!', performed well. The Republicans then held gatherings in the Irish Catholic district of Kensington. And, following clashes in April, there erupted a full-scale nativist attack on Kensington in May. The riots led to the destruction of property and the loss of at least sixteen lives. Nativist anger had not, however, run its course. According to Laurie, 'Nativism surged through the summer and American Republican helmsmen adroitly steered it into displays of political might.'

The nativist upsurge was felt throughout the North. In New York City, for example, butchers, carpenters and others little affected by industrialisation and with a strong sense of the interests of 'the Trade', were prominent in the American Republican Party. The latter, formed in 1843 and independent of both 'the priest-ridden Democrats and the ineffectual Whigs', performed extremely well in the elections of 1844 – a feat repeated throughout the North – and led to 'an outpouring of popular nativism' in the early summer months.[170]

Nativism had two major effects upon workers and radicalism. First, heightened ethnic tensions and conflicts undermined working-class solidarity and attached workers to largely middle-class leaders within their own ethnic groups. In Philadelphia, for example, Irish Catholic weavers who were engaged in bitter industrial conflict with Irish Catholic bosses in 1843, sided with those very same bosses in response to nativist attacks during the mid 1840s. Likewise, Protestant weavers, who had made common cause with Catholic weavers in Philadelphia during the 1830s, were firmly ensnared within nativist structures by 1844.

Second, nativism effectively negated any potential to develop independent working-class political radicalism. Up to its rapid demise in 1845 American Republicanism was the main institutional expression for the nativist politics of Protestant workers. After the mid 1840s the Whigs cut the nativist ground from under the American Republicans, at least down to the mid 1850s when the 'Know Nothings' enjoyed spectacular, if brief, popularity. On the other side of the political divide the Democrats cultivated a style of politics revolving around support for immigration, defence of diverse life-styles, religions and drinking habits, commitment to the concerns of the 'common man' and, not infrequently, racism. On both counts, therefore, the class feelings and attachments of the 1830s suffered.

A further source of fragmentation was the escalation of racism. Anti-abolitionist sentiments (especially in New York City), Democrats' defence of states' rights, and outright racism were, of course, not new to the 1840s. In earlier decades whites in both the North and the South had sought to drive blacks from the docks and other areas of employment. New York City and Washington in the mid 1830s, Baltimore as early as 1812, and many more places had experienced ugly race riots.[171] But, as Laurie informs us, the riots in Cincinnati, Philadelphia, the South and elsewhere in the 1840s were, 'unlike the flare-ups in the past . . . orgies of brutality that stretched over several days, claimed several lives and scores of injuries, and left black ghettos in charred ruins'. By the end of the 1840s, concludes Laurie:

> the Irish had muscled most blacks off the Philadelphia docks. In Deep South cities Irish toughs forced blacks out of dray work and other hauling trades, and in New Orleans they even took over the traditional black work of serving customers in pubs and restaurants . . . Racial violence helped destroy what remained of a black artisan class in both regions by the 1850s. Only in Charleston did black artisans hold their own.[172]

As seen in the above quotation, increased competition in the job market provided an impetus to racism. In Philadelphia, for example, unemployed weavers and new immigrants searched for sources of employment. And 'the exodus from weaving to the docks and construction sites irritated racial antagonisms and touched off another round of rioting between the hungry Irish and hungry but employed Black dockers'.[173] But racism could not be reduced to economic competition alone: it pervaded most aspects of life. The depression, economic competition and, less directly, nativism provided the sparks. Even those workers in New York City and elsewhere who prided themselves upon their rationalism and radicalism, and who expressed anti-slavery sentiments, were frequently indifferent or hostile to blacks themselves (as seen, for example, in their exclusion from the trade unions). And, as noted by Wilentz, most craft workers and white labourers in New York (and, we might add, elsewhere) 'retained a deep distrust of the small, unskilled black community as a class of supposedly abject dependents'.[174]

THE 1840s US LABOUR MOVEMENT AND NATIVIST PRODUCERISM

It was thus in the context of protracted depression, nativism and racism that rationalist radicals attempted to reconstruct the impressive labour movement of the 1830s. Given such a daunting context, it was no surprise that such attempts had extremely limited effects and that 1830s style radicalism remained very much a minority or 'subterranean' influence for most of the 1840s. This is not to argue, however, that radicalism disappeared. Trade unions, 'the sole institutional survivals of the old radicalism with emphatic working-class membership', persisted and industrial conflict was a feature of the early 1840s, but less so for the remainder of the decade. During the 1840s trade unionism was concentrated largely in those trades badly hit by capitalist transformation, and was mainly the preserve of men. But there were instances of women's organisation. Women were extremely active in Lowell and other centres of ten-hours agitation in New England; and in 1845 workingwomen from a number of trades in New York City formed the Ladies' Industrial Association, an organisation which placed a premium upon female self-reliance and which advocated trade-union organisation and higher wages for the female trades.[175]

Such examples of trade-union activity could not, however, mask the severe overall decline in the fortunes of trade unionism in the post-depression years. In Philadelphia, New York, Cincinnati, Boston and hosts of other centres, 1840s trade unionism was but a pale shadow of the robust General Trades' Unionism of the 1830s. Militancy ebbed, sectionalism increased (in Philadelphia, 'Artisan combinations regressed to their pre-thirties form and rarely drafted the semiskilled or expressed solidarity with one another, with industrial workers, or with the unskilled'),[176] organisation tended to be sporadic and shortlived (the Ladies' Industrial Association, for example, soon suffered from an influx of bourgeois women, disunity of purpose and by 1846 was effectively dead), the general appeal and social base of trade unionism were greatly diminished (the vast majority of unions founded in the 1830s did not survive the depression), and the trade-union movement, at least up to the late 1840s revival, was dwarfed by revivalism, nativism and ethnic conflict.[177]

Rationalists and other radicals did, despite their minority standing, channel their energies into a variety of other causes during the 1840s. The issue of land reform, for example, attracted a wide and varied following. As noted in Part One, George Henry Evans' National Reform Association, established in New York City in 1844, and with its rallying cry of 'Vote Yourself a Farm', built up a considerable following among tenants, labourers and marginal farmers in the Midwest. Those eastern artisans undergoing proletarianisation and foreign-born radicals (such as John Campbell of Philadelphia and other former Chartists) were also attracted by land reform. In addition to schemes for co-operative production (which maintained an existence throughout the 1840s and were especially popularised by Wilhelm Weitling) and for Fourierist phalanxes (between 1843 and 1853 more than forty Fourierist socialist communities were established, the most famous being Brook

Farm in Massachusetts), land ownership held the twin appeals of personal and collective independence. As with O'Connor's Land Plan in Britain, land reform cannot simply be seen as a reactionary and romantic craving for a past idyll of 'peasant' proprietorship. Independence, as the direct antidote to 'wage-slavery', was at the heart of working-class radicalism on both sides of the Atlantic and assumed a variety of forms. In addition, it was believed that the increased availability of land would draw off surplus labour from the urban, industrial areas and so reduce the supply of labour and increase wages.[178]

As noted earlier, the Ten Hours Movement, especially in New England, was an important focus for labour radicalism. Indeed, as Thomas Dublin has observed, the 1840s labour movement in New England, especially Massachusetts, was an exception to the general rule in that it was stronger and more solidly organised than in the 1830s.[179] Organisations such as the Lowell Female Labor Reform Association (1844) and the New England Workingmen's Association (1845) conducted impressive campaigns for a ten-hour statute. As Theresa Murphy has demonstrated, the campaigns were deeply coloured by a form of radical Protestantism which emphasised the importance of community and co-operation, which criticised long hours of work and the unlimited individualism and profit-maximising endeavours of the employers as 'un-Christian', and which sought by means of moral persuasion rather than class conflict (ten-hour campaigners were opposed to strikes) to achieve a working day compatible with the full performance of material, Christian and republican duties.[180] In the event such tactics were not successful. Legislators in Massachusetts were reluctant to intervene in market relations between consenting individual workers and employers. In New Hampshire and Pennsylvania ten-hour laws were passed. But their results were less than effective: whilst the legislatures stipulated ten hours as a legal day's work, they simultaneously allowed individual workers to work overtime.

More secular and strident anti-capitalist sentiments were to be found inside the 1840s Democratic Party. The latter was fond of presenting itself as the 'true home of the working classes'.[181] The rhetoric of 'equality, liberty and workerism' was most loudly articulated inside the party during the 1840s and early 1850s by Mike Walsh and his 'shirtless Democrats' of New York City's Bowery district.[182] The son of a cabinet-maker and veteran of the United Irishman uprising of 1798, the flamboyant Walsh became a journalist, the 'radical Bowery B'Hoy politician', and, in 1846, an elected representative to the state assembly. Within the Democratic Party Walsh saw himself as the defender of the immigrant against the 'paltry and bigoted principles' of the nativists, the representative of Bowery bravado and toughness, and the champion of workers

and small 'honourable' masters. But, as noted by Wilentz, what differen-
tiated Walsh from mainstream Democrats was his 'increasingly vitriolic
anticapitalism'. Walsh was opposed to 'the slavery of wages' and 'all
forms of capitalist greed and power'. In the state assembly he introduced
legislation to end butchers' and builders' monopolies, to abolish contracting on public building projects, and to regulate conditions of
apprenticeship.

Increasingly, however, Walsh's anti-capitalism was subsumed within
his defence of the South and slavery. From the mid 1840s to the mid
1850s the Democratic Party was deeply divided upon the issues of
Southern domination of the party and the non-extension of slavery.
Walsh, critical of those northern abolitionists who enforced capitalist
domination and 'wage-slavery' and yet who simultaneously denounced
chattel slavery, sided with southern interests. He regarded political interference with slavery as 'a violation of democratic rights by Yankee
entrepreneurs and as a diversion from the war on capital'. Nominated
to Congress in 1852, Walsh emerged as 'a northern champion of southern rights'. He continued to defend states' rights, to act as apologist for
slavery, and denounced emerging Republican opposition to the Kansas-
Nebraska Bill as deference to the wishes of 'the barons of wage
slavery'.[183] In effect Walsh had become a pawn of Southern political
power-brokers in their search for northern Democratic allies. As Wilentz
observes, by the mid 1850s Walsh's political departure was inevitable.
Given the expansionary aims of the 'Slave Power', many radical workers
in the North transferred their anger from the immigrant to the arrogant
and imperialistic Southern planter. And the main beneficiary was the
newly formed Republican Party.[184]

Walshites, National Reformers, utopian socialists, ten-hour campaigners and trade unionists were thus present during the 1840s. But
they lacked major influence, their victories were small and isolated and
their radicalism generally lacked the work-place-based class-conscious
bite of the 1830s. Indeed, we can go further, to endorse the claims of
Wilentz and Laurie that the dominant form of popular radicalism in the
1840s was that of 'radical revivalism', a form of protest which embraced
both 'producerism' and revivalism/nativism. Simultaneously anti-immigrant, anti-accumulator and pro 'honest' producers, radical revivalism
marked a major retreat from the class-based developments of the
1830s.[185]

Radical revivalism took root in those nativist fraternal orders which
'spread like wildfire' during the mid 1840s. Despite the rapid demise of
the American Republican Party in 1845, plebeian nativism continued to
flourish, especially in the Mechanics Mutual Protective Association and
the Order of United American Mechanics. The former, formed in 1841,

'raged through the upper Midwest and extended into some Eastern cities after 1845'. The latter, created in the aftermath of the Kensington riots in Philadelphia, and largely led by veteran Washingtonians and American Republicans, 'shot up in the North and even reached into the South'. Of particular interest were the social composition and ideologies of these orders. Both were dominated by journeymen artisans (especially from those trades in which mutualism between master and artisan was still strong and in which an immigrant presence was relatively weak) and small masters. Indeed, both orders officially excluded 'non-producers' (merchants, professionals and financiers) as well as immigrants from membership. In practice merchants and lawyers were sometimes admitted but only upon the condition of paying 'due homage to productive labor'.

In contrast to the 'catch-all' nativism of the early 1840s, the middle to late years of the decade thus saw the emergence of a strong nativist movement which sought to recapture the 'producerism' of the 1820s and 1830s. But now producerism was fashioned in nativist mould. The immigrant and the 'accumulator' – cast as, respectively, cheap, unproductive and frequently drunken destroyer of 'honest' American standards and customs, and parasitical financial drone – constituted the foes of sober, honest and upright native-born workers and employer producers. 'Blasphemy, brothels, and drink' were to be the sworn enemies of nativists: 'honesty, industry and sobriety' were their watchwords.

Massive post-Famine immigration from Ireland and from Germany provided fertile soil for the further growth of producerist nativism in 1847. Ironically, however, immigration was also instrumental in the revival of trade unionism and labour radicalism at the end of the 1840s and the beginning of the 1850s. For a start nativist and other employers were quick to attempt to use the immigrants as a source of de-skilling and cheap labour, an act which immediately laid them open to the charge of 'dishonourable' behaviour, and which placed increasing strains upon the 'community-of-interest' ideal of radical nativists. Furthermore, despite economic growth and a rise in earnings from the mid 1840s onwards, money wages generally failed to keep pace with the cost of living. Capitalist transformation also continued to adversely affect conditions at work, to undermine the artisan's desire for economic independence, and to produce employers totally opposed to collective worker organisation.[186] In effect, therefore, economic factors once again began to place strains upon the notion of harmonious producerism beloved of nativists and to resurrect questions of class and class conflict.

Moreover, the immigrants themselves were often not as opposed to radicalism and labour organisation as is sometimes supposed. Contained within German immigration, for example, was a strong 'Forty-eighter' presence, artisans who had fled their homelands in the wake of the failure of the 1848 revolutions, and who brought to America strong radical credentials, as reflected in their republicanism, their militant rationalism, and support for socialism and co-operative production.[187] Large numbers of the post-Famine Irish immigrants were, of course, poverty-stricken Catholic peasants, concentrated in New York City and elsewhere at the bottom rung of the occupational ladder, increasingly embroiled in the politics of Tammany, drink, 'roughness' and racism, and in their desperate search for work and general fatalism unlikely candidates for labour radicalism. But a picture of a uniformly downtrodden, resigned and 'traditionalist' Irish Catholic mass is far from complete. Wilentz's observations in relation to New York City are instructive:

> On labour questions . . . neither the city's Irish press nor the rank and file showed any of the deference and pessimism usually ascribed to the famine refugees. The shoemakers' union, still active through the late 1840s, was kept alive almost entirely by Irish outworkers. In 1843, Irish building laborers helped organize the first mutual-aid society for the city's unskilled . . . The most celebrated strike in the New York area involved, not native journeymen artisans, but Irish labourers who struck their jobs on the Brooklyn waterfront in 1846.[188]

Cultural stereotypes, whether of a 'traditional' or 'modern' kind, can, therefore, be most misleading. Rather than 'reading off' a series of personal characteristics from a particular (idealist) 'type', we should begin by an examination of people in their concrete historical contexts, both material and non-material.[189]

THE 1850s REVIVAL OF CLASS

Given the changing context of the late 1840s, formerly nativist artisans, immigrants and sometimes the non-craft native-born found themselves in increased conflict with employers. After all, speculators and bankers could hardly continue to be seen as the omnipotent masters of those printing employers who replaced the small shop with the large sweatshop or factory, and who eagerly de-skilled and 'dishonoured' journeymen printers; or of those employers in shoemaking, clothing, the building trades and bookbinding who resisted demands for wage increases and decent conditions of work.[190]

The revival of class was reflected in a variety of ways: in the decline in the language of nativist producerism and in the renewed emphasis upon conflicts between labour and capital; in the more proletarian-based constituency of the labour movement in New York and elsewhere during the early 1850s; in the breaking down of ethnic divisions (in 1852 the National Typographical Association sought to organise all printers, native- and foreign-born alike); in the formation of Industrial Congresses by trade unionists, land reformers and co-operators in the early 1850s in an attempt to heighten labour solidarity and mutual support; and, in a few scattered instances (Cincinnatti in 1850 and Philadelphia in 1851) in the development of independent labour politics.[191] And in the frontier lands, as seen in Chapter one, the mid–late 1850s saw mounting radicalism.

The influences of class- and non-class-based forces upon politics during the 1850s have been usefully delineated by Amy Bridges.[192] As Bridges shows, by the 1850s most workers were part of the Democratic and Republican structures of partisan politics (the Republicans having arisen in 1854 out of a merger of Free-Soil, Whig and nativist elements). Issues of class were present in both local and national politics, but in the overall scheme of things were overshadowed by ethnocultural issues concerning prohibition, temperance and anti-temperance, bible reading in schools, Sunday closing laws, prostitution, gambling, immigration and nativism (as seen especially in the rise of 'Know-Nothingism'), the spread of Catholicism, and, increasingly, by the actions of the 'aristocratic' Slave Power and its desire to extend slavery. Furthermore, given that workers had political aims (such as the ten-hour working day, the election of judges, extended public education and so on), possessed the vote, if white adult males, and constituted an urban minority of the population, they were 'inevitably drawn into electoral politics and party politics' and cross-class coalitions. Experience usually demonstrated that they were more likely to gain their demands by means of pressure exerted upon the established political parties and groups than by means of independent labour politics. Bridges thus demonstrates that by the mid 1840s most states had 'abolished imprisonment for debt, made their militia systems less oppressive, expanded their public school systems, and enacted lien laws' – all key demands of labour radicals. And we can endorse Bridges' conclusion that, 'Workers became Republicans and Democrats not as the result of "symbolic" or "ritualistic" activities but in the service of quite objective working-class goals.'

In keeping with this perspective of rational political behaviour, we simply cannot attach crude labels of 'social control' and 'false consciousness' to political structures and workers' preferences. Given the wide suffrage and strong traditions of republican citizenship, political parties were dependent upon the support and involvement of working men to a much greater extent than in nineteenth-century Britain. In turn, parties took at least part of their organisational characteristics and ideological colouring from working-class influences, especially at the local level. Thus, the rise of political machines and 'boss' politics in New York City and elsewhere 'all bore the imprint of the working classes'. In view of the rapid growth of machine politics which catered to the needs of specific ethnic and working-class communities, and in which positions of power and influence were not infrequently filled by workingmen, we must also endorse Bridges' claim that American political organisations were far less the creatures and possessions of the middle and upper classes than in Britain. American workers enjoyed greater political clout and control than their British counterparts.

In so far as working-class influence was class-based in character, it constituted, however, one determination among many in the overall character and direction of politics. And other considerations and determinations often overshadowed that of class. Thus Bridges:

> The workingman's advocate, the boss, and local parties, then, all bore the imprint of the working classes. Like other social forces, though, their political will was mediated by the rules of the political order and disciplined by the logic of electoral politics. The boss, for example, despite the concessions and despite the militance of his stance, was more politician than workingman's advocate; electoral victory was more compelling than the solidarities of class. Although party success required, on the one hand, endorsing some working-class demands, it required on the other resources for organization building and ties to state and national governments ... Alternative political organizations of the working classes ... were always to be opposed ... if the Democracy was the 'true home of the working classes' in New York City, it was surely not a labor party. Indeed, rather than making of the party a workers' party, the party made of the workers, Democrats.[193]

Political alliances and allegiances were not, however, set in tablets of stone. To a much greater extent than in mid-Victorian Britain tensions, squabbles, contradictions and popular insurgencies, sometimes rooted in class conflicts, characterised mid-century American political organisations. In a theme which was to become all too familiar in the post-Civil War decades, the rhetoric of Democratic or Republican support for workingmen in the 1850s often related more to ethnocultural concerns than to militant trade unionism and the primacy of radical class-based demands. And, especially in the context of industrial conflict, political differences could, as had been demonstrated in the case of the 1830s Workingmen's Parties, develop into popular revolts against the status quo.

Popular political insurgencies in New York City, Cincinnati and Lynn between 1850 and 1860 illustrated the volatile nature of politics. In 1850 a number of New York's trades decided that they could not entrust their political fortunes to the 'sinister influences', 'wire pullers' and 'needy or ambitious politicians' in the major parties. Rather than create 'a separate organization of workingmen', the Industrial Congress decided to adopt an independent non-partisan approach. Major party candidates were to be judged by the Congress on the basis of their support for a reform programme. It was thus hoped to purify and reform rather than repudiate the main parties, especially the Democrats. In the event the Congress's chosen candidates did reasonably well in the 1850 elections. But, as had often been the case in the past, and as would happen again in the future, Tammany leaders managed to gain control of the Congress and to re-organise it in the manner of the 'old political parties'.[194] Thereafter, the Democratic machines run by Fernando Wood (who created public works during the depression of 1857) and 'Boss' William Tweed (in the post-bellum years) secured the allegiances of the majority of New York's workers into the 1870s.

The revolts in Cincinnati and Lynn were also shortlived. In the former there were attempts in the early 1850s to resurrect the style of independent labour politics which had been briefly popular during the previous decade. But Democratic promises of reform and more public offices for journeymen, and the adoption of popular radical working-class leaders as regular party candidates stopped the independent movement in its tracks. And the causes of political and industrial working-class unity in Cincinnati were shattered by anti-German riots in 1855.[195] Independent labour's prospects in Lynn seemed, at least in the short term, to be much brighter. Following the defeat of the great shoemakers' strike of 1860 workers organised a Workingmen's Party to, 'wreak vengeance on the politicians who had connived with officials of the state militia and the Boston police to defeat the workers'. The campaign was successful. The city elections of 1860 saw the Republicans lose the office of mayor to the insurgent Workingmen. The new mayor replaced the former city marshall (who had called out the militia during the strike) with a man who had played a leading role in the strike. But the new administration, its task of retribution successfully completed, made no attempt to introduce a labour-based programme. By the end of 1861 the Workingmen, notes Dawley, had vanished. Lynn's Republicans, running for office on a patriotic anti-secessionist ticket, were triumphant. And:

> The stunning impact of Civil War lifted the Republican party from a minority organization to the dominant force in city politics; it won every local election during the war and held the upper hand for the next thirteen years after it was over.[196]

The pattern of popular revolt described above – of short-term insurgency followed by realignment and integration within the dominant political structures – was to become a familiar feature of America's post-bellum political landscape. Such a scenario was neither lawed nor functionally 'necessary' (in the interests of consensus and stability). And stability *and* change, consensus *and* conflict, were continuing features of American politics during the post-1860 decades. But the very frequency and ephemeral nature of popular political insurgencies must be underlined. Explanations will be offered in due course.

In the fields of work-place relations and trade unionism the influence of class was more pronounced. In contrast to the generally somnolent years between 1843 and 1847, the late 1840s and early 1850s saw industrial unrest in printing, the building trades, clothing, shoemaking and a host of other occupations. In Cincinnati, for example, the accelerated pace of capitalist transformation, the formation of new employers' associations and wage stagnation gave rise to a mass upsurge in trade unionism and the hardening of divisions between workers and employers. Insisting that 'the increasing degradation of labor, which is now taking place throughout the city, under the wages system', could be remedied only by 'a united and determined effort', over sixty-seven different groups of Cincinnati's workers organised new unions between 1850 and 1861.[197] Similar patterns were evident elsewhere. In New York, Philadelphia, Boston, Newark, Pittsburgh, Milwaukee and less populous areas artisans were joined by labourers, clerks, drivers, porters and even domestics in the great union upsurge of 1850. In the course of this movement many workers abandoned the craft benefit societies – open to masters and journeymen and devoted to mutual aid – in favour of more militant trade unionism.[198]

Between 1852 and the onset of the Civil War there were further significant advances. Some eight or ten national unions were formed (the vast majority of unions being local in character) and more extensive collective bargaining developed. There was also heightened militancy in 1859 and 1860. In the former year, for example, Irish and native-born workers in Lowell conducted their first joint strike action. In the following year some 20,000 native- and foreign-born workers in New England shoemaking suppressed their ethnic animosities to wage one of the greatest ante-bellum strikes.[199]

CONTINUED WEAKNESSES

Trade-union and other advances made from the late 1840s onwards could not, however, conceal the overall retreats and defeats suffered by class-based labour radicalism since the 1830s. Both in the 1840s and

1850s the constituency of trade unionism was, despite the presence of immigrant and other newly organised workers, generally more narrowly based than during the 'heroic' 1830s. Organisation, especially for the non-skilled, tended to be shortlived. And for the most part, as noted by Foner, the trade unions of the 1850s were 'exclusive craft unions composed of skilled mechanics'. Despite periodic upsurges, 'unskilled workers found it almost impossible to join these unions, and several of them such as printers, hotel waiters, shoemakers, and tailors excluded women from the unions'.[200] Indeed, Stansell observes that during the 1850s women's labour activity 'narrowed to a few flurries in family-based trades', and that, as epitomised by the actions of male Industrial Congress, 'the mutualist, egalitarian strains of union thought in the 1830s were missing, and paternalism had hardened into rigid notions of woman's place'.[201] The Industrial Congresses did attempt to unify the male craft sections of the labour movement, but women, blacks and the unskilled were excluded. The impressive social embrace achieved by the General Trades' Unions was not repeated on any stable or durable basis.

The achievements of the 1840s and 1850s were more sporadic, uneven and less durable than those of the 1830s; and in overall terms the labour movement was weaker. Thus only three national unions – the typographical, the hat finishers and the stone-cutters – survived the 1850s. Most local and national unions had been destroyed in the depressions of 1854 and 1857, and the revival of unionism in the late 1850s was impeded by secession and the outbreak of the Civil War.[202] The Industrial Congresses of the early 1850s likewise lacked durability, falling victims to internal labour movement divisions between trade unionists and land reformers (as in New York), to the divisive issue of ethnicity (as in Philadelphia), or becoming an adjunct to the Democratic Party.[203] The uneven nature of Labour's development was reflected in an extremely limited presence in the South and in 'the long silence of labour' and the industrial calm which characterised, respectively, Philadelphia's and New England's textiles during the 1850s.[204]

In terms of conflict, as reflected in the articulation of anti-capitalist ideas, we have seen that 1840s producerist revivalism generally marked a retreat from the articulation of the more specifically class-based ideologies of the 1830s. We have, however, proceeded to trace the decline of producerist revivalism during the 1850s in favour of a sharper sense of specific worker consciousness. The latter did not, however, signify outright opposition to the capitalist system. Rather, the 1850s saw the decline of 'Utopianism' and the wider acceptance of a more restricted, pragmatic and accommodating stance on the part of workers. It was recognised, especially by trade unionists, that many employers were anti-union, but the strike weapon was, in the opinion of many unions, to be used judiciously. Advancement was to lie more in the perfection of organisation and formal procedures and in the development of an institutionalised system of collective bargaining, than in 'wild and vision- ary' schemes to either bypass or overthrow the system. In practice, of course, labour's moderation, as in Britain, was often not reciprocated by employers and the courts: the upshot was a highly volatile structure of 'industrial relations'. But continued industrial conflict could not con- ceal, again as in Britain, a greater acceptance of the 'wages system' and desires to achieve equity and protection within the confines of that system.

Finally, labour's capacity to act as an independent class-conscious body was, throughout the 1840s and 1850s, more restricted than in the 1830s. We have noted the profoundly divisive influences of ethnic, racial and other cultural conflicts during the 1840s. And such conflicts continued to erupt at inopportune moments throughout the 1850s. Thus labour's revival in the early years of the latter decade was undercut not only by economic depression but also by the extensive revival, in both North and South, of nativism. During the 1850s over 2 million immi- grants arrived in the United States. And the 'Know Nothing' Party, spouting a familiar mixture of nativism, temperance and concern for the grievances of the workingman, won landslide victories in the elections of 1854 and beyond.[205]

Ethnic and racial conflicts exerted a profoundly debilitating influence upon class. In Cincinnati, for example, the advances recorded by the Labor and Labor Reform Party (1850) and the General Trades' Union (1853–4) were shattered by the rise of 'Know Nothingism' in 1854 and three days and nights of rioting against the city's German community in the spring of 1855. Labour unity in Cincinnati revived in the winter of 1861 with the formation of a new Workingmen's Party which success- fully enlisted the support of native- and foreign-born workers. But the firing of the first shots at Fort Sumter presaged the overshadowing of class by nationalist loyalties.[206] In the South, and despite the intensifi- cation of class conflicts within white society and the rise of 'Free Soilist' sentiments, pervasive racism and continuing job competition (in Baltimore and elsewhere) between black and white erected insuperable barriers to class solidarity.[207] And throughout the country independent labour politics had never fully recuperated from the defeats suffered by the Working Men in the 1830s. The co-optation of labour's leaders and programmes (repeated in Philadelphia and Cincinnati in the 1850s) and a wider ideological appeal based upon cultural diversity, religious toler- ation, support for workers' economic grievances and racism had enabled the Democratic Party to make deep inroads into the working class.

Some anti-slavery Democrats bolted to the Free Soil Party in 1848. And anti-slavery and the ideology of free labour, complete with republican emphasis, underlay the impressive rise in working-class support for the new Republican Party during the late 1850s and throughout the Civil War. Class-based issues, as we have seen in the case of Mike Walsh, continued to surface *within* the official party structure. But strong working-class political consciousness, as reflected in the creation of independent and radical institutions, had fallen by the wayside. Thus, in contrast with the 1830s, the American labour movement and American workers on the eve of the Civil War generally lacked a strong sense of class consciousness.

BRITAIN: CONTINUITIES AND DISCONTINUITIES

Changes or 'discontinuities' were also much in evidence in the mid-Victorian labour movement in Britain. It is highly doubtful that discontinuities were so great or sharp as suggested by the Webbs (whose 'watershed' thesis posited a more or less complete break between the allegedly class-conscious, even revolutionary, pre-1850 period and the collaborationist, capitalist-minded and consensual third quarter of the nineteenth century).[208] Indeed, some historians, such as A. E. Musson, have gone to the other extreme to suggest that 'continuity', as reflected in trade unionists' limited class consciousness, sectionalism, moderation, aloofness from the unskilled, and the stubborn pursuit of moderate goals constituted the key to labour's true character throughout the nineteenth century. According to Musson, the Webbs and their followers have exaggerated both the radical and class-based character of the pre-1850 labour movement and its collaborationist and capitalist character in the post-1850 years.[209]

We will suggest that elements of both continuity and discontinuity were present in the post-Chartist period, and that a simple, dichotomous picture of either revolutionary/class-based or moderate/sectionalist action does scant justice to the full complexities of the early- and mid-Victorian periods. We will, nevertheless, proceed to argue that on balance and, as in the United States, change greatly outweighed continuity during the third quarter of the century in Britain. To argue in this manner is to endorse the thesis of modified discontinuity propounded by Hobsbawm, Harrison and others.[210]

The latter view does incorporate the notion of continuity. For example, independent working-class politics were less completely eclipsed than is sometimes supposed. Chartism, as we have seen, recovered some of its former strength in 1847 and 1848, and persisted up to 1858.

Beyond the late 1850s the various Manhood Suffrage associations and, to some extent, the Reform League kept alive the tradition of independent radicalism. Furthermore, as in the United States, class-based political issues (concerning, for example, hours of labour and safety conditions) were conducted inside the mainstream parties. Similarly, the 'Age of Equipoise' witnessed the outbreak of a significant number of protracted and bitter industrial disputes (in, for example, engineering in 1851–2, cotton 1853–4, in the building trades 1859–60 and in the iron industry in 1866) which belie notions of total class harmony and pervasive consensus. Large numbers of employers remained resolute in their anti-unionism, displaying as noted by Hobsbawm, a 'fundamental reluctance to accept the existence of a labour movement at all'.[211] And Musson is right to claim, in opposition to the Webbs, that the 'new model' craft unions which dominated the trade-union movement during the third quarter were neither so novel nor so pacifistic and capitalist-minded as is often thought.

Furthermore, in their 'respectable' life-styles (revolving around industry, thrift and sobriety) working-class activists and others did not passively accept and practise 'bourgeois' values and norms. 'Respectability' assumed a variety of meanings, and in the context of the general insecurity of working-class life could signify self-respect, a necessary safeguard against poverty and dependence, and a stimulus to collective self-help (as seen in the trade unions and co-operative societies), even class pride, rather than 'embourgeoisement'. Accelerated middle-class initiatives to 'reach' and transform workers into practitioners of 'rational recreation' and due deference to their social betters, often met with little success. The institutions of the labour movement continued to welcome genuine offers of friendship and help from many quarters, but remained steadfast in their proud independence and their opposition to being 'petted, pampered and patronized' by self-appointed middle-class tutors.[212] Class feelings thus continued to inform leisure activities as well as those at the work-place.

Simultaneously we must, however, evaluate the extent and typicality of such class-based feelings and conflicts. The suggestion made here is that, in comparison with the Chartist period, class diminished in importance at mid century and change outweighed continuity.

Trade Unionism

From the perspective of labour radicals change manifested itself in both positive and negative ways. In terms of positive achievements, there is no doubt that the more narrowly based labour movement made major institutional advances between the mid 1840s and the early 1870s. For example, despite considerable opposition, trade unionism achieved significant progress. Membership increased during the third quarter of the century from approximately one-quarter to half a million people. And as a result of the introduction of the Trade Union Act of 1871 and the Conspiracy and Protection of Property Act and the Employers and Workmen Act of 1875, the trade-union movement acquired seemingly secure legal status and official state recognition (peaceful picketing was made indubitably legal and workers and employers placed upon a more equal contractual footing).[213]

Trade-union gains were particularly marked among craft and skilled workers. Just as the failure and defeats of Chartism closed the door upon politics as the primary means of working-class emancipation, so the 'Mid-Victorian Boom', complete with its expansion of export markets and the capital goods industries and its great demand for skilled workers, provided a highly favourable context for the growth of trade unionism and other economic and social means of working-class advancement. And, as is well known, increasing numbers of skilled workers turned to the moderate, pragmatic, conciliatory, cautious, respectable, sectional, centralised and bureaucratic principles and practices of 'new model' unionism in order to achieve their goals.[214] In fact, 'new model' characteristics and aims were far less novel than claimed by the Webbs. But during the mid-Victorian years 'new model' features became more pronounced, extensive and effective within British trade unionism.

The fortunes of the most famous 'new model' union, the Amalgamated Society of Engineers, formed in 1851, illustrate the general observations made in the previous paragraph. Militantly moderate, the ASE nevertheless suffered a major defeat at the hands of the employers over the issues of overtime, piecework, the employment of semi-skilled machine operators and the principle of trade-union membership itself during the extensive conflicts of 1851–2. However, resourcefulness, determination, prudent financial management, and accentuated respectability and conciliation soon enabled the ASE to become the most powerful trade union of its day. Membership of the ASE grew from 9,737 in 1852 to 21,000 in 1860. By the mid 1870s the union had 44,000 members, a figure which increased to 54,000 by 1888 and to 72,221 in 1891. The mid-Victorian economy's insatiable demand for skilled metal trades' labour, and the remarkable tenacity and strength of the skilled turners' and fitters' collective loyalties at the point of production, meant that wages for the skilled and informal workplace controls were restored and strengthened alongside formal trade-union membership. Thus Zeitlin:

an ASE survey taken in 1861 shows that the principle of the standard working day had become well established and systematic overtime contained in most districts. Similarly, the hated institution of subcontracted piecework . . . was tending to disappear, and piecework itself was confined to 10.5 per cent of ASE members . . . The union was likewise able to insist on the payment of the district rate for work it considered to be skilled, and often to organise those who had entered the industry as handymen but who had been promoted to skilled positions.[215]

Pushing the 'frontier of control' in favour of workers necessitated, in the eyes of the ASE leadership, strict and proper attention to the principles of craft/skilled unionism (labourers and others deemed insufficiently skilled were excluded from membership of the ASE); systematic bookkeeping and dues collection; increasingly centralised controls over publicity, finance and the sanctioning of strikes; favourable publicity (the union as a 'reasonable' promoter of the interests of employer and employed, consumer and producer); caution (especially in relation to the drain on funds necessitated by strikes); prudence (an emphasis upon the friendly benefits provided by the union); and, if possible, good relations with employers and those influential members of the public (such as the Positivists) sympathetic to the union cause and anxious to heal social divisions in the wake of Chartism.

'Before long', notes Hunt, 'the ASE became a symbol of permanency and respectability. Its constitution and policies were widely adopted [and] its virtues were much publicized'. In the building trades the Amalgamated Society of Carpenters and Joiners modelled its constitution upon that of the ASE, and the union leaders of both the carpenters and bricklayers were, especially in the wake of the failure of the London building unions' fight for the nine-hour day in 1859, quick to advocate moderation and caution. In printing, the iron trade and shipbuilding the skilled unions sought to regulate apprenticeship (in order to maintain a scarcity of skills in the labour market), to jealously and zealously defend their members' relatively privileged positions at work (against the threats of technological change, de-skilling and enhanced competition from the non-skilled), and to counsel firm moderation in relation to employers. Rewards were forthcoming. 'By the 1870s', note McClelland and Reid, 'boilermaking was probably the best organised trade in the country and certainly the best organised in this industry.'[216]

Metals, engineering, shipbuilding, building and printing – these were the industries in which 'new model' influence, at least among craft and skilled workers, was at its strongest. But it is important to remember that neither the principles nor the practices of 'new model' trade unionism were so influential, successful or straightforwardly simple as maintained by the Webbs. The majority of British workers remained outside formal trade-union organisation throughout the nineteenth century. And even in the well-organised mid-Victorian trades – such as engineering – the mass of workers were not members of a union. Furthermore, as highlighted by Hunt, there were a number of unions that 'made no pretence to be part of "new model" unionism'. In London for example, George Potter acted as a spokesman for a group of small, militant unions which were critical of the conciliatory policies of the 'new model' leaders (the Webbs' so-called 'Junta') who controlled the London Trades Council.

As noted in Part One, we must, moreover, be careful to differentiate between, on the one hand, the stated intentions and public face presented by the 'new models' and, on the other hand, their actual daily practices and the ambiguities at the heart of their utterances. Above all we must remember that trade unions were, at least during the 1850s and for much of the 1860s, operating within a generally hostile climate of public opinion. The fears aroused in the minds of many of the 'respectable' classes by the protests of the 1840s, the continued widespread hostility of employers to trade unionism and the 'wrongheadedness' attributed to the unions by political economists and many politicians, created an atmosphere which was hardly conducive to the easy acceptance and smooth progress of trade unionism, however moderate the latter may have been. In addition, the 'Sheffield Outrages' of 1866 (the employment of physical violence against non-unionists in the metal trades at Sheffield), the ruling in the case of Hornby versus Close in 1867 (which established that trade unions were not entitled to protection of their funds under the Friendly Societies Act of 1855), and the appointment of the Royal Commission on Trade Unions in 1867 (to investigate both the events at Sheffield and trade unionism in general) created a crisis in which the trade-union leadership was hardly likely to parade the virtues of radical militancy. The 'Junta', composed of Applegarth of the Amalgamated Society of Carpenters and Joiners and Allan of the ASE, supported by Guile of the Ironfounders, Coulson of the Operative Bricklayers' Society, and Odger of the Shoemakers, accordingly, and in the event successfully, presented a very favourable account of trade unionism to the public and to members of the Commission, highlighting the self-helping, friendly society, moderate and conciliatory features of the movement.

As a number of historians have argued, we must adopt a critical approach to the study of the language and image of trade unionism presented by the 'Junta'. The latter were employing words and images to achieve a desired end – greater public and state acceptance of trade unionism. A purely formal and one-dimensional interpretation of the

'Junta's' statements, as partly reflected in the work of the Webbs, results in a skewed and misleading view of 'new model' trade unionism. The many-sided meanings and strategic purposes of language merit renewed emphasis, especially in view of the recently fashionable post-structuralist 'turn to language'.[217] Trade-union leaders could, for example, denounce strikes and militancy while simultaneously condoning 'action' against 'unreasonable' employers. Hunt makes the telling point that the ASE secretary who declared before the Royal Commission that strikes were, 'the very last thing that we would think of encouraging', had, during the previous thirteen years, 'distributed 179 separate grants to support strikes by other unions'. Similarly, the development of bureaucratisation, centralisation and accommodation among unions should not mask the great extent to which local branches continued to exert the 'screw' upon employers in relation to demands concerning wages and conditions. Unions adopted, when necessary, the language of orthodox political economy. But they also continued to insist upon the strong effects of collective organisation upon wage levels. Especially in periods of economic upswing, the 'invisible' hand of market forces required a firm push from the visible force of trade unionism to ensure that employers paid the 'just' market rate.

Proven sectionalism and aloofness from the 'masses' were, further-more, sometimes offset by demonstrations of inter-trade co-operation and financial support (as seen during the engineers' lockout in 1852, the 'Ten Per Cent' campaign in cotton during 1853–4, and the 1859–60 building strike), even occasional support for the non-skilled (as wit-nessed in organised union support for the agricultural labourers' cause during the early 1870s), and rank-and-file opposition to the caution of the 'new model' leaders (as reflected in the successful mass campaign, launched against the wishes of the national leadership, for the nine-hour day in 1871–2).

Opposition to the Webbs' oversimplified account of 'new model' unionism should not, however, lead to an underestimation of the sig-nificant changes which occurred in the British trade-union world around 1850. We have earlier seen that attitudes and policies revolving around caution, moderation, sectionalism, class conciliation and aloofness from the unskilled were not invented by the 'new models', being present among many of the more secure and privileged 'aristocratic' trades during the first half of the nineteenth century. However, unlike the more class-conscious 1830s and 1840s when the trade-union 'pukes' frequently ran for cover in the face of militant and mass-based industrial and political protest, 'aristocratic' attitudes became far more extensive, even dominant, during the less charged 1850s and 1860s. During the latter decades the boundaries and social composition of trade unionism

considerably narrowed. But it is highly significant that the future dominant forces within trade unionism, the cotton operatives and the miners,
assumed many of the features of the 'new models' during the more
balmy mid-Victorian years. Conflict did not expire in cotton, and,
especially in weaving, many employers remained in fundamental opposition to the claims of trade unionism; but both the 'open', mass unions
in weaving and the more closed and sectional unions in spinning became
more self-consciously moderate and conciliatory in their dealings with
employers. The non-skilled weaving unions adopted the 'new model'
title of 'Amalgamated', and their leaders increasingly set themselves
against 'reckless' outbursts of strike activity. The spinners, recovering
from the traumas of the 1830s and early 1840s, successfully repaired
and strengthened their unions and avidly cultivated a responsible and
conciliatory image.[218] And in coalmining Alexander Macdonald's
National Miners' Association opposed militancy and similarly preached
the virtues of moderation and class harmony.[219] (Detailed case studies
of mining and cotton are to be found in Chapter 2 of Volume Two.) In
both mid-Victorian cotton and coal trade unionism registered important,
if uneven, advances in terms of membership and recognition.

Co-ops, Friendly Societies and Socio-Political Advances

Other sectors of the labour movement also showed marked advances in
comparison with the 1830s and early 1840s. From the mid 1840s
onwards the co-operative movement recorded striking successes. The
formation of the Rochdale Pioneers in 1844 provided the spark. By
1850 there existed more than 200 co-operative societies run according
to the Rochdale principle of the 'divi' (whereby members received a
dividend upon purchases made). The vast majority of these societies
were located in the north of England. During the following two decades
Co-operation flourished in terms of both consumer and producer
societies. Indeed we can suggest that Co-operation was *the* great success
story of the (especially northern) labour movement at mid century – a
veritable tribute to the powers of collective self-help. 'Success', 'progress'
and 'improvement' became the watchwords of the co-operative leadership: co-operators were no longer outsiders but respectable citizens with
a stake in the social system. In 1861 the *Co-operator* (the main organ
of the movement) joyfully proclaimed, 'Englishmen have much to be
thankful for inasmuch as there is probably no country on the face of
the globe where sober, industrious young men can so soon raise themselves to ease and comfort, as in England.' 'Thousands of men' had,
according to the *Co-operator*, achieved, as a result of Co-operation, 'that
independence and contentedness of mind which is the happiest state the

natural man can feel, having plenty of clothes and food, and something to spare for the needy'.[220] This was a far cry from the language of discontent, poverty, bitterness and alienation which had characterised the Chartist years. By 1872 industrial and provident co-operative societies in Britain had at least 301,157 members. And advances were to be both more spectacular and widespread during the final quarter of the century when Co-operation established a national presence beyond its northern strongholds.[221]

By the 1860s friendly societies had also established a very strong presence throughout the ranks of the working class. No longer regarded as subversive and secretive but as respectable and sound institutions, the friendly societies, especially the affiliated orders (the Oddfellows and Foresters being the most prominent), experienced heady growth rates from the 1830s onwards. In 1874 the Royal Commission on Friendly Societies calculated that there were 4 million members of friendly societies in Britain and approximately 8 million interested in them as beneficiaries. And as promoters of industry, thrift and sobriety, both co-operative and friendly societies benefited from legislative protection. The Industrial and Provident Societies Acts of 1852 and 1862 established a legal context conducive to the growth of the co-ops, and friendly societies received legal protection from the legislation of 1850, 1855 and 1875.[222]

Finally, and despite the decline of Chartism, the Reform Act of 1867 extended the parliamentary franchise in the boroughs to all adult male owners and occupiers of dwelling houses, if resident for at least twelve months. In effect, the upper sections of the urban working class, the 'labour aristocracy', were rewarded for their self-help, moderation and 'restraint' by admission to political citizenship. The creation of a mass electorate was, however, to await the reform bills of 1884 and 1918.[223]

The greatly enhanced achievements and recognition achieved by the British labour movement during the mid-Victorian period were of profound importance in moulding the nation's labour traditions. Along with Hobsbawm,[224] we should first emphasise the significance of the early official (i.e. state) recognition of the labour (and especially trade-union) movement in Britain as opposed to the United States and, indeed, most European countries. Second, as we will see in more detail below, advancement and recognition were of crucial importance in promoting the more widespread acceptance of 'labourist' or 'reformist' ideas – in effect the philosophy that labour's emancipation was not to be achieved by the 'wild and visionary' schemes of Owenism or Chartism but essentially by patient, step-by-step advancement within the confines of the system. And such piecemeal gradualism and general opposition to 'theory' were, arguably, to be of greater importance in moulding the future character of British labour than the more ambitious and radical pre-1850 traditions.

As such, the mid-Victorian labour movement merits far more attention from labour historians than has traditionally been the case. All too often the 1845–75 period has been one-dimensionally categorised as a 'retreat', as a somnolent interlude between the 'heroics' of Chartism and 'new' unionism/socialism. In effect crucial, and in some ways very positive, developments took place at mid century.

But the latter did not constitute the total picture. And for Chartist stalwarts such as Ernest Jones and left-wing thinkers such as Marx and Engels, the positive features of labour's mid-century discontinuities were outweighed by more negative changes. It is to an examination of these more negative features that we will now turn.

The Retreat of Class

In terms, for example, of constituency, the social composition of the post-1850 labour movement was far more narrowly based than during the 1830s and 1840s. Many of the depressed artisan and outworking groups which had supplied much of the radical, indeed insurrectionary impetus behind Chartism and trade unionism, fell by the wayside – the victims of technological revolution and general capitalist transformation. During the years of mid-Victorian economic expansion craft and skilled workers came to the fore. Enjoying regular and well-paid work and, during the 1850s and 1860s increasingly finding a niche within, rather than being downgraded by, industrial capitalism, these relatively privileged workers in engineering, the metal trades in general, the building trades and the more traditional 'luxury' sectors assumed control of the labour movement. Coal and cotton were also represented; but, as noted, their domination of organised labour lay in the future. In any event, we have observed trends towards caution, moderation and conciliation in most sectors of the trade-union world.

The friendly and co-operative societies, and the activists' culture of 'respectability' did enjoy much longer social tails than many advocates of the 'labour aristocracy' thesis have suggested. But such deep penetration could not conceal the overall domination of the institutions of workers (especially at leadership levels) by the relatively prosperous and moderate craft and skilled workers, the increased divorce between 'respectables' (mainly regularly employed) and 'non-respectables' (mainly the poor) within the mid-Victorian working class, and the general indifference, and at times hostility, of organised craft and skilled workers to the unorganised and unskilled.[225] Sectionalism and craft superiority also became far more marked during the third quarter.

The institutions of the labour movement continued to pride themselves upon their capacities for self-determination and corporate, even
class, pride. But whilst the trade unions were more or less wholly run
by workers in the interests of workers, working-class independence was
in general terms less marked than during the Chartist years. Especially in
its heartlands of Lancashire and Yorkshire, the co-operative movement
did attract not only middle-class support (unlike the 'wrongheaded'
trade unions, the co-ops were seen as promoters of individualism and
capitalist values), but also significant membership among small
employers, managers, overlookers, agents of one kind or another and
teachers. Middle-class reformers were also sometimes prominent as
leaders in the more established and larger friendly societies.[226]

It was, however, in the area of politics that the decline of class-based
independence was most marked. The continued existence of Chartism
during the 1850s could not disguise the sharp decline in support of the
movement and the shift away from political to social and economic
means of advancement. By 1853 national Chartism was a very pale
shadow of its former self. And the remainder of the 1850s and 1860s
were to witness the greater integration of labour movement figures into
the two-party structure. By the elections of 1868 former Chartists were
for the most part strong supporters of Gladstonian Liberalism. And the
Conservative Party had created a mass working-class following,
especially in Lancashire on the basis of its 'No Popery' and populist
appeals. Symptomatic of such changes were the anti-Catholic Murphy
Riots which swept the former Chartist strongholds of Ashton and Stalybridge during 1868, and the adoption of Marx and Engels' former
socialist protégé, Ernest Jones, as a Liberal candidate at Manchester in
the 1868 parliamentary elections.[227]

Anti-capitalist ideas did not expire during the third quarter. Especially
during periods of industrial unrest, employer 'tyranny' was roundly
condemned. And, as Hobsbawm has observed, 'the labour aristocrat
might wear a top-hat and think on business matters exactly like his
employer, but when the pickets were out against the boss, he knew
what to do'. Attempts to establish better working relationships with
employers were combined with a strong sense of being a wage earner
and having interests and ideas specific to that position. To refer, once
again, to Hobsbawm's 'labour aristocrat': 'he developed, if on a narrow
basis, a solidarity and class consciousness, a belief that so long as a man
worked for wages his interests were exclusively determined by that
fact: a conviction which has become a valuable part of British labour
tradition'.[228] Given such a context, the appeal of 'producerism' in mid-
Victorian Britain was extremely limited.

But growing wage-earning consciousness was simultaneously combined with the widespread development of the narrowed, reformist outlook and spirit noted earlier. 'Rising in society' and obtaining a 'stake' therein took precedence over the Chartist belief that working-class emancipation necessitated a 'revolving of the whole system'. As I have written elsewhere:

> Class conflict did not suddenly disappear with the demise of Chartism, but root-and-branch criticisms of society did decline in frequency, intensity and appeal. Energies were increasingly channelled into the more limited and narrowed directions of the co-op., trade union and educational 'improvement' society. Industrial capitalism came, in practice, to be accepted as a fact of life, as a system to be lived with, or modified and reformed from within rather than frontally challenged.[229]

By the 1860s conscious commitment to reformism had become widespread. Thus leading co-operators openly contrasted the 'utopian' and 'dark and incomprehensible' schemes of Owenism with the material successes of a movement rooted in the 'divi', and practical day-to-day business management. Social levelling was frowned upon. Co-operation sought to prosper, 'not by pulling down the rich – excepting those who are rich with ill-gotten gains – but by lifting up the poor'. There was to be no attempt to 'set class against class', but rather, 'to build up and promote that sympathy and friendship which is of such vital importance to the national welfare'. Workers were thus exhorted to 'rise' without infringing the property rights of others.[230] Trade unionists might attack the 'tyranny' of specific capitalists, but the capitalist system, rooted in the wage labour–capital relationship, was largely accepted. Trade unionists also placed greater emphasis upon the role of market forces (as opposed to custom) in the determination of wages, and the importance of learning and abiding by the 'rules of the [capitalist] game'.[231] And, as Royden Harrison has long insisted, independent working-class politics during the third quarter came into being in relation to much more limited aims – to enable workers to 'rise in the social scale' rather than to 'knock property on the head' – than during the Chartist period.[232]

Along with the reformism of the institutions of labour there developed a more conservative and status-conscious working class. Patriotism, of an increasingly non-radical character, had, notes Cunningham, established a strong presence among workers by the late 1870s.[233] The rise to dominance of the craft and skilled élite was accompanied by a hardening of gender-based divisions, a much quickened retreat of married working-class women into the home, and a much stronger emphasis upon male superiority and female inferiority. Within the labour movement notions of the 'family wage' and a 'woman's place' assumed central importance at the expense of the Chartist emphases upon mutuality and shared (if unequal) relationships.[234] The state was increasingly seen less as an implacable foe than as a neutral umpire, keen to create a legislative framework and climate of opinion receptive to the progress of a plurality of social interests.[235]

Such changes suggested that notions of alternative ways of living and organising life, so prominent during the 1830s, were in serious decline. However much mediated by the awkward facts and conflicts of life, bourgeois hegemony became the established reality in mid-Victorian Britain.

Finally, the ability of the workers to mount an effective challenge to bourgeois ideas and practices was greatly impeded by the development of a far more fragmented working class, a pulling apart of formerly unified groups and individuals, during the third quarter. Such fragmentation revealed itself in a host of ways. Reference has already been made to a hardening of gender-based divisions and ascendant patriarchal attitudes within the working class. In addition, and whilst not passively accepting bourgeois ideas, many 'respectable' (and especially skilled 'aristocratic') workers did increasingly dissociate themselves from the 'non-respectable' (especially the poor and unskilled). Unlike the Chartists, who had explained the root causes of poverty in terms of economic structure and exploitation and political exclusion, mid-Victorian 'labour aristocrats' increasingly saw poverty as the main result of character failings. The poor were exhorted to help themselves, to follow the example of successful co-operators and other 'respectables', rather than passively to await external help or structural change. This was the smug, self-righteous, and far from admirable side of working-class 'respectability'.[236]

The values and practices associated with 'respectability' – the emancipatory powers of education, collective and personal self-help, respect, independence, advancement, restraint, discipline, moderation, sobriety and so on – could, as in the Chartist period, be perfectly consistent with a strong sense of class pride. But what happened during the mid-Victorian period was that such practices were increasingly divorced from the class-based, mutualistic and genuinely collective and democratic context of Chartism, and allied to more privatised and status-conscious ends. 'Respectability' thus became more of a divisive status symbol than a unifying bond of class. As in the United States, questions concerning 'respectable' status were increasingly linked to the issue of ethnicity. The post-Famine immigration into mainland Britain brought in its wake greatly intensified ethnic and religious conflicts. Immigrant Irish Catholics were not only widely seen as a source of labour market and housing competition, but also in both countries as puppets of a despotic and irrational Papacy intent upon universal domination. And, despite the weaker formal attachment of British workers to organised religion, they, in keeping with their American counterparts, saw the Irish Catholics as threats to both their material and spiritual wellbeing and reacted with hostility. Conflict was more widespread in the United States. But in Liverpool, western Scotland and those parts of Lancashire in which Chartism had constituted a hegemonic force (such as Ashton-under-Lyne), anti-Catholic riots and mass support for Orange and Conservative cries of 'No Popery' became staple features of the popular politics of the post-1850 years. As in America, the politics of class-based radicalism were largely lost in the outpourings of ethnic, religious and chauvinistic hatred.[237]

The dominant trends in the mid-Victorian labour movement and class relations lay, therefore, in the ebbing of class, the rise of a more fragmented labour force, and the triumph of reformist impulses.

These trends were viewed in widely contrasting ways by contemporaries. Enraptured by the self-helping activities of co-operators and others, and the newfound 'discipline', 'moderation' and 'restraint' of the upper sections of the working class, Gladstone was moved to declare that workingmen had become, 'our fellow-subjects, our fellow-Christians, our own flesh and blood.'[238] – a view endorsed by many establishment figures. Attention has already been drawn to the positive and self-satisfied stance of the co-operative movement. Others were, however, less pleased. In 1845 Engels had predicted that, 'The approach to Socialism cannot fail, especially when the next crisis directs the working-men by force of sheer want to social instead of political remedies.' But in 1858 Engels was delivering his pessimistic judgement that,

> the English proletariat is actually becoming more and more bourgeois, so that this most bourgeois of all nations is apparently aiming ultimately at the possession of a bourgeois aristocracy and a bourgeois proletariat *as well as* a bourgeoisie.[239]

And in 1870 the former Chartist, Thomas Cooper, recorded his 'sorrowful impressions' that, despite improvements in their 'physical condition' since the days of Chartism, Lancashire workmen had 'gone back, intellectually and morally':

> In our old Chartist time, it is true, Lancashire working men were in rags by thousands; and many of them often lacked food. But their intelligence was demonstrated wherever you went. You would see them in groups discussing the great doctrine of political justice... Now, you will see no such groups in Lancashire. But you will hear well-dressed working men talking, as they walk with their hands in their pockets, of 'Co-ops'... and their shares in them, or in building societies. And you will see others, like idiots, leading small greyhound dogs, covered with cloth, on a string![240]

THE ROOTS OF FRAGMENTATION: THE UNITED STATES AND BRITAIN

In order to discover the underpinnings of the weakened class presence of mid-century labour in both countries, of the more reformist movement in Britain, and of the generally evanescent nature of labour's development in the United States, we can first of all usefully consider changes in the social composition of the working class on both sides of the Atlantic.

Changes in Social Structure

As Gutman and Berlin have pioneeringly observed,[241] the period between 1840 and 1880 saw the growth of both an older and larger American working class (it has been estimated by Montgomery that by 1870 wage earners represented more than 50 per cent of those gainfully employed)[242] and, simultaneously, a failure of that class to reproduce itself. Thus, relatively few of those largely native-born artisans and others who had *formed* the working class in the decades up to 1840 were to play a central role in its *development* up to 1880. It is true, note Gutman and Berlin, that native white workers of native-born parents remained numerous in small- and middle-sized New England towns, in eastern Pennsylvania and in the Hudson and Mohawk valleys (Montgomery adds that a large majority of urban teamsters and clerical employees, and many of those in the building and railroad carrying trades were drawn from workers of native stock.)[243] But increasingly the working class of the towns and cities of the Midwest, West and Southwest was made up of foreign-born immigrants and their native-born children; and by 1880 immigrants and their children 'dominated the wage-earning population in most Middle Atlantic cities of size'.

Two major conclusions emerge. First, as noted by Gutman, 'Over the entire nation, native white workers of native white parents composed a small percentage of the developing American working class.' Second, as observed by Montgomery, 'immigrants and their children were not intruders on the working class and the labor movement. They *were* the working class, and they made the labor movement.'[244]

Such far-reaching developments were, of course, in their early stages during the 1840s and 1850s, our period of immediate concern. But of major significance was the arrival of some 2 million European immigrants (largely from the United Kingdom, Ireland and Germany) on American shores between 1847 and 1858. The vast majority of these immigrants joined the ranks of the urban working class in both the North and the South, and radically transformed the largely native-born, white and Protestant labour force of the pre-1837 era. As Laurie has written:

> The huge inflow of immigrants at midcentury transformed the ethnic composition and occupational configuration of the work force in both regions. Native-born whites hung on to the best-paid handicrafts ... the 'honorable trades'. Women and immigrants succeeded white workmen in semiskilled jobs within the declining handicrafts, and Irish women replaced Yankees in the textile industry. Blacks and Irish shared unskilled work. What had been an ethnically homogeneous working class had become a polyglot group by the 1850s.[245]

Greater ethnic and cultural diversity within the working class did not *necessarily* induce heightened divisions and conflicts. Much of Gutman's research has, for example, clearly demonstrated that feelings of class solidarity and ethnic allegiance are by no means incompatible. We have observed earlier in Part Two that during the late 1840s and early 1850s German and other immigrants involved themselves in labour movement activity. However, we have seen that the *dominant* patterns to emerge during the mid-century decades were those of chronic ethnic tensions and conflicts and upsurges of nativist politics and sentiments which effectively undermined attempts to develop working-class unity, and which attached workers to the framework of bourgeois politics. Given the profundity of the 1837–42 depression, further depressions in 1854 and 1857, intensified competition in the labour and housing markets, accelerated employer attempts to utilise cheap immigrant labour to de-skill and 'dishonour' the native born, the growing clash of religions and cultures (especially between white native-born Protestants and immigrant Catholics), and the ability of nativist, Democratic and Whig politicians to whip up and exploit divisions among workers, the politics of class solidarity stood little chance of lasting success.

We have also seen that changes in the social composition of the British working class also had a debilitating effect upon class solidarity and militancy. The reader's attention has been drawn to the decline of many of those outworking and artisanal groups which stood at the heart of radicalism. Similarly, massive post-Famine Irish Catholic immigration to Britain triggered hostile responses from workers as geographically separate as Lancashire cotton operatives, Lanarkshire miners and Liverpudlian dock workers. Above all, the voracious demand of the dynamic mid-Victorian economy for skilled labour greatly reinforced, rather than created, a moderate, cautious and sectional 'labour aristocracy' which sought to distance itself from the poor and 'non-respectable'. Ironically, these various manifestations of weakness and fragmentation occurred precisely at that point in time when 'manual labour class' had come to embrace the great majority of British citizens.[246]

Economic Changes

Weakened class presence and enhanced fragmentation were rooted not only in changes in social composition but also in changing economic structures and processes. At first sight, such a statement might appear misleading, if not perverse. There now exists a solid body of evidence to suggest that significant improvements in living standards – for many years the standard explanation for the demise of Chartism and the growth of 'moderation' – did not take place for the *mass* of British workers until the early 1860s, long after the beginning of the movement's demise in the 1840s.[247] Similarly, most recent works on American labour history are united in the belief that, despite considerable economic growth and improvements in money wages from the early–mid 1840s onwards, wage increases failed to keep pace with the cost of living.[248] And, heeding Edward Thompson's strictures against the adoption of a narrow economic reductionism (whereby politics, ideas and values are simply assumed or 'read off' from economic factors), many historians are now careful not to assume that economic improvement will, of itself and of necessity, lead to political and social moderation. Rather, it is a consideration of the interaction of relatively autonomous social forces which merits the closest scrutiny.

To argue in this manner is not, however, to dismiss the importance of material factors. In terms, first, of Britain there were undoubtedly intimate connections between reformism and the growth of a more stable and dynamic economy at mid century. More secure and enlarged employment opportunities and the newfound stability and seeming permanence of industrial capitalism (up to the early 1840s the fate of the system had seemed to many to hang in the balance), not only gave workers a stake in the smooth and efficient workings of the economy (unemployment and instability loomed large in recent memory), but also generated more widespread faith in 'progress' and 'success'.

The very solidity of the system meant that it could no longer realistically be bypassed by communitarian experiments and so forth. The stark choice presented to labour was reform or revolution; and given labour's newly acquired moderation and the very successes achieved by gradualism, revolution was out of the question. Finally, as noted earlier, economic expansion greatly increased the demand for skilled labour. And, unlike the mass of workers, the 'labour aristocratic' élite did enjoy a significant rise in living standards from the mid–late 1840s onwards. Relatively privileged and affluent, and able to find a secure place, indeed enhanced recognition, within a booming economy, the mid-Victorian 'labour aristocrat' thus presented a stark contrast to the beleaguered and transformed artisans and others of the Chartist period. It is hardly surprising, in view of the changed material context, that reformism appeared to be increasingly commonsensical, indeed 'natural' to such people.

Contrary to an influential viewpoint within British labour history,[249] it is not suggested that the emergence of this aloof and privileged 'labour aristocracy' constituted *the key* to the reformism of mid-Victorian labour. As various historians have observed, an élite of craft and skilled workers had existed prior to the 1840s, and labour aristocratic influence varied greatly from one geographical area to another. Moreover, the labour aristocracy thesis is too narrowly based to constitute a sufficient explanation of the many discontinuities which occurred in the labour movement and class relations at mid century. Nevertheless, there is little doubt that the newfound domination of the labour movement by a moderate and cautious 'labour aristocracy' did constitute an important and necessary factor in the overall growth and triumph of reformism.

In the United States there was also greater stability and less rapid and concerted capitalist transformation than during the 1830s. As Gordon, Edwards and Reich have informed us,[250] the long economic boom between the mid 1840s and mid 1870s, as reflected in the creation of a national communications network and dramatic increases in demand, output and employment, was generally rooted in proletarianised rather than fundamentally transformed (i.e. greatly sub-divided, de-skilled, alienated and largely factory-based) labour. There were selected advances in factory production (the shoe industry constituting the classic site of the transition from independent artisan to dependent and specialised factory operative), and in New York, Philadelphia and elsewhere capital-ists continued to attack customary controls and standards. Furthermore, as seen in the upsurge in trade unionism during the late 1840s and early 1850s, in the shoeworkers' strike of 1860 and the phenomenal rise of the Knights of St Crispin in 1860s Massachusetts, such capitalist initiatives continued to spark off labour militancy and solidarity.[251]

In *overall* terms, however, the advance of the factory was limited and capitalist transformation as a whole proceeded far less evenly and profoundly than during the 1830s. As observed by Gordon, Edwards and Reich, the consolidation of the social structure of accumulation forged during the pre-1850 decades (the proliferation of capitalist prac-tices and values, the defeats suffered by labour, mass immigration as a source of labour, the spread of waged labour and so on), rather than the widespread creation of a new structure, formed the basis for the 1840s–70s boom.[252] As in Britain, the consolidation and extension of

existing techniques rather than the wholesale introduction of qualitat-
ively new methods of production constituted the key to the economic
history of America's mid-century decades.

Most significantly, the very diversity of methods of production and
the uneven nature of capitalist transformation, allied to the increased
fragmentation of the American working class, meant that labour's
response was less unified and less profoundly radical than during the
1830s. Only during the last quarter of the century would capitalists in
both countries (albeit to varying degrees) make concerted efforts to
create a radically different social structure of accumulation (involving,
especially in the United States, fundamentally transformed labour) in
response to increased competition and declining rates of growth, prices
and profit margins. Significantly, the last quarter of the century would
see a corresponding upsurge in worker militancy and radicalism in both
countries.

The Sociological and Institutional Roots of Accommodation

This is, however, to run ahead of our story. To return to the 1850s and
1860s, sociological factors accompanied economic causes of both the
decline of class and the accommodation of labour to capitalism. In
terms, first, of the United States there exists the celebrated 'mobility
thesis' which, associated most closely with Stephan Thernstrom,[253] main-
tains that high rates of geographical and social (occupational improvement and/or property ownership) mobility in the United States have
unlike many European countries, severely limited the appeal of class-
based radicalism to workers.

In reference to the specific decades of the 1840s and 1850s, many of
the younger American labour historians have seriously questioned the
adequacy of the mobility thesis. Laurie, for example, has suggested
that population volatility and class consciousness, 'were not necessarily
incompatible and might even have been quite consonant'. Laurie admits
that the ebb and flow of population, 'could have upset the process
of building confidence among workers and undermined their social
organisations', but that, in reality, 'Every ... kind of institution and
association' took root among Philadelphia's workers. In Laurie's opinion
'meager resources and hard times, not unstable memberships' constituted
the main reasons for the lack of durability of labour's institutions.
Furthermore, argues Laurie (a view endorsed by Ross and Wilentz), it
was the language of *diminished* opportunities for upward occupational
mobility and economic independence which most characterised artisans
and skilled workers of this period. Thus whilst, we are told, some
workers did rise out of their class, accumulate modest holdings and

subscribe to liberal individualism, such workers were, 'exceptional in an age of receding opportunities for men of humble origins and it is doubtful that their less fortunate brothers subscribed to the mobility ethic'. For example, 'traditionalist' Irish Catholic immigrants of the 1840s 'valued survival above all else and were a decade or two away from endorsing the idea of accumulating the income for a house – the goal that they achieved with such frequency in the post-Civil War period'. For Laurie, therefore, the mobility thesis has 'limited explanatory power': the 'Revivalists were alone in paying homage to the mobility ethic and they were but a single cultural group in a larger aggregate.'[254]

We must also heed Henretta's cautionary note that the mobility thesis all too often assumes a cosy and insufficiently supported correspondence between 'improvement' and the adoption of liberal-individualistic values. Given the central importance within mid-nineteenth-century working-class communities of familialistic, mutualistic and class-based values and practices, it would be both ahistorical and erroneous to assume that individual mobility *necessarily* constituted the key motivating force in workers' lives and that mobility signified the triumph of individualism over collectivism. It is thus important not only to record patterns of mobility but also to evaluate their meanings in a variety of contexts over time.[255]

Notwithstanding the empirical and theoretical reservations presented above, mobility did have a significant, if limited, impact upon the strength and durability of labour radicalism. Thus we have earlier observed in relation to the studies of Prude (of New England's factory villages), Scranton (Philadelphia's textiles) and Dublin (Lowell's factories), that extremely high rates of labour turnover prevailed in a variety of contexts and were, for the most part, not conducive to the creation and consolidation of class-based labour institutions. Laurie himself has noted that some of the city's leading activists had left Philadelphia by the early 1840s. We desperately need further studies of geographical mobility, labour turnover and migrant attitudes and behaviour, especially of a comparative character. But we can suggest, on the basis of limited evidence, that the mid-century British pattern of considerable *short-distance* mobility which was seemingly conducive to continued attachments to class and community, was probably less prevalent in the United States.[256]

In terms of occupational mobility, Laurie and Wilentz are quite right to emphasise the heightened perception among labour radicals that opportunities to become an independent producer were diminishing and that the Republic was being undermined by the growth of rigid class divisions and 'wage slavery'. Equally, however, we must be careful not

to present an unbalanced and uniformly negative picture. Industrialisation could expand opportunities and create new skills at the same
time as undermining custom and opportunity: much depended upon the
sector of the economy in which one was involved. Thus, despite
the growth of mechanised agriculture and tenancy, western farmers
greatly benefited from the transportation revolution and the rise in
demand in the two decades before the Civil War. And as Foner observes
of the small town North and West, the veritable heartlands of Republicanism, 'A well-organised, persistent person could expect to achieve
economic success, and a skilled wage earner could reasonably look
forward to the day he acquired enough capital to start a small business
of his own.'[257] Ross has similarly noted that the adverse effects of
capitalist growth in Cincinnati were not uniformly spread across the
working class; newer workers in the metal trades constituted a 'labour
aristocracy', enjoying higher living standards and greater control at work
than depressed tailoring and furniture workers; and of the top 10 per
cent of Cincinnati's manufacturers in 1850, 74.5 per cent had 'worked
their way up through the ranks, either in the same or in different
crafts'.[258]

In the longer term, industrialisation offered opportunities for home
ownership among the poverty-stricken immigrants of the 1840s and,
especially in smaller- and medium-sized manufacturing centres, avenues
to employer status, especially among the craft and skilled.[259] As conclusively demonstrated by Gutman and Berlin, by 1880 between 35 and 45
per cent of native white males of old stock 'no longer had working-
class occupations' (working 'far more often as clerks, bookkeepers, and
salesmen than as day laborers and factory workers'). In short, native
white Americans 'experienced little of the pain associated with the
expansion of American capitalism after 1840'.[260] Beyond the ranks of
labour's mid-century radicals the constituencies of enhanced social
mobility and status (upwardly mobile native-born whites ascending
above immigrant proletarians) and social integration may well, therefore,
have been far larger than we initially suggested.

Given the widespread belief among Americans in the rigidity of
the British class structure, it is ironic that there occurred considerable
advancement and social mobility among sections of the British working
class during the third quarter of the century. The scattered and uneven
nature of the evidence renders statements concerning the pace and the
extent of occupational mobility between the first and second halves of
the nineteenth century extremely hazardous. We do know that financial
barriers and the increasing size of units of production meant that 'rags
to riches' mobility probably diminished after the 1840s.[261] But, as
Hobsbawm and others have observed, the small scale of many industries

and the universal prevalence of sub-contracting ensured a continued and plentiful supply of better-off workers into the middling employer ranks. Advancement into the lower middle class, especially for the sons and daughters of the 'labour aristocracy', became increasingly common. The introduction of compulsory elementary education and the growth of the tertiary and government sectors during the last quarter of the century greatly increased the numbers of clerks, teachers and other white-collar workers who had been born into the skilled working class.[262]

However, as noted by Hunt, most working-class mobility at mid century took place within the working class.[263] We have thus already noted that the mid-Victorian boom brought with it more stable and regular employment. Better-paid work also accounted for a growing amount of all employment. And the 'labour aristocracy' was particularly privileged. Thus Hobsbawm:

> It is quite probable that, relatively speaking, the position of the skilled British artisan has never been higher than in the 1860s, nor his standard of living and access to education, culture and travel (by contemporary standards) so satisfactory, nor the gap between him and the small local manufacturers who employed him so narrow, nor that between him and the mass of 'labour' so wide.[264]

The labour movement's language of 'success' and 'improvement' was, in part, a mirror-image of the values of the skilled and craft élite. But such language also reflected the new-found gains made by the wider band of 'respectable' workers embraced by the institutions of labour. In the cotton districts of Lancashire and Cheshire, for example, not only did the co-ops, friendly societies and, to a lesser extent, the trade unions prosper in the mid-Victorian years but local labour leaders, including former Chartists, made considerable gains. The latter took a variety of forms – advancement within the organisations of labour, the attainment of managerial or ownership status and, commonly, the achievement of municipal prominence as councillors, justices of the peace, Poor-Law guardians, aldermen, mayors, or members of school or hospital boards – and led to a marked softening of attitudes. Protests against immiseration and outsider status became increasingly rare: 'success' became the watchword of labour. Significantly, enhanced success and moderation extended throughout England, Scotland and Wales.[265]

New-found social advancement and recognition for labour leaders were accompanied by more widespread worker accommodation to the structures of everyday life under industrial capitalism. We have noted that the economic system became more solid and routinised, a (to use Stedman Jones' term) seemingly 'irremoveable horizon'. The shocks of the factory, of new work disciplines, patterns of authority and of industrial capitalist culture, became less profound. This is not to argue that people became 'incorporated'. Battles and conflicts were still in evidence, but they functioned within narrowed terms of reference and an overall acceptance of bourgeois hegemony. The labour leaders and their institutions were in the process of developing a 'stake', albeit ambiguous, in the existing system. As Edward Thompson has written:

> Each advance within the framework of capitalism simultaneously involved the working class far more deeply in the *status quo*. As they improved their position by organization within the workshop, so they became more reluctant to engage in quixotic outbreaks which might jeopardize gains accumulated at such cost. Each assertion of working-class influence within the bourgeois-democratic state machinery, simultaneously involved them as partners (even if antagonistic partners) in the running of the machine. Even the indices of working-class strength – the financial reserves of trade unions and co-ops. – were secure only within the custodianship of capitalist stability.[266]

Changes from Above

The achievement of a 'stake' required, however, more than changes in working-class experience. It also necessitated more sympathetic treatment of workers' and organised labour's claims by Britain's employers, the state, the established political parties and by other controlling influences in society. During the mid-Victorian years there were significant, accelerated and in many cases novel, if generally uneven, attempts on the part of those in positions of power and authority to make concessions, to 'reach' workers, to build or strengthen inter-class institutions and cultural forms, and above all to give workers a new-found sense of being 'understood'. Such concessions and initiatives took place within culture, at the workplace and in politics.

The third quarter of the century saw important shifts in middle-class (and especially liberal middle-class) cultural attitudes and practices towards workers. The widespread fears around in middle-class circles by 'physical-force' Chartism, the (albeit greatly exaggerated) threat of European-style revolution in Britain, and the 'wild and unruly' habits of the 'masses', relief concerning the growth of 'moderation and responsibility' within the ranks of post-1848 labour and the working class, and genuinely humanitarian and religious desires to build bridges across the massive class divide – these were some of the key underpinnings to quickened middle-class efforts to 'reach and refine' post-Chartist workers. Increasingly the working class was not seen as a uniform and undisciplined 'mob', lacking in 'culture' and 'civilised' behaviour. In contrast to the Chartist years, growing sections of the middle class 'adopted an increasingly positive evaluation of the habits and customs of a sizeable section of the working class'. In particular there was a growing appreciation of the 'improving' endeavours of the 'respectable' workingman and his family. As I have written:

> To be sure, there was continued and loud opposition to the 'wrong-headedness' of trade unions, and the supposed growth in the size of the 'residuum' in the major cities aroused the fears and anxieties of respectable opinion. Nevertheless, there was a growing recognition, most marked among Liberal politicians and the Liberal press, that the working class was not an undifferentiated mass, and that large numbers of operatives were daily becoming more 'moderate' and 'temperate', more 'reasonable' and 'responsible', both in their domestic lives and in their outlook upon the world.

Attempts to reach and cultivate working-class 'respectables' accordingly quickened and multiplied. For example, in the cotton towns:

> Members of the middle class busily established lecture and reading rooms for workers, opened public libraries with much self-congratulation and public fanfare and patronised mechanics institutes, lyceums, mutual improvement societies, co-ops and temperance societies.

The leaders of St Paul's Mutual Improvement Society in Manchester were acutely conscious of the pressing interest of local dignitaries in Manchester and elsewhere in the lives of working-class members of 'respectable' societies:

> Peers, philanthropists, men of science, art and literature now take a deep interest in all their doings, and in most of our large towns there are working men's societies. Nothing is kept sacred from them. They are taken up and down the country to view the scenery. They are constantly invited to visit gentlemen of note at their residences, thus being brought into touch with the classes above them.[267]

The middle classes hoped that increased contact with, tutelage of, and provision (in the form of libraries, parks and so on) for workers would 'assuage grudges' and promote inter-class harmony and understanding. But, as shown by Tholfsen, middle-class efforts to provide workers with 'a stake in society' did not involve fundamental changes to a hierarchical and grossly unequal social order. Workers were to be 'instructed', made more 'rational' and 'civilised' by their middle-class tutors. 'Dangerous' and 'wrongheaded' attitudes towards political economy and the basic unfairness of the system were to be abandoned. The notion of *equality* between the classes was entirely alien to the thinking of the vast majority of the middle class. Workers were to be led into an acceptance of the acquisitive individualism of bourgeois society; and 'respectable' workingmen would 'turn their backs upon the crude and debilitating influences of the public house and . . . gambling, brawling and general bawdiness'.

As demonstrated by several historians, neither the Chartists nor the mid-Victorian labour activists passively imbibed the values and behavioural prescriptions of the bourgeoisie. Commitments to education, thrift, sobriety and other tenets of 'respectability' had, as earlier noted, an *independent* existence within the working class irrespective of middle-class cultural intervention and implantation. We have observed that key elements of the 'respectable' Chartist's democratic and egalitarian social vision were at odds with the middle-class ideals of competition and individualism. But we have also seen that during the third quarter working-class 'respectability' frequently became more privatised and status-conscious in character. 'Respectables' did divorce themselves from 'non-respectable' workers, and did experience greater contact and empathy with middle-class 'respectables' (whether in the co-ops, friendly societies and mutual improvement societies, or in more general political and social movements in favour of reform and improvement). Inter-class bridge building and harmony became more pronounced. In these various ways middle-class hegemony was subtly and 'commonsensically' (rather than forcibly) constructed and consolidated.

In the pre-1850 decades it seemed highly unlikely that class co-operation and harmony would be widely constructed at the work-place. Capitalist transformation, the pressures placed upon capital accumulation by the Industrial Revolution, acute competition in the market-place, sharp cyclical fluctuations, the growth of employers fiercely committed to the ideology of *laissez-faire* and totally opposed to collective worker interference in their concerns, allied to the new time and work discipline demanded by the new order and the growing rebelliousness of workers – all combined, as seen in this volume, to make the 1830s and 1840s periods of acute and chronic industrial and class conflicts. We have further noted that both fierce industrial conflicts and employer opposition to trade-union recognition remained in strong evidence throughout the third quarter.

The latter period did, nevertheless, simultaneously witness the emergence of a 'new spirit', more conciliatory and relaxed, among a minority of, especially the more wealthy, employers. As Royden Harrison has shown,[268] a number of 'new model' employers increasingly held out the hand of friendship to mid-Victorian trade unions primarily in the belief that union recognition would enhance harmony, moderation and improved production within the work-place. Many employers, and particularly those small employers situated in acutely competitive markets and attempting to cut unit costs of labour to the bone, could often ill afford the 'luxury' of trade-union recognition. But pragmatic concerns could also induce greater accommodation to the claims of organised labour. In the cotton districts, for example, most employers retained their profound ideological opposition to unions. But a number of practical experiences – the tenacity of trade unionism, its increasingly moderate and conciliatory stance, its opposition to unauthorised militancy, its useful function of regulating and stabilising markets by means of the establishment of district rates of pay and uniform price lists, and the loss of production and vital markets attendant upon chronic industrial conflict – did lead to much more extensive toleration of unions by the late 1860s. In addition, the export-led boom in cotton during the third quarter, the massive fortunes acquired and the general easing of pressures upon capital accumulation, the routinisation of factory labour among workers, and widespread desires to avoid a resurgence of the class conflicts of the Chartist era did induce a partial 'change of heart' among cotton employers. It was among the wealthy cotton dynasties, frequently cushioned against the worst effects of market competition, that the 'new spirit' was most prominent.[269]

The accumulation of large fortunes in cotton and elsewhere provided the solid material foundation for the 'mighty reassertion' (Patrick Joyce) of employer paternalism in the post-Chartist years. As I have noted elsewhere:

> From the mid-1850s onwards we find that an increasing number of employers cast aside their parsimonious attitudes of the 1830s and 1840s. The annual works dinner, trips to the countryside and seaside, and the provision of libraries and reading rooms, canteens and baths at the workplace – all financed by the employer – became an increasingly notable characteristic of employer policies in this period.[270]

Provision was sometimes both lavish and pregnant with the symbolism of reciprocal employer and worker rights and duties. The flavour of paternalism and worker responses was demonstrated on the occasion of the outing of Robert Platt's workers (Platt was a leading cotton manufacturer and Liberal in Stalybridge) to their employer's estate in Cheshire:

> In August 1858, 900 workers, carrying banners bearing inscriptions such as 'Long Life to our Employers', and 'Britannia Rules the Waves', congregated in front of Platt's mills, which were decorated with flags. The procession, headed by the Stalybridge Old Band, walked through the town to the railway station, where they boarded the special trains hired by Platt. On their arrival at 'Deanwater', Platt's stately mansion, they were greeted by salvos of artillery fire. The day was spent in sports, competitions and eating and drinking. The food bill in itself was astronomical. In 1858 300 pounds of beef, 160 pounds of ham, 250 pounds of assorted meats,

600 pounds of potatoes, 300 pounds of plum pudding, 100 pounds of rice, and 144 gallons of ale were consumed at one sitting. In Platt's opinion, the attainment of social harmony took precedence over financial considerations: 'He didn't like to treat workers as inanimate machinery', and 'it mattered little to him whether he acquired a few thousands more or a few thousand less than ordinary, so that those under him did their duty, and were contented and happy'.[271]

This was indeed a far cry from the hard and impersonal language used by employer 'tyrants' during the Chartist years; workers had been transformed from 'mere instruments, items of cost', to real people with characters, cares and needs.

Sentiments similar to Platt's became commonplace in the cotton districts during the late 1850s and 1860s (surviving even the disastrous years of the Cotton Famine between 1861 and 1865). In April 1860 the *Ashton Standard* enthused, 'scarcely a week passes, but we chronicle a treat to the workpeople in some part of the district'. Many paternalistic employers came to accept and praise factory legislation: some even accepted trade unions.

Funded by the huge profits from the export of mid-Victorian cotton, and not infrequently informed by religious and humanitarian concerns, paternalism sought to promote company loyalty and harmony between workers and employers. And there is no doubt that, despite articulated and symbolic worker protests against total employer control and worker dependency, many workers did, as claimed by Joyce, respond positively and warmly to employer initiatives. Thus on several occasions workers made presentations to their employers and toasted the 'new found employer spirit'. We can quote a single example to demonstrate what was becoming a widespread phenomenon in the cotton districts. In 1857 the operatives at the Old Mill in Dukinfield invited their employer to dine with them, and presented him with a gold pen and an address which read:

> As an employer of labour you have been kind ... and have completely divested yourself of those petty acts that give so much uneasiness to working people, and lead to the worst feelings between employers and employed. We earnestly hope that the influential class of men, who have so many hearts beating in their employ ... will follow your noble example, and endeavour to improve the moral and social conditions of the people.

Within the field of politics a range of experiences taught 'lessons' which served to diminish the appeal of independent working-class political action and to give workers a greater 'stake in society'. A number of important legislative measures – the repeal of the Corn Laws, Peel's reduction of taxes on consumption and his general aim to 'remove the material sources of popular discontent', the massively important Ten Hours Act of 1847, the 1867 Reform Act and the trade-union legislation of the 1870s – had extremely damaging implications for the viability of continued commitment to independent political action. As Stedman Jones has argued in relation to the legislation of the 1840s, the state, in direct opposition to Chartist ideology, was no longer to be perceived as an implacable foe of popular interests and, contrary to Chartist predictions, reforms and improvements had been achieved prior to the enactment of universal manhood suffrage.[272] (Such reforms and improvements were to gather pace in the post-1840s decades).

Furthermore, reductions in wages had not, contrary to the Chartist argument, followed the repeal of the Corn Laws (the 'cheap loaf' proved not to have as its corollary the 'cheap wage'): single-issue campaigns and pressure-group politics had (as maintained by the Anti-Corn-Law League) been seen to pay dividends; moderate, piecemeal reform, as advocated by many middle-class reformers, had demonstrated its superior efficacy to the more ambitious 'all-or-nothing' strategy of the Chartists; and, as argued by Bright and Cobden, free trade and self-help were increasingly widely perceived to be the 'natural' prerequisites of economic and social advancement. In truth, Chartism had been gravely affected not only by the coercive actions of the state, but also by the latter's softened visage and the movement's ultimate failure to win the battle of ideas with the free-trade Liberals.

Many evils and grievances – lack of the vote, appalling housing and general environmental conditions, instances of employer 'tyranny', poor wages and so on – remained to be tackled. Stedman Jones has probably exaggerated both the extent to which the state mellowed its practice (as opposed to increasing its promises) during the 1840s and the degree to which Chartist ideology failed to address itself to the factory operative as well as the artisan. But he is surely right to highlight the growing weakness of an independent political strategy, the demonstrable superiority of pressure-group politics, and, by the early 1850s, the overall triumph of liberal ideology. We might add, in support of Ross McKibbin, that during the second half of the nineteenth century the British state, buttressed by the monarchy, would increasingly lay claim to 'class neutrality', to representation of the interests of the nation as a whole rather than a particular section of society.[273]

Despite the continued absence of a mass electorate, the established political parties made far more strenuous efforts in the mid-Victorian years to build up popular support. The nature of those efforts and the characteristics of post-1850 popular Liberalism and Conservatism will be fully investigated in Chapter 3 of the second volume of this work. A few brief observations are, however, in order at this juncture. The mid-Victorian Liberals attempted, with increasing success, to enlist the support of workers and labour-movement activists by presenting their party as 'the organ of the people, the true embodiment of progress and enlightenment'. The Liberals also tried to come to terms with the trade unions and other working-class institutions which had formerly been seen as largely 'wrongheaded' and dangerously collectivist in character. On a national level Chartism merged into Liberalism and liberal-radicalism became the dominant political characteristic of organised labour. Simultaneously, the Conservative Party had succeeded, by the 1870s, in building mass working-class support on the basis of its policies of 'No Popery', opposition to the 'Manchester School' Liberals, and attachments to patriotism, paternalism and deference, 'traditionalism', and a robust and chauvinistic popular culture. In these various ways there occurred a 'liberalisation' of attitudes and practices 'from above' in post-1850 British society which helped to attach workers more firmly to the 'system'.

In the United States concessions and initiatives to organised labour on the part of the rich and powerful were much less in evidence than in Britain. The mounting pressures placed by increasingly rapid industrialisation (from the 1840s onwards) upon capital accumulation, the powerful position of industrial capital within northern society and its fierce commitments to *laissez-faire* and 'free labour' ideologies, the central importance within American society of individualism and the great opposition to collectivism, the minority position of wage earners within the population, the largely heterogeneous character of the working class and (certainly as compared with Britain) the relatively weak standing of organised labour, the decentralised nature of political power in the country and the weakness of effective countervailing political (and other) influences to the massive powers exercised by anti-union employers, courts and planters – all placed severe limitations upon the extent to which there could be 'liberalisation' from on high in the ante-bellum years. Scranton has noted instances of mid-century paternalism in Philadelphia. But neither the latter phenomenon nor that of the British 'new model' employers was much in evidence in the United States. Continued and widespread employer and state opposition to trade unionism remained the norm.[274] This (largely successful) opposition is of crucial importance in explaining both the comparative weakness of American labour and the unstable and chronically conflict-ridden nature of work-place relations. As we shall observe in Chapters 1 and 2 of Volume Two, employer and state hostility to organised labour in America remained at extremely high levels down to the 1920s and beyond. Only from the mid 1930s onwards would a more 'British-style' compromise between the state, employers and organised labour (painfully) develop in America (see Chapter 5 of Volume Two).

Attempts to go some way towards accommodating the interests of organised labour in ante-bellum America were not, however, absent. Indeed, we have repeatedly observed that the mainstream parties were highly adept at nipping popular insurgencies and third-party movements in the bud by adopting planks in the insurgents' programmes and offering labour leaders the promise of office, wealth and mobility within the 'official' structure of politics.[275] Simultaneously, the very diversity of the American working class and the key importance of ethnocultural issues were often more conducive to political division rather than political unity. In the long run the Whigs/Republicans and the Democrats proved to be far more skilful at tapping such ethnocultural concerns than did third parties. As we shall see in Volume Two (Chapters 3 and 4), cultural divisions among American workers continued to greatly weaken the long-term appeal of independent labour and socialist politics from the period of the Civil War down to the onset of the Second World War. For much of that long period patterns established during the ante-bellum years – especially cultural, political and industrial battles between the forces of class solidarity and fragmentation – would continue to centrally shape the fortunes of American labour and American society.

Conclusion

On the eve of the Civil War in the United States and at the height of the mid-Victorian boom in Britain the working classes of both countries were thus characterised more by diversity and divisions than by unity and solidarity. A minority of workers in Britain had nevertheless created a relatively strong labour movement anchored in organisation at the work-place, and to a lesser extent in the community rather than in independent political organisation. In America the 1850s had seen the revival of the trade-union movement from the disasters of the 1840s, but in overall terms the American movement lacked both the strength and official recognition enjoyed by its British counterpart. In comparison with the 'heroic' days of Chartism and the General Trades' Unions, 1850s labour movements and working classes in both countries were mainly in retreat from the fierce conflicts and large constituencies, if not independence, born of class.

The Civil War years, the period of Reconstruction (down to 1877), and thoroughgoing capitalist transformation and rapid industrial expansion between the 1870s and the early 1920s were to set much of the new agenda for the post-1860 American labour movement. The post-bellum years would see the rise of a national labour movement and, especially between the 1880s and 1920s, fierce and prolonged ideological conflicts as to the 'true' direction and character of American workers and organised labour. The 'Great Depression' (1873–96), intensified foreign competition and relative economic decline would provide the economic context in Britain for the rise of 'new' unionism, the growth of socialism and the 'Rise of Labour'. Simultaneously, however, more moderate and conservative forces would continue to exert significant influence within the ranks of British workers and the labour movement. The multifaceted development of post-1860 workers and labour movements constitutes the subject matter of Volume Two. A proper appreciation of such development necessitates, however, initial attention to the broad economic and related structures and processes which exerted profound influences upon patterns of worker thought and behaviour. Above all, the crisis of competitive capitalism in both countries during the final quarter of the nineteenth century and the (albeit very uneven) moves from competitive to monopoly capitalism constitute the starting point of analysis. It is, therefore, to developments and changes within the broad features of capitalism in Britain and America that we must turn at the beginning of Volume Two.

Notes

Introduction

1. E. J. Hobsbawm, *Worlds of Labour: Further Studies in the History of Labour* (1984), Preface; D. Brody, 'The Old Labor History and the New: In Search of an American Working Class', *Labor History*, 20 (Winter 1979).
2. See, for example, S. Perlman, *A Theory of the Labor Movement* (1928); E. J. Hobsbawm, 'Labour Traditions', in his *Labouring Men* (1964); and David Montgomery's influence as the former editor of *International Labor and Working Class History*.
3. G. M. Holmes, *Britain and America: A Comparative Economic History* (1976); P. S. Bagwell and G. E. Mingay, *Britain and America: A Study of Economic Change 1850–1939* (1970).
4. Two of the best are J. Rule, 'Artisan Attitudes: A Comparative Survey of Skilled Labour and Proletarianization Before 1848', *Society Study Labour History Bulletin*, 50 (Spring 1985), and J. Breuilly, 'The Labour Aristocracy in Britain and Germany: A Comparison', in ibid., 48 (Spring 1984). There has developed a strong tradition of comparative work in relation to continental Europe. See, for example, D. Geary, *European Labour Protest 1848–1939* (1981); P.N. Stearns, *Lives of Labour: Work in a Maturing Industrial Society* (1975). For more general comparative labour history see, J. Breuilly, 'Comparative Labour History', *Labour History Review*, 55, 3 (1990); F. Lenger, 'Beyond Exceptionalism: Notes on the Artisanal Phase of the Labour Movement in France, England, Germany and the United States', *International Review of Social History*, XXXVI (1991); and C. Eisenberg, 'The Comparative View in Labour History: Old and New Interpretations of the English and German Labour Movements Before 1914', *International Review of Social History*, 34 (1989). In terms of specific comparisons between Britain and the United States, see the essays by Holt (trade unionism in steel) and Morgan (women's suffrage) in C. Emsley (ed.), *Essays in Comparative History: Economy Politics and Society in Britain and America 1850–1920* (1984). The collection of essays edited by Margaret Jacob and James Jacob, *The Origins of Anglo-American Radicalism* (1984), is very helpful to students of the seventeenth and eighteenth centuries.
5. See, for example, W. J. Mommsen and H.-G. Husung (eds.) *The Development of Trade Unionism in Great Britain and Germany 1880–1914* (1985). In their *Working Class Formation: Nineteenth Century Patterns in Western Europe and the United States* (1986) I. Katznelson and A. R. Zolberg (the editors) do attempt to provide an explicitly comparative method of class analysis (revolving around structure, ways of life, dispositions, and collective action). But the majority of essays in this very useful collection apply this method of analysis to a single country.

6. B. Moore, *Social Origins of Dictatorship and Democracy* (1967), I and III; C. Emsley, op. cit., Introduction.

7. For a stimulating discussion of the 'exceptionalist' question see S. Wilentz, 'Against Exceptionalism: Class Consciousness and the American Labor Movement', *International Labor and Working Class History*, 26 (Fall 1984), and the ensuing debates between Wilentz, Salvatore, Hanagan and Sapolsky in ibid., nos. 26, 27 (Spring 1985), and 28 (Fall 1985). See also the essay by A. R. Zolberg ('How Many Exceptionalisms?') in I. Katznelson and A. R. Zolberg (eds.), op. cit.; S. Berger, 'The British and German Labour Movements before the Second World War: The Sonderweg Revisited', *Twentieth-Century British History*, Vol. 3, no. 3 (1992), pp. 219–248.

8. J. Potter, 'Atlantic Economy 1815–1860: The U.S.A. and the Industrial Revolution in Britain', in A. W. Coats and R. M. Robertson (eds.), *Essays in American Economic History* (1969); D. J. Jeremy, *Transatlantic Industrial Revolution: The Diffusion of Textile Technologies Between Britain and America 1790–1830s* (1981); M. A. Jones, *The Limits of Liberty: American History 1607–1980* (1983), Ch. 1. For the important contribution made by British immigrants to the formation and development of labour movements in the United States see C. K. Yearley, Jr., *Britons in American Labour: A History of the Influence of United Kingdom Immigrants on American Labour 1820–1914* (1957); R. T. Berthoff, *British Immigrants in Industrial America 1907–1950* (1953).

9. D. Montgomery, *The Fall of the House of Labor: The Workplace, the State and American Labor Activism 1865–1925* (1987), p. 1.

10. See, for example, R. Glen, *Urban Workers in the Early Industrial Revolution* (1984), Ch. 1 and Conclusion; A. E. Musson, *British Trade Unions 1800–1875* (1972); R. Roberts, *The Classic Slum: Salford Life in the First Quarter of the Century* (1974), Ch. 1; P. Johnson, *Saving and Spending: The Working Class Economy in Britain 1870–1939* (1985), especially Conclusion; K. D. Brown, *The English Labour Movement 1700–1951* (1982), Ch. 2.

11. See the introduction to J. M. Winter (ed.), *The Working Class in Modern British History* (1983); G. S. Jones, *Languages of Class: Studies in English Working Class History 1832–1982* (1983).

12. D. Montgomery, op. cit., pp. 1–2.

13. Ibid., p. 4.

14. Ibid., p. 2.

15. D. M. Gordon, R. Edwards and M. Reich, *Segmented Work Divided Workers: The Historical Transformation of Labor in the United States* (1984), p. 20.

16. T. Bennett, 'Popular Culture and the Turn to Gramsci', in T. Bennett, C. Mercer and J. Woollacott (eds.) *Popular Culture and Social Relations* (1986), xvi.

17. N. Kirk, *The Growth of Working Class Reformism in Mid Victorian England* (1985), Ch. 5.

18. For a useful summary of the views of Thompson and his critics see J. Rule, *The Labouring Classes in Early Industrial England 1750–1850* (1986), pp. 383–93. See also P. Anderson, *Arguments Within English Marxism* (1980), Ch. 2; and E. M. Wood, 'Falling Through the Cracks: E. P.

Thompson and the Debate on Base and Superstructure', in H. J. Kaye and K. McClelland (eds.), *E.P. Thompson: Critical Perspectives* (1990).

As I hope to demonstrate in the pages of this book, Thompson's historical materialism retains a vitality and relevance, indeed centrality, to the historian insufficiently appreciated by many of those on the post-structuralist Left. Similarly, J. C. D. Clark's view from the Right, that historical materialism and 'socialist' historiography are largely defunct and discredited, carries little weight in relation to the historical-materialist tradition represented by Thompson, Hobsbawm and Montgomery. For such matters see the essays by G. Eley, W. H. Sewell and R. Gray in ibid; J. C. D. Clark, 'National Identity, State Formation and Patriotism: The Role of History in the Public Mind', *History Workshop Journal*, 29 (Spring 1990); N. Kirk, 'Social Theory Engages E. P. Thompson', *Labour History Review*, 56, 3 (Winter 1991).

19. E. P. Thompson, *The Making of the English Working Class* (1968), p. 8.

20. Ibid., p. 9. Given the multiplicity of usages and confusions surrounding the terms 'experience' and 'structure', it is important to clarify the definitions offered in this book. I employ the terms experience and structure synonymously, to refer to deep and objective forces and structures (e.g. economic and social systems consisting of patterned social relationships, modes of production, distribution, exchange and so on) which: (i) take place 'behind the backs' of human consciousness and/or intention, but which are nevertheless; (ii) 'lived' or 'experienced' by people in their daily lives; and which (iii) are by no means *necessarily* beyond the powers of human perception, comprehension and change. In sum, I suggest both that there is a reality 'out there' (in part beyond immediate 'commonsense' and perception), and that people, as conscious (and unconscious) beings, modify and change that reality. To argue in this way is to support 'critical realist' attempts to investigate the interactions between 'culture' and 'structure', agency and conditioning, at specific points in time and over periods of time. See E. P. Thompson, 'The Politics of Theory', in R. Samuel (ed.), *People's History and Socialist Theory* (1981), especially pp. 405–6; E. V. da Costa, 'Experience versus Structure: New Tendencies in the History of Labor and the Working Class in Latin America – What do We Gain? What do We Lose?', *International Labor and Working Class History*, 36 (Fall 1989); and the 'Response' by Perry Anderson in ibid.; R. Bhaskar, *Reclaiming Reality: A Critical Introduction to Contemporary Philosophy* (1989), especially Chs. 1 and 9.

21. See, for example, the very useful essay by Catherine Hall ('The Tale of Samuel and Jemima: Gender and Working-Class Culture in Nineteenth-Century England') in H. J. Kaye and K. McClelland (eds.), op. cit.; J. W. Scott, *Gender and the Politics of History* (1988), Chs. 2, 3 and 4. See also the criticisms of Scott's arguments by B. Palmer and C. Stansell in *International Labor and Working Class History*, 31 (Spring 1987); A. Baron (ed.), *Work Engendered: Toward a New History of America Labor* (1991).

22. A. Przeworski, 'Proletariat into a Class: The Process of Class Formation from Karl Kautsky's *The Class Struggle* to Recent Controversies', *Politics and Society*, 7,4 (1977).

23. Two recent attempts to largely define class in terms of the post-structuralist emphases upon language and ideas (especially political ideas) have been

made by Gareth Stedman Jones (*Languages of Class*, op cit., especially the Introduction and Ch. 3) and Joan Wallach Scott (*Gender and the Politics of History*, op. cit., especially the Introduction and Chs. 1 and 4). Both these attempts pay insufficient attention to the effects of material conditions upon ideas and language. In turn, Stedman-Jones underestimates the changed meanings of words, and Joan Scott falsely portrays E. P. Thompson's model of class as unitary, deterministic and teleological. See E. P. Thompson, 'Eighteenth-century English Society: Class Struggle Without Class?', *Social History*, 3, 2 (May 1978), p. 150; E. P. Thompson, *The Making*, op. cit., pp. 937, 939; N. Kirk, 'In Defence of Class: A Critique of Recent Revisionist Writing Upon the Nineteenth-Century English Working Class', *International Review of Social History*, XXXII (1987–1).

24. A. Przeworski, op. cit., p. 343.
25. E. P. Thompson, *The Making*, op. cit., pp. 8–9.
26. E. P. Thompson, 'Eighteenth-century English Society', op. cit., p. 150.
27. For example, the Democratic Party in mid nineteenth-century New York City attempted to both incorporate and transcend class-based issues, and to create inter-class support and participation. See A. Bridges, 'Becoming American: The Working Classes in the United States before The Civil War', in I. Katznelson and A. R. Zolberg (eds.), op. cit., pp. 182–9.
28. For Sean Wilentz (*International Labor and Working Class History*, 26 (Fall 1984), p. 6), class consciousness is defined, 'not as any particular set of ideas, doctrines, or political strategies but far more broadly as the articulated resistance of wage workers (and, in certain situations, of those from other strata who have allied with them, chiefly small producers and radical intellectuals) to capitalist wage-labor relations'. While providing a welcome corrective to the narrow equation of class consciousness with socialism, Wilentz's definition is, nevertheless, arguably too elastic to carry total conviction. Wilentz is vague concerning levels (as opposed to necessary stages), types and the extent of articulated worker opposition to capitalist wage-labour relations. The relationship between class and politics is also defined too loosely. However, when moving from the realm of definitions to the area of concrete investigation and explication, Wilentz's treatment of class (as seen especially in his *Chants Democratic*) is far more nuanced and interesting.
29. A. Marwick, 'Images of the Working Class Since 1930', in J. M. Winter (ed.), op. cit., especially pp. 220–1; M. Savage, *The Dynamics of Working Class Politics: The Labour Movement in Preston 1880–1940* (1987), Introduction; I. Katznelson and A. R. Zolberg (eds.), op. cit., pp. 19–20.
30. D. Montgomery, op. cit., p. 7.
31. E. Olssen, 'The Case of the Socialist Party That Failed, Or Further Reflections on an American Dream', *Labor History*, 29, 4 (Fall 1988), pp. 418, 449. Olssen's interesting article concerns itself with political developments in Australia, New Zealand and Britain as well as the United States.

Part One

1. For general studies of early nineteenth-century popular radicalism in the United States see B. Laurie, *Artisans into Workers: Labor in Nineteenth-Century America* (1989), Chs. 1–3; R. B. Morris (ed.), *A History of the American Worker* (1983), Ch. 2; P. Buhle and A. Dawley (eds.), *Working for Democracy: American Workers from the Revolution to the Present* (1985), Chs. 1 and 2; N. Ware, *The Industrial Worker 1840–1860* (1924); J. R. Commons and Associates, *History of Labor in the United States* (1916), Vol. 1; P. S. Foner, *History of the Labor Movement in the United States* (1972), Vol. 1; E. Pessen, *Most Uncommon Jacksonians: Radical Leaders of the Early Labor Movement* (1967). For slave resistance and slave revolts see E. D. Genovese, *Roll Jordan Roll: The World the Slaves Made* (1976), pp. 587–98; id., *From Rebellion to Revolution* (1979), Ch. 1.

2. For general surveys of early nineteenth-century British popular radicalism see J. F. C. Harrison, *The Early Victorians 1832–1851* (1973), Ch. 6; J. Rule, op. cit. Part 4 and Conclusion; E. H. Hunt, *British Labour History 1815–1914* (1985), Chs. 6 and 7; J. Stevenson *Popular Disturbances in England 1700–1870* (1979); R. Glen, op. cit., Ch. 1; A. E. Musson, op. cit.; E. P. Thompson, *The Making*, op. cit., Ch. 16; K. D. Brown, op. cit.; R. Price, *Labour in British Society* (1986), Ch. 2; J. Belchem, *Industrialization and the Working Class: The English Experience 1750–1900* (1990), Chs. 5 and 6.

3. See, for example, B. Laurie, *Working People of Philadelphia 1800–1850* (1980), especially Chs. 4 and 5; S. Wilentz, *Chants Democratic: New York City and the Rise of the American Working Class 1788–1850* (1986), especially Chs. 5–7; S. J. Ross, *Workers on the Edge: Work Leisure and Politics in Industrializing Cincinnati 1788–1890* (1985), Ch. 3; S. E. Hirsch, *Roots of the American Working Class: The Industrialization of Crafts in Newark 1800–1860* (1978); H. B. Rock, *Artisans of the New Republic: The Tradesmen of New York City in the Age of Jefferson* (1979); S. Wilentz, 'Artisan Origins of the American Working Class', *International Labor and Working Class History* 19 (Spring 1981); D. Thompson, *The Chartists* (1984); J. A. Epstein and D. Thompson (eds.), *The Chartist Experience* (1982).

4. D. Montgomery, *Beyond Equality: Labor and the Radical Republicans 1862–1872* (1967), especially Ch. 4.

5. N. Kirk, op. cit., especially Ch. 1; E. H. Hunt, op. cit., Ch. 8; R. Q. Gray, *The Aristocracy of Labour in Nineteenth-century Britain c1850–1914* (1981), especially Chs. 6 and 9.

6. K. Marx, *Capital*, I (1970), pp. 176, 302, 356, 441, 453, 509, 540–1, 595, 645; K. Polanyi, *The Great Transformation* (1957); M. Dobb, *Studies in the Development of Capitalism* (1968), Ch. 1.

7. R. Johnson, 'Reading for the Best Marx: History-writing and Historical Abstraction', in R. Johnson, G. McLennan, B. Schwarz and D. Sutton (eds.), *Making Histories* (1982).

8. E. P. Thompson, 'The Poverty of Theory', in *The Poverty of Theory and Other Essays* (1978), pp. 273–6, 288–90; R. Williams, *Marxism and Literature* (1977), pp. 75–89.

9. The following section, concerning merchant and industrial capital and patterns of protest, draws heavily upon: D. Montgomery, unpublished

correspondence, July 1989; G. Rodgers Taylor, *The Transportation Revolution 1815–1860* (1951), 1; M. Dobb, *Studies in the Development of Capitalism* (1968), Ch. IV; E. J. Hobsbawm, *Industry and Empire* (1969), Chs. 2 and 3; M. Rediker, *Between the Devil and the Deep Blue Sea* (1987), Chs. 1 and 2; the Foreword by Elizabeth Fox and E. D. Genovese to A. Kaufman, *Capitalism, Slavery and Republican Values: Antebellum Political Economists 1819–1848* (1982); P. Linebaugh, *The London Hanged: Crime and Civil Society in the Eighteenth Century* (1993), Chs. 2 and 12.

10. G. Rodgers Taylor, op. cit., p. 10.

11. D. Montgomery, unpublished correspondence, July 1989.

12. For the nature of 'Old Corruption' see E. P. Thompson, *The Making*, op. cit., pp. 507–14.

13. N. W. Thompson, *The People's Science: The Popular Political Economy of Exploitation and Crisis* (1984), pp. 87–8, 96–102, 108–9, 145.

14. M. Berg, *The Age of Manufactures 1700–1820* (1985), Introduction, p. 316; N. Crafts, 'British Economic Growth, 1700–1831: A Review of the Evidence', *Economic History Review*, xxxvi (1983); D. Cannadine, 'The Past and the Present in the English Industrial Revolution 1880–1980', *Past and Present*, 103 (1984). Jonathan Prude ('Protoindustrialization in the American Context', *International Labor and Working Class History*, 33 (Spring 1988)), rightly reminds us that the absence of a sudden and complete transition to 'machinofacture' should not obscure the fact of uneven capitalist transformation taking place within workshops and other units of production in both town and countryside. See also for the European context, C. Tilly, 'Did the Cake of Custom Break?', in J. Merriman (ed.), *Consciousness and Class Experience in Nineteenth-Century Europe* (1979).

15. R. Samuel, 'Workshop of the World: Steam Power and Hand Technology in mid-Victorian Britain', *History Workshop Journal*, 3 (1977); M. Berg, op. cit., pp. 20, 316–19, and Ch. 3; D. M. Gordon, R. Edwards and M. Reich, op. cit., pp. 13–14, 79–80.

16. For a good critique of the continuity thesis see P. Hudson, *The Industrial Revolution* (1992), especially Introduction and Ch. 1.

17. E. J. Hobsbawm, *Industry and Empire*, op. cit., p. 154.

18. D. Montgomery, *Beyond Equality*, op. cit., pp. 26–7; *id.*, *The Fall*, op. cit., pp. 46, 48–9; H. G. Gutman and I. Berlin, *Power and Culture* (1987), Ch. 11.

19. I have employed the term 'customary' to refer to a cluster of 'moral'/regulatory practices and values variously held by all manner of (and often seemingly unconnected) labouring people and petty producers located largely (rather than exclusively) within petty-commodity and semi-subsistence modes of production. The looser descriptive term of cluster is preferred to the notion of system. The latter is too suggestive of rigour, uniformity, and clearly articulated and closely shared consciousness on the part of historical actors to accurately describe our more tenuously connected historical subjects. I suggest, in effect, that artisans, women of the labouring population, industrial workers and others were connected in important ways by 'custom' and opposition to free-market capitalism, even though that unity of interests often lacked the clarity, force and depth of expression articulated by increasingly class-conscious nineteenth-century workers. The term 'moral economy', at least as employed in the pioneering work of E. P. Thompson, assumes a far more specific meaning

than the general term customary. Thompson's 'moral economy' refers to confrontations in the eighteenth-century English market-place between those (especially food rioters) advocating a customary paternalist model of food marketing (based upon market regulation in times of dearth, longstanding statute law and the paramount importance of the needs of the whole community versus those of the profiteering few) and those, such as the followers of Adam Smith, urging the adoption of 'the new political economy of the free market in grain'. Thompson warns against loose and decontextualised application of his usage of 'moral economy'. E. P. Thompson, *Customs in Common* (1991), pp. 260–1, 336–51; W. Reddy, *The Rise of Market Culture: The Textile Trade and French Society 1750–1900* (1984). Karl Marx's observations on the mainsprings of the economic behaviour of workers and capitalists (*Capital*, Vol. 1, op. cit., pp. 84–155) can still be read with interest and reward, and should be recommended to all those who falsely separate values, norms and ideas on the one hand and material reality on the other.

20. The quotations are from E. Countryman, 'The Uses of Capital in Revolutionary America: The Case of the New York Loyalist Merchants', *William and Mary Quarterly*, XLIX (Jan. 1992). I am indebted to the author for a copy of his article. See also E. Foner, *Tom Paine and Revolutionary America* (1976), p. 47 and Ch. 5; the essays by G. B. Nash ('Artisans and Politics in Eighteenth-century Philadelphia'), A. F. Young, ('English Plebeian Culture and Eighteenth-century American Radicalism') and R. W. Malcolmson, ('Workers' Combinations in Eighteenth-century England'), in M. and J. Jacob (eds.), op. cit.; C. G. Steffen, *The Mechanics of Baltimore* (1984), Chs. 5 and 6; S. Wilentz, *Chants Democratic*, Ch. 3; id., 'Artisan Republican Festivals and the Rise of Class Conflict in New York City 1788–1837', in M. H. Frisch and D. J. Walkowitz (eds.), *Working Class America* (1983); A. F. Young (ed.), *The American Revolution: Explorations in the History of American Radicalism* (1976). For the importance of the free market see, J. Appleby, *Capitalism and a New Social Order: The Republican Vision of the 1790s* (1984).

21. M. Berg, op. cit., Ch. 7. There is, however, a tendency in Berg's approach to rigidly separate and compartmentalise what may well have been more overlapping and interrelated work-, gender- and community-based experiences and forms of consciousness. See A. J. Randall, 'The Industrial Moral Economy of the Gloucestershire Weavers', in J. Rule (ed.), *British Trade Unionism 1750–1850: The Formative Years* (1988), especially pp. 46–9, for an important and largely convincing argument in favour of a widespread, community-based commitment to customary values and practices; id., *Before the Luddites: Custom Community and Machinery in the English Woollen Industry* (1991). Forms of consciousness and language as between workers in different sectors of the eighteenth-century economy, between men and women, skilled and non-skilled, and different kinds of community merit further investigation.

22. For the notion of a 'moral economy' among slaves, ex-slaves and freedpeople in the southern states see B. Fields, *Slavery and Freedom on the Middle Ground: Maryland During the Nineteenth Century* (1985), pp. 28–39, 70–1, 151–8; G. D. Jaynes, *Branches Without Roots: Genesis of the Black Working Class in the American South 1862–1882* (1986), Chs. 1 and 4; J. S. Strickland, 'Traditional Culture and Moral Economy: Social

and Economic Change in the South Carolina Low Country 1865–1910', in S. Hahn and J. Prude (eds.), *The Countryside in the Age of Capitalist Transformation: Essays in the Social History of Rural America* (1985). The essays in ibid. by Hahn, Kulik, Prude, Faragher and McMath examine the importance of 'custom' for white southern yeomen farmers, northeastern rural dwellers and western and southwestern settlers.

23. As noted by Patrick Joyce ((ed.), *The Historical Meanings of Work* (1987), pp. 26–7), it is important to remember that 'later eighteenth-century workers had for long been involved in a market economy, one that was very much capitalist in character', and that custom was 'a way of living the market and was not a resource sealed in hermetic opposition to it'. See also E. P. Thompson, *Customs*, op. cit., p. 272.

24. A static identification of 'customary' with 'backward looking' does scant justice to the changed meanings and contexts of popular protest. As Hobsbawm has observed, 'artisans who began simply by trying to defend or re-establish the old 'moral economy' could find themselves driven, under the pressure of the economic transformations of the early nineteenth century, to envisage a new and revolutionary way of re-establishing the moral social order as they saw it, and in doing so to become social innovators and revolutionaries' ('Artisan or Labour Aristocrat?', *Economic History Review*, Second series, XXXVII (1984), p. 362).

25. For the importance of cultural influences see, for example, H. Gutman and I. Berlin, op. cit., pp. 18–25. For recent emphases upon the importance of politics and ideas in moulding worker consciousness and behaviour see G. S. Jones, 'Rethinking Chartism', in his *Languages of Class*, op cit.; A. J. Reid, 'Marxism and Revisionism in British Labour History', *Society Study Labour History Bulletin*, 52, 3 (Nov. 1987), pp. 46–8.

26. For the revived debate concerning landed-aristocratic-city or manufacturing-bourgeois hegemony in modern Britain see P. Anderson, 'The Figures of Descent', *New Left Review*, 161 (Jan.–Feb. 1987); C. Barker and D. Nicholls (eds.), *The Development of British Capitalist Society: A Marxist Debate* (1988); M. J. Daunton, ' "Gentlemanly Capitalism" and British Industry 1820–1914', *Past and Present*, 122 (1989); J. Seed and J. Woolf (eds.), *The Culture of Capital: Art Power and the Nineteenth Century Middle Class* (1988).

27. J. Saville, 'Some Notes on Perry Anderson's "Figures of Descent" ', in C. Barker and D. Nicholls (eds.), op. cit.; P. Joyce, *Work Society and Politics* (1980), pp. 2–4, 40–1; A. Howe, *The Cotton Masters 1830–1860* (1984); S. Gunn, 'The "Failure" of the Victorian Middle Class: A Critique', in J. Seed and J. Woolf (eds.), op. cit.

28. B. Moore, *Social Origins of Dictatorship and Democracy*, op. cit., Ch. III; S. Thernstrom, *Poverty and Progress* (1969), Ch. 3.

29. P. S. Bagwell and G. E. Mingay, op. cit., p. 5.

30. Ibid., p. 5.

31. M. Berg, op. cit., Ch. 6, and pp. 169–74; A. Kessler-Harris, *Out To Work: A History of Wage-Earning Women in the United States* (1983), Chs. 1 and 2.

32. R. W. Malcolmson, *Life and Labour in England 1700–1780* (1981), pp. 23–5, 45–55; J. Rule, *The Labouring Classes*, op. cit., pp. 10–11; E. Pessen, 'Builders of the Young Republic', in R. B. Morris (ed.), op. cit.,

p. 47; J. Prude, 'Town-Factory Conflict in Antebellum Rural Massachusetts', in S. Hahn and J. Prude (eds.), op. cit., p. 75.

33. J. Prude, 'Protoindustrialization in the American Context', op. cit., p. 23; S. Hahn, 'The "Unmaking" of the Southern Yeomanry: The Transformation of the Georgia Upcountry 1860–1890', in S. Hahn and J. Prude (eds.), op. cit., pp. 179–80; W. B. Rothenberg, 'The Market and the Massachusetts Farmer 1750–1855', *Journal of Economic History*, 41 (June 1981), and 'The Market and Massachusetts Farmers: Reply', Ibid;, 43 (June 1983); M. A. Bernstein and S. Wilentz, 'Marketing, Commerce and Capitalism in Rural Massachusetts', ibid., 44 (March 1984); W. B. Rothenberg, 'The Emergence of Farm Labor Markets and the Transformation of the Rural Economy: Massachusetts 1750–1855', ibid., 3 (Sept. 1988), especially p. 538.

34. D. E. Williams, 'Morals, Markets and the English Crowd in 1766', *Past and Present*, 104 (Aug. 1984). For an effective critique of Williams' thesis see A. Charlesworth and A. J. Randall, 'Morals, Markets and the English Crowd in 1766', *Past and Present*, 114 (1987). For emphasis upon the predominantly individualistic, economically 'rational', market-orientated and acquisitive nature of English society see, A. Macfarlane, *The Origins of English Individualism* (1978), pp. 163, 198–200.

35. A. Charlesworth and A. J. Randall, op. cit., p. 201.

36. A. J. Randall, 'The Industrial Moral Economy', op. cit., pp. 40–6. For Owenism see G. Claeys, *Machinery Money and the Millenium: From Moral Economy to Socialism 1815–1860* (1987), and the review of Claeys' book by Noel Thompson in *Society Study Labour History Bulletin*, Vol. 53, 1 (Spring 1988), pp. 32–6.

37. A. J. Randall, op. cit., p. 41.

38. Ibid., pp. 44, 47.

39. C. H. Dahnhof, *Change in Agriculture: The Northern United States 1820–1870* (1969), Ch. 1; R. A. Gross, 'Culture and Cultivation: Agriculture and Society in Thoreau's Concord'. *Journal of American History*, 69, (1982); S. Hahn and J. Prude (eds.), op. cit., pp. 27–8, 74–5, 144, 179–80, 183.

40. J. Prude, *The Coming of the Industrial Order: Town and Factory Life in Rural Massachusetts 1810–1860* (1985), pp. 10–17.

41. J. Prude, 'Town-Factory Conflicts', op. cit.

42. This section on western agriculture is heavily indebted to P. W. Gates, *The Farmers Age: Agriculture 1815–1860* (1960), pp. 50, 66–9, IV, VIII, IX, XIII; G. Rodgers Taylor, op, cit., V; C. H. Dahnhof, op. cit., pp. 14–15, 20–1, 114–29, 149–54; S. Hahn and J. Prude (eds.), op. cit., Part III; M. Walsh, *The American Frontier Revisited* (1981); A. G. Bogue, *From Prairie to Corn Belt* (1963). Reeve Huston, of Yale University, has given very helpful advice concerning developments in agriculture.

43. J. M. Faragher, 'Open-Country Community: Sugar Creek Illinois 1820–1850', in S. Hahn and J. Prude (eds.), op. cit.; id., *Sugar Creek: Life on the Illinois Prairie* (1986).

44. R. C. McMath Jr., 'Sandy Land and Hogs in the Timber: (Agri)cultural Origins of the Farmers' Alliance in Texas', in S. Hahn and J. Prude (eds.), op. cit.; L. Goodwyn, *Democratic Promise: The Populist Moment in America* (1976).

45. For the view that there did exist a strong commitment to capitalist values

and practices among large sections of the western farming population (including tenants) and a correspondingly low level of class conflict see R. P. Swierenga, *Pioneers and Profits: Land Speculation on the Iowa Frontier* (1968), and D. Winters, *Farmers Without Farms: Agricultural Tenancy in Nineteenth Century Iowa* (1978).

46. The following section on slavery is heavily reliant upon E. D. Genovese, *The World the Slaveholders Made: Two Essays in Interpretation* (1969); id. *Roll Jordan Roll*, op. cit., especially Book One, Part 1 and Book Four; B. Fields, op. cit; and P. J. Parish, *Slavery* (1979).

47. E. D. Genovese and E. Fox Genovese in A. Kaufman, op. cit., xiii.

48. G. D. Jaynes, op. cit., Ch. 4.

49. B. Fields, op. cit., pp. 70–1, 87–9.

50. Ibid., p. 163.

51. E. D. Genovese, *Roll Jordan Roll*, op. cit., pp. 3–7, 587–98; H. G. Gutman and I. Berlin, op. cit., pp. 42–59.

52. J. S. Strickland 'Traditional Culture and Moral Economy: Social and Economic Change in South Carolina Low Country 1865–1910', in S. Hahn and J. Prude (eds.), op. cit., p. 144.

53. Ibid., pp. 145–6.

54. Ibid., pp. 152–4; B. Fields, op. cit., p. 159.

55. S. Hahn, 'The "Unmaking" of the Southern Yeomanry', in S. Hahn and J. Prude (eds.), op. cit., p. 180.

56. R. W. Malcolmson, op. cit., Ch. 2, pp. 102–7.

57. See, for example, S. J. Ross, op. cit., Ch. 1; I. Prothero, *Artisans and Politics in Early Nineteenth Century London: John Gast and His Times* (1979), especially Conclusion; and the articles by Behagg and Sykes in J. A. Epstein and D. Thompson (eds.), op. cit.

58. For such changes see J. Rule, *The Labouring Classes* op. cit., Introduction, and Ch. 4; S. Wilentz, 'Against Exceptionalism', op. cit. pp. 6–9.

59. M. Berg, op. cit., pp. 157–8; C. Stansell, *City of Women: Sex and Class in New York 1789–1860* (1987), Chs. 5 and 7; A. Kessler-Harris, op. cit., Ch. 3; D. Thompson, 'Women and Nineteenth-Century Radical Politics: A Lost Dimension', in J. Mitchell and A. Oakley (eds.), *The Rights and Wrongs of Women* (1976), especially pp. 136–8; J. W. Scott, 'Gender: A Useful Category of Historical Analysis', *American History Review* (Dec. 1986).

60. C. Stansell, 'The Origins of the Sweatshop: Women and Early Industrialization in New York City', in M. H. Frisch and D. J. Walkowitz (eds.), *Working Class America* (1983), p. 50; S. Alexander, 'Women's Work in Nineteenth-Century London', in J. Mitchell and A. Oakley (eds.), op. cit.

61. R. Price, op. cit., p. 18; C. Stansell, 'The Origins', op. cit., p. 79.

62. R. Price, op. cit., pp. 19–22; S. Wilentz, *Chants Democratic*, op. cit., pp. 5–12.

63. E. P. Thompson, *The Making*, op. cit., p. 344; J. Rule, *The Labouring Classes*, op. cit., p. 3.

64. S. Wilentz, op. cit., pp. 113–14; B. Laurie, *Working People of Philadelphia*, op. cit., p. 15; J. Prude, *The Coming*, op. cit., pp. xiv–xvi; T. Dublin, *Women at Work: The Transformation of Work and Community in Lowell Massachussets 1826–1860* (1979), Ch. 2.

65. J. Prude, op. cit., Ch. 3; S. Wilentz, op. cit., pp. 12, 31, 115–29; B. Laurie, op. cit., pp. 14, 30; C. Stansell, *City of Women*, op. cit., Ch. 6.

66. P. G. Faler, *Mechanics and Manufacturers in the Early Industrial Revolution: Lynn Massachusetts 1780–1860* (1981), Ch. 2; A. Dawley, *Class and Community: The Industrial Revolution in Lynn* (1982), p. 8.
67. P. G. Faler, op. cit., p. 148.
68. Ibid., pp. 22–3.
69. A. Dawley, op. cit., pp. 5, 17–18.
70. Ibid., pp. 5, 62–3, 82–5; P. G. Faler, op. cit., pp. 24, 85.
71. P. G. Faler, op. cit., Ch. 3; A. Dawley, op. cit., pp. 2–3, 58–66.
72. A. Dawley, op. cit., pp. 25–9, 51–8; P. G. Faler, op. cit., p. 26, Ch. 4.
73. A. Dawley, op. cit., p. 57.
74. Ibid., pp. 60–6, 82–5.
75. Ibid., p. 84; P. G. Faler, op. cit., pp. 42–4, 75–6.
76. P. G. Faler, op. cit., pp. 75–6.
77. Ibid., p. 99.
78. Ibid., pp. 97–9.
79. E. P. Thompson, *The Making*, op. cit., pp. 326, 340.
80. Ibid., p. 299.
81. Ibid., pp. 305–6.
82. Ibid., pp. 307–9; D. Thompson, *The Chartists*, op. cit., p. 208.
83. E. P. Thompson, op. cit., pp. 299–303, 310–14, 316; A. J. Randall, op. cit.; P. Hudson, 'Proto-industrialization: The Case of the West Riding', *History Workshop Journal*, 12 (Autumn 1981); P. Linebaugh, op. cit. (Ch. 8) for the deteriorating conditions of 18th-century London silk weavers.
84. E. P. Thompson, op. cit., pp. 344–5.
85. For a summary of the 'optimistic' case see J. Rule, *The Labouring Classes*, op. cit., Ch. 1, especially pp. 36–7.
86. E. P. Thompson, op. cit., Chs. 6, 8 and 9.
87. Ibid., p. 330.
88. M. Berg, op. cit., Ch. 6; A. Kessler-Harris, op. cit., Ch. 2; C. Stansell, 'The Origins of the Sweatshop', op. cit., pp. 80–3; J. Rendall, *The Origins of Modern Feminism* (1985), Ch. 5; P. Hudson and W. R. Lee, *Women's Work and the Family Economy in Historical Perspective* (1990), Ch. 1.
89. M. Berg, op. cit., p. 158.
90. D. Thompson, 'Women and Nineteenth-Century Radical Politics', op. cit., pp. 137–8; N. Kirk, *The Growth of Working Class Reformism*, op. cit., pp. 216–20; A. Kessler-Harris, op. cit., pp. 46–53.
91. A Kessler-Harris, op. cit., pp. 46–7.
92. E. H. Hunt, op. cit., pp. 17–18; J. Rule, *The Labouring Classes*, op. cit., p. 14.
93. S. Alexander, op. cit., p. 78.
94. E. H. Hunt, op. cit., pp. 19–25; A. V. John, *Unequal Opportunities: Women's Employment in England 1800–1918* (1986), Introduction; A. Kessler-Harris, op. cit., pp. 70–2, Ch. 4.
95. A. Kessler-Harris, op. cit., pp. 77; C. Stansell, *City of Women*, op. cit., pp. 12–15.
96. S. Wilentz, *Chants Democratic*, op. cit., pp. 24–25, Ch. 3.
97. S. Wilentz, 'Artisan Republican Festivals and the Rise of Class Conflict in New York City 1788–1837', in M. H. Frisch and D. J. Walkowitz (eds.), op. cit., p. 41.
98. C. Stansell, 'The Origins of the Sweatshop', op. cit., p. 82.
99. Ibid., p. 80.

100. S. Alexander, op. cit., pp. 86–8, 97–107.

101. Ibid., p. 98.

102. J. Liddington and J. Norris, *One Hand Tied Behind Us: The Rise of the Women's Suffrage Movement* (1984), Ch. V.

103. The Lancashire female cotton operatives' reputation for 'boldness', 'independence' and a marked lack of deference towards their 'betters' probably being the exception rather than the rule, at least in England. See N. Kirk, op. cit., p. 220.

104. C. Stansell, 'The Origins of the Sweatshop', op. cit., p. 95.

105. J. Rule, *The Labouring Classes* op. cit., (pp. 35–7) for a useful summary of the main lines of debate.

106. R. A. Sykes, 'Trade Unionism and Class Consciousness', in J. Rule (ed.), *British Trade Unionism*, op. cit., p. 183; A. E. Musson, op. cit.; R. A. Sykes, 'Early Chartism and Trade Unionism in South-East Lancashire', in J. A. Epstein and D. Thompson (eds.) op. cit., pp. 154, 181–4; S. Wilentz, *Chants Democratic*, op. cit., pp. 32, 141–2.

107. E. P. Thompson, *The Making*, op. cit., p. 269.

108. S. Wilentz, op. cit., especially Part II.

109. S. J. Ross, op. cit., pp. xvii, 3–24, Chs. 2 and 3 for Cincinati's artisans.

110. Ibid., Part II.

111. B. Laurie, *Working People of Philadelphia*, op. cit., p. 4.

112. Ibid., Chs. 4 and 5.

113. E. J. Hobsbawm, 'Custom, Wages and Work-load', in his *Labouring Men* (1974 edition); D. A. Reid, 'The Decline of Saint Monday', *Past and Present*, 71 (1976); W. Hamish Fraser, *Conflict And Class:.Scottish Workers 1700–1838* (1988), pp. 10, 23–38, Chs. 5 and 7; K. J. Logue, *Popular Disturbances in Scotland 1780–1815* (1979); J. D. Young, *The Rousing of the Scottish Working Class* (1979), Chs. 2 and 3; D. J. V. Jones, *The Last Rising: The Newport Insurrection of 1839* (1986) Chs. 1 and 2.

114. R. A. Sykes, 'Trade Unionism and Class Consciousness', op. cit.; id., 'Early Chartism and Trade Unionism', op. cit.

115. D. Goodway, *London Chartism 1838–1848* (1982), pp. 6–7.

116. Ibid., p. 9.

117. C. Behagg, 'An Alliance With the Middle Class: The Birmingham Political Union and Early Chartism', in J. Epstein and D. Thompson (eds.), op. cit., p. 72; id., *Politics and Production in the Early Nineteenth Century* (1990), Chs. 4 and 5.

118. C. Behagg, 'An Alliance With the Middle Class', op. cit., p. 69.

119. D. McNulty, 'Bristol Trade Unionism in the Chartist Years', in J. Rule (ed.), *British Trade Unionism*, op. cit., p. 222.

120. G. Crossick, *An Artisan Elite in Victorian Society: Kentish London 1840–1880* (1978), Ch. 10; R. Q. Gray, *The Labour Aristocracy in Victorian Edinburgh* (1976), pp. 155–64.

121. R. Price, op. cit., p. 27; C. R. Dobson, *Masters and Journeymen: A Prehistory of Industrial Relations 1717–1800* (1980), Chs. 1 and 2.

122. J. Rule, *The Labouring Classes* op. cit., p. 10.

123. J. K. Walton, *Lancashire: A Social History 1558–1939* (1987), p. 202; J. Rule, op. cit., p. 10.

124. For textiles in Philadelphia County see A. F. C. Wallace, *Rockdale: The Growth of an American Village in the Early Industrial Revolution* (1978), pp. 125–239; D. Montgomery, 'The Shuttle and the Cross: Weavers and

Artisans in the Kensington Riots of 1844', *Journal of Social History* 5 (1972), p. 47; B. Laurie, *Working People of Philadelphia*, op. cit., pp. 14–30; P. Scranton, Proprietary Capitalism: The Textile Manufacture at Philadelphia 1800–1885 (1983), pp. 10, 45–7, 418, Chs. 4 and 5.

125. For example, Fall River, one of the most prominent manufacturing centres of the country, had a population of only 4,159 in 1830. See, T. A. Murphy, 'Labor, Religion and Moral Reform in Fall River, Massachusetts 1800–1845', unpublished Ph.D. thesis, Yale University (1982), pp. 42–4; D. A. Zonderman, 'The Quest for the Middle Ground: Factory Operatives and the Concept of Community in Antebellum New England', paper presented at the AHA (Chicago, Dec. 1986), pp. 3–4. I am grateful to these authors for copies of their unpublished research.

126. E. J. Evans, *The Forging of the Modern State 1783–1870* (1985), p. 407; N. Kirk, *The Growth of Working Class Reformism*, op. cit., Ch. 2.

127. J. Prude, *The Coming of the Industrial Order*, op. cit., pp. xiv-xv.

128. J. Prude, 'The Social System of Early New England Textile Mills', in M. H. Frisch and D. J. Walkowitz (eds.), op. cit., p. 7.

129. T. Dublin, op. cit., pp. 77–8.

130. J. Prude, *The Coming*, op. cit., p. xv.

131. Ibid., pp. 82–7.

132. T. Dublin, op. cit., pp. 74, 86 and Ch. 5.

133. J. Prude, *The Coming*, op. cit., p. 96.

134. J. Prude, 'The Social System', op. cit., p. 7.

135. B. Laurie, *Working People of Philadelphia*, op. cit., pp. 28–30; D. Montgomery, 'The Shuttle and the Cross', op. cit., p. 48; P. Scranton, op. cit., pp. 38, 87, 94, 167 and Ch. 6.

136. J. K. Walton, op. cit., Ch. 6; N. Kirk, op. cit., p. 35.

137. D. A. Farnie, *The English Cotton Industry and the World Market 1815–1896* (1979), p. 209.

138. N. Kirk, op. cit., pp. 33–6.

139. E. P. Thompson, op. cit., p. 341.

140. N. Kirk, op. cit., p. 35.

141. J. K. Walton, op. cit., p. 124; M. Anderson, *Family Structure in Nineteenth-Century Lancashire* (1971).

142. J. K. Walton, op. cit., pp. 123–4.

143. Ibid., p. 132.

144. H. I. Dutton and J. E. King, 'The Limits of Paternalism: The Cotton Tyrants of North Lancashire 1836–54', *Social History*, 7, 1 (Jan. 1982), pp. 59–60; J. K. Walton, op. cit., pp. 132–3.

145. D. Thompson, *The Chartists*, op. cit., pp. 62, 133.

146. Ibid., p. 62 and Chs. 6 and 11; M. Jenkins, *The General Strike of 1842* (1980).

147. D. Thompson, op. cit., pp. 14–15, 106, 208–33 and Ch. 11; R. A. Sykes, 'Early Chartism and Trade Unionism', op. cit.; J. K. Walton, op. cit., Ch. 8.

148. E. P. Thompson, op. cit., p. 221; N. Kirk, 'In Defence of Class: A Critique of Gareth Stedman Jones', *International Review of Social History* XXII (1987), pp. 18–32.

149. N. Kirk, op. cit., p. 22.

150. Ibid., p. 27.

151. Ibid., p. 28.

152. Ibid., p. 28.
153. R. A. Sykes, 'Early Chartism and Trade Unionism', op. cit., p. 180.
154. Ibid., p. 181.
155. T. Dublin, op. cit., p. 86.
156. J. Prude, 'The Social System', op. cit., p. 3.
157. Ibid., p. 18.
158. T. Dublin, op. cit., pp. 89–107, Ch. 7.
159. D. Montgomery, 'The Shuttle and the Cross', op. cit., pp. 49–51.
160. P. Scranton, op. cit., pp. 124, 149–56.
161. Ibid., pp. 38, 166–7, 227ff., 240–71, 418.
162. T. Dublin, op. cit., p. 59.
163. Ibid., p. 35.
164. Ibid., pp. 31, 34, 38, 40.
165. J. Prude, 'The Social System', op. cit., pp. 10–11.
166. It is important to remember that large numbers of former farm labourers and servants entered factory employment. See J. Rule, *The Labouring Classes* op. cit., p. 174; M. Anderson, op. cit., pp. 37–9.
167. T. Dublin, 'Women and Outwork in a Nineteenth-century New England Town', in S. Hahn and J. Prude (eds.), op. cit., pp. 53–4; J. Prude, *The Coming* op. cit., p. 73; T. A. Murphy, op. cit., (p. 36) for the lack of an established system of cottage weaving in Fall River.
168. J. Prude, 'The Social System', op. cit., pp. 10–11, 19–21; id., *The Coming* op. cit., pp. 21–4, 54–5, 70–1, 89, 92, 93, 96.
169. J. Prude, 'The Social System', op. cit., pp. 10–12, 25.
170. T. Dublin, *Women At Work*, op. cit., pp. 23, 31, 88–9.
171. P. Joyce, *Work Society and Politics: The Culture of the Factory in Later Victorian England* (1980), p. 105.
172. Ibid., p. 116; N. Kirk, 'Cotton Workers and Deference', *Society Study Labour History Bulletin* 42 (Spring 1981).
173. J. Prude, 'The Social System', op. cit., p. 3; D. A. Zonderman, op. cit., for the wide variety of operative responses to the coming of the factory.
174. J. Prude, 'The Social System', op. cit., p. 17.
175. Ibid., p. 27.
176. S. Hahn and J. Prude (eds.), op. cit., p. 248.
177. P. W. Gates, op. cit., p. 275.
178. R. P. Swierenga, 'Agriculture and Rural Life: The New Rural History' in J. B. Gardner and G. R. Adams (eds.), *Ordinary People and Everyday Life: Perspectives on the New Social History* (1983), p. 97.
179. P. J. Parish, op. cit., p. 27.
180. See above, pp. 31–38.
181. For such tensions see the essays by Kulik, Prude and McMath in S. Hahn and J. Prude (eds.), op. cit.
182. R. M. Brown, 'Back Country Rebellions and the Homestead Ethic', in R. M. Brown and D. E. Fehren-Bacher (eds.), *Tradition Conflict and Modernization: Perspectives on the American Revolution* (1977).
183. H. Christman, *Tin Horns and Calico: A Decisive Episode in the Emergence of Democracy* (1945). Reeve Huston has also kindly given me access to chapters in his forthcoming (Yale) Ph.D. thesis on the Anti-Rent Wars.
184. M. A. Lause. 'Voting Yourself a Farm in Antebellum Iowa: Towards an Urban, Working-Class Prehistory of the Post Civil War Agrarian Insurgency', *Annals of Iowa*, 49 (1988), pp. 171–3.

185. Ibid., pp. 178–86.
186. P. W. Gates, op. cit., pp. 67–8, 75–6, 86–9; A. G. Bogue, 'The Iowa Claim Clubs: Symbols and Substance', in V. Carstensen (ed.), *The Public Lands: Studies in the History of the Public Domain* (1963); D. E. Schob, *Hired Hands and Plowboys: Farm Labor in the Midwest 1815–1860* (1975).
187. E. D. Genovese, *From Rebellion to Revolution*, op. cit., p. 6.
188. J. Oakes, 'The Political Significance of Slave Resistance', *History Workshop Journal*, 22 (1986), p. 89.
189. E. D. Genovese, *Roll Jordan Roll*, op. cit., pp. 22–5.
190. I. Berlin and H. G. Gutman, 'Natives and Immigrants, Free Men and Slaves: Urban Workingmen in the Antebellum South', *American Historical Review*, 88 (1983), p. 1197.
191. B. Fields, op. cit., pp. 35–6, 68–9, 71–82.
192. J. Rule, *The Labouring Classes* op. cit., p. 9.
193. Ibid., p. 353.
194. P. Horn, *Life and Labour in Rural England 1760–1850* (1987), p. 145; M. Reed and R. Wells (eds.), *Class Conflict and Protest in the English Countryside 1700–1850* (1990), Ch. 1.
195. E. J. Hobsbawm, *Industry and Empire* (1971), p. 296.
196. Ibid., pp. 301–5; J. D. Young, op. cit., pp. 27, 74, 83, 89–96; E. Richards, *The Highland Clearances* (1982).
197. R. Wells, 'Tolpuddle in the Context of English Agrarian Labour History', in J. Rule (ed.), *British Trade Unionism*, op. cit., p. 100; M. E. Turner, *British Parliamentary Enclosure* (1983).
198. R. Wells, op. cit., pp. 101–7; K. D. M. Snell, *Annals of the Labouring Poor: Social Change and Agrarian England 1660–1900* (1985).
199. R. Wells, op. cit., p. 108.
200. Ibid., pp. 109–12.
201. Ibid., p. 112.
202. Ibid., p. 118; J. Rule (*The Labouring Classes* op. cit., pp. 353–63) for a survey of the literature. J. Bohstedt, *Riots and Community Politics in England and Wales 1790–1810* (1983); M. Reed and R. Wells (eds.), op. cit.; J. E. Archer, *By A Flash and A Scare: Incendiarism Animal Maiming and Poaching in East Anglia 1815–1870* (1990); B. Reay, *The Last Rising of the Agricultural Labourers: Rural Life and Protest in Nineteenth-Century England* (1990).
203. J. Rule, op. cit., p. 356.
204. M. Berg, op. cit., Ch. 7; A. J. Randall, op. cit., pp. 44–8. In the United States successive waves of immigration and the attachment of many immigrant groups to 'traditional' customs and beliefs ensured the persistent, if uneven, appeal of aspects of the 'customary economy'. For example, food rioting and price fixing occurred in New York City in 1837, 1857, 1902 and 1917. The protests of 1902 and 1917 were initiated by immigrant Jewish women. The same degree of ethnic homogeneity was not present in the riots of 1837 and 1857. See H. G. Gutman, *Work Culture and Society in Industrializing America* (1977), pp. 59–63; A Bridges, *A City in the Republic: Antebellum New York and the Origins of Machine Politics* (1987), pp. 9–11; D. Frank, 'Housewives, Socialists and the Politics of Food: The 1917 New York Cost-of-Living Protests', *Feminist Studies*, 11, 2 (Summer 1985).
205. D. Thompson, *The Chartists*, op. cit., p. 240.

206. Ibid., p. 253.
207. R. D. Storch, 'The Problem of Working-Class Leisure', in A. P. Donajgrodzki (ed.), *Social Control in Nineteenth Century Britain* (1977), pp. 139–42.
208. N. Kirk, 'In Defence of Class', op. cit., pp. 35–7, 43.
209. A. Dawley, op. cit., pp. 70–2; P. G. Faler, op. cit., Ch. 3; S. J. Ross, op. cit., p. xix and Ch. I; E. Foner, op. cit., Ch. 4; G. Nash, op. cit., p. 70; S. Wilentz, *Chants Democratic*, op. cit., pp. 14–15, Ch. 2.
210. S. J. Ross, op. cit., p. xix; see also A. Dawley (op. cit., p. 70) for the view that the ballot box was 'the coffin of class consciousness' in Lynn.
211. S. J. Ross, op. cit., pp. xix, 49–55; S. Wilentz, op. cit., pp. 14–15.
212. S. J. Ross, op. cit., pp. 55–9, 169–71; S. Wilentz, op. cit., pp. 145–50.

Part Two

1. S. Wilentz, ' A Reply to Criticism', *International Labor and Working Class History*, 28 (Fall 1985), pp. 46–55; id., *Chants Democratic*, op. cit., pp. 15–19.
2. A. Bridges, 'Becoming American', in I. Katznelson and A. R. Zolberg (eds), op. cit., p. 162; M. Davis, 'Why the U.S. Working Class is Different', *New Left Review*, 123 (Sept.–Oct. 1980), pp. 12–16.
3. B. Laurie, *Artisans into Workers*, op. cit., p. 63.
4. A. Bridges, op. cit., p. 165; id., *A City in the Republic*, op. cit., Ch. 6.
5. P. S. Foner, *The History of the Labor Movement*, Vol 1, op. cit., p. 122.
6. B. Laurie, *Working People of Philadelphia*, op. cit., p. 75.
7. B. Laurie, *Artisans into Workers*, op. cit., p. 66.
8. S. Wilentz, *Chants Democratic*, op. cit., pp. 190–9.
9. Ibid., pp. 176–89.
10. B. Laurie, *Artisans into Workers*, op. cit., p. 79.
11. Ibid., pp. 68–72; id., *Working People of Philadelphia*, op. cit., pp. 77–8, 94–5.
12. A. Dawley, *Class and Community*, op. cit., pp. 65, 68; A. Bridges, 'Becoming American', pp. 163–6; S. Wilentz, op. cit., pp. 188–96; B. Laurie, *Artisans into Workers*, op. cit., pp. 58, 68–9, 72–3, 80–1.
13. B. Laurie, *Working People of Philadelphia*, op. cit., p. 76.
14. A. Bridges, *A City in the Republic*, op. cit., p. 22.
15. Ibid., p. 22.
16. S. Wilentz, op. cit., p. 195.
17. B. Laurie, *Working People of Philadelphia*, op. cit., p. 76.
18. A. Bridges, op. cit., p. 23.
19. P. S. Foner, op. cit., pp. 144–9.
20. S. Wilentz, op. cit., pp. 14–19, 188, 207–8, 214; B. Laurie, *Artisans into Workers*, op. cit., pp. 68–73.
21. S. Wilentz, 'Against Exceptionalism', op. cit., pp. 10–12.
22. B. Laurie, *Working People of Philadelphia*, op. cit., p. 77.
23. S. Wilentz, *Chants Democratic*, op. cit., pp. 214–15.
24. S. Wilentz, 'Against Exceptionalism', op. cit., pp. 3–4.
25. S. Wilentz, *Chants Democratic*, op. cit., p. 214.
26. P. S. Foner, op. cit., p. 126.

27. B. Laurie, *Artisans into Workers*, op. cit., p. 81.
28. J. Prude, *The Coming of the Industrial Order*, op. cit., pp. 218–19.
29. B. Laurie, op. cit., p. 80.
30. S. Wilentz, op. cit., pp. 201–13.
31. B. Laurie, op. cit., p. 82; id., *Working People*, op. cit., p. 111.
32. B. Laurie, *Artisans into Workers*, op. cit., p. 80.
33. P. S. Foner, op. cit., pp. 154–5.
34. S. Wilentz, op. cit., pp. 292–3.
35. P. S. Foner, op. cit., pp. 157–62.
36. A. Bridges, *A City in the Republic*, op. cit., p. 109.
37. S. Wilentz, op. cit., pp. 235, 293–4.
38. S. J. Ross, *Workers on the Edge*, op. cit., pp. 42–51.
39. Ibid., p. 54.
40. R. Huston, unpublished paper (Yale University, 1989), p. 25.
41. E. Pessen, 'Builders of the Young Republic', in R. B. Morris (ed.), op. cit.; C. G. Steffen, *The Mechanics of Baltimore*, op. cit., xiii, Chs. 5 and 10; A. F. Young, 'Revolutionary Mechanics', in P. Buhle and A. Dawley (eds.), op. cit.
42. S. Wilentz, op. cit., p. 254.
43. Ibid., p. 219.
44. B. Laurie, op. cit., p. 83.
45. Ibid., p. 85.
46. S. Wilentz, op. cit., pp. 220–1.
47. S. J. Ross, op. cit., pp. 47–8.
48. B. Laurie, op. cit., p. 84.
49. B. Laurie, *Working People*, op. cit., pp. 90–1.
50. C. Stansell, *City of Women*, op. cit., p. 133.
51. Ibid., pp. 137–41.
52. Ibid., p. 141.
53. B. Laurie, *Artisans into Workers*, op. cit., p. 88.
54. S. Wilentz, op. cit., p. 286.
55. B. Laurie, op. cit., p. 84; id., *Working People*, op. cit., p. 87; S. Wilentz, op. cit., pp. 224–30.
56. B. Laurie, *Working People*, op. cit., pp. 73–84, 88, 94–5.
57. S. Wilentz, op. cit., pp. 221–3; B. Laurie, op. cit., pp. 88–9; id., *Artisans into Workers*, op. cit., p. 88.
58. B. Laurie, *Working People*, op. cit., p. 94; id., *Artisans into Workers*, op. cit., pp. 71–3, 83–4, 87–8.
59. B. Laurie, *Working People*, op. cit., pp. 99–100; S. Wilentz, op. cit., pp. 248–54.
60. B. Laurie, *Working People*, op. cit., pp. 89, 98–9; S. Wilentz, op. cit., p. 270.
61. B. Laurie, *Working People*, op. cit., pp. 60–1.
62. S. Wilentz, op. cit., pp. 263–71.
63. B. Laurie, *Artisans into Workers*, op. cit., p. 84.
64. S. Wilentz, op. cit., p. 241.
65. Ibid., pp. 241–2.
66. Ibid., pp. 242–3.
67. Ibid., pp. 243–8.
68. S. J. Ross, op. cit., pp. 45, 59.
69. D. Montgomery, 'The Shuttle and the Cross', op. cit., p. 51.

70. B. Laurie, *Working People*, op. cit., Part 3.
71. B. Laurie, *Artisans into Workers*, op. cit., pp. 56–7.
72. Ibid., pp. 54, 82; id., *Working People*, op. cit., pp. 110–11.
73. B. Laurie, op. cit., p. 111.
74. Ibid., pp. 114–15.
75. A. Bridges, *A City in the Republic*, op. cit., pp. 27–9, 62, 68–70; id., 'Becoming American', op. cit., pp. 186–8.
76. A. Bridges, *A City in the Republic*, op. cit., p. 67.
77. E. P. Thompson, *The Making*, op. cit., p. 782; for popular radicalism during the first quarter of the nineteenth century see J. Belchem, *Industrialization and the Working Class*, op. cit., Ch. 6; *Manchester Region History Review* (1989 'Peterloo' issue).
78. J. Rule, *The Labouring Classes*, op. cit., p. 307.
79. E. H. Hunt, *British Labour History*, op. cit., pp. 210–12.
80. E. P. Thompson, op. cit., p. 896.
81. Ibid., pp. 898–9.
82. D. Thompson, *The Chartists*, op. cit., p. 40.
83. E. J. Hobsbawm and G. Rude, *Captain Swing* (1973), p. xxi; quoted in J. Rule, op. cit., p. 357. See also J. P. D. Dunbabin, *Rural Discontent in Nineteenth-century Britain* (1974), Chs. II and III.
84. R. Wells, 'Tolpuddle in the Context of English Agrarian History', in J. Rule (ed.), *British Trade Unions*, op. cit., p. 119.
85. E. Richards, 'Patterns of Highland Discontent, 1790–1860', in J. Stevenson and R. Quinault (eds.), *Popular Protest and Public Order: Six Studies in British History 1790–1920* (1974); R. H. Campbell and T. M. Devine, 'The Rural Experience', in W. H. Fraser and R. J. Morris (eds.), *People and Society in Scotland, 1830–1914*, Vol. II (1990).
86. D. J. V. Jones, *Before Rebecca: Popular Protest in Wales 1793–1835* (1973), Ch. 4; G. Rude, *The Crowd in History 1730–1848* (1964), Ch. 10; D. J. V. Jones, *Rebecca's Children: A Study of Rural Society, Crime and Protest* (1989).
87. J. Rule (ed.), *The Labouring Classes*, op. cit., pp. 357–8; E. Richards, op. cit., p. 76.
88. J. Rule, op. cit., pp. 285–309.
89. Ibid., pp. 290–2, 294–8.
90. R. A. Sykes, 'Trade Unionism and Class Consciousness: the "Revolutionary" Period of General Unionism, 1829–1834', in J. Rule (ed.), *British Trade Unions*, op. cit., p. 181.
91. Ibid., pp. 186–7.
92. Ibid., pp. 186–93; J. Rule, 'The Formative Years of British Trade Unionism: An Overview', in ibid., pp. 16–17.
93. E. H. Hunt, op. cit., pp. 192–3; A. E. Musson quoted in J. Rule (ed.), *The Labouring Classes*, op. cit., p. 290.
94. B. Taylor, *Eve and the New Jerusalem: Socialism and Feminism in the Nineteenth Century* (1983), pp. 110–11.
95. I. Prothero, *Artisans and Politics*, op. cit., Conclusion; G. S. Jones, *Languages of Class*, op. cit., pp. 110–11, 137, 143–5, 153–4, 168–9.
96. R. A. Sykes, op. cit., pp. 178–80.
97. Ibid., p. 184.
98. B. Taylor, op. cit., p. 269.
99. M. I. Thomis and J. Grimmett, *Women in Protest* (1982); C. Stansell, *City*

of Women, op. cit., Ch. 7; E. P. Thompson, *Customs in Common*, op. cit., (pp. 305–36) for a stimulating review of the literature relating to women's involvement in food riots; B. Hill, *Women Work and Sexual Politics in Eighteenth-Century England* (1989).

100. R. Wells, op. cit., pp. 121–4.
101. N. W. Thompson, *The People's Science*, op. cit., pp. 110, 148–50, 219–28.
102. N. Kirk, 'In Defence of Class', op. cit., p. 17.
103. D. Thompson, op. cit., pp. 35–6.
104. Ibid., pp. 30–2.
105. Ibid., Preface. Thompson's book is the most rewarding general study of Chartism. See also id., *The Early Chartists* (1971); D. J. V. Jones, *Chartism and the Chartists* (1975); J. T. Ward, *Chartism* (1973); A. Briggs (ed.), *Chartist Studies* (1959); J. A. Epstein and D. Thompson (eds.), op. cit.
106. D. Thompson, *The Chartists*, op. cit., p. 11.
107. G. S. Jones, *Languages of Class*, op. cit., pp. 101–4.
108. D. Thompson, op. cit., Preface.
109. M. I. Thomis and J. Grimmett, op. cit., p. 123.
110. R. A. Sykes, 'Physical-Force Chartism: The Cotton District and the Crisis of 1839', *International Review of Social History*, XXX (1985, II).
111. Ibid.; D. Thompson, op. cit., p. 83; D. J. V. Jones, *The Last Rising*, op. cit., Chs. 4 and 5, pp. 203–11; I. Wilks, *South Wales and the Rising of 1839* (1984).
112. D. Thompson, op. cit., pp. 258–70, 273–5, 288–90.
113. Ibid., pp. 281–98; M. Jenkins, *The General Strike of 1842*, op. cit., especially Ch. 11.
114. N. Kirk, *The Growth of Working Class Reformism*, op. cit., p. 57.
115. D. Thompson, op. cit., p. 306.
116. Ibid., Ch. 13; J. Belchem, '1848: Feargus O'Connor and the Collapse of the Mass Platform', in J. A. Epstein and D. Thompson (eds.), op. cit.; J. Saville, *1848: The British State and the Chartist Movement* (1987).
117. N. Kirk, op. cit., pp. 67–70; K. Tiller, 'Late Chartism: Halifax, 1847–58', in J. A. Epstein and D. Thompson (eds.), op. cit.
118. A. Briggs, op. cit., p. 3.
119. D. Thompson, op. cit., pp. 5–6.
120. Ibid., Ch. 6, pp. 173–9; J. Foster, *Class Struggle and the Industrial Revolution: Early Industrial Capitalism in Three English Towns* (1974); T. Koditschek, *Class Formation and Urban-Industrial Society: Bradford 1750–1850* (1990), Ch. 17.
121. D. Thompson, op. cit., pp. 179–230.
122. See, for example, R. A. Sykes, 'Early Chartism and Trade Unionism', in J. A. Epstein and D. Thompson (eds.), op. cit., especially pp. 176–85.
123. D. Thompson, 'Ireland and the Irish in English Radicalism', in J. A. Epstein and D. Thompson, op. cit.; J. Belchem, 'English Working-Class Radicalism and the Irish, 1815–1850', *North West Labour History Bulletin*, 8 (1982–3).
124. D. Thompson, *The Chartists*, op. cit., pp. 231–2; J. D. Young, *The Rousing of the Scottish Working Class*, op. cit., pp. 92–3; A. Campbell, 'Honourable Men and Degraded Slaves: A Comparative Study of Trade Unionism in Two Lanarkshire Mining Communities c1830–1874', in R. Harrison (ed.), *Independent Collier: The Coal Miner as Archetypal Proletarian Reconsidered* (1978); R. Colls, *The Pitmen of the Northern Coalfield: Work*

Culture and Protest 1790–1850 (1987); R. Fyson, 'The Crisis of 1842: Chartism, the Colliers' Strike and the Outbreak in the Potteries', in J. A. Epstein and D. Thompson (eds.), op. cit.; D. J. V. Jones, *The Last Rising*, op. cit., pp. 20–1, 41–5, Ch. 2.

125. R. Wells, 'Tolpuddle', op. cit., pp. 126–7; J. D. Young, op. cit., p. 93.
126. J. Schwarzkopf, *Women in the Chartist Movement* (1991); D. Thompson, *The Chartists*, op. cit., Ch. 7; M. I. Thomis and J. Grimmett, op. cit., Ch. 6; J. A. Epstein, 'Some Organisational and Cultural Aspects of the Chartist Movement in Nottingham', in J. A. Epstein and D. Thompson (eds.), op. cit. For women's involvement in popular radicalism in the pre-Chartist period see J. A. Epstein, 'Understanding the Cap of Liberty: Symbolic Practice and Social Conflict in Early Nineteenth-Century England', in *Past and Present*, 122 (1989), especially pp. 100–7; C. Hall, 'The Tale of Samuel and Jemima: Gender and Working-Class Culture in Early Nineteenth-Century England', in T. Bennett, C. Mercer and J. Woollacott (eds.), *Popular Culture and Social Relations* (1986); J. Bohstedt, 'Gender, Household and Community Politics: Women in English Riots, 1790–1810', *Past and Present*, 120 (1988); B. Harrison, 'Class and Gender in Modern British Labour History', *Past and Present*, 124 (1989); A. Clark, 'The Rhetoric of Chartist Domesticity: Gender, Language and Class in the 1830s and 1840s', *Journal of British Studies*, 31, 1 (1992).
127. D. Thompson, *The Chartists*, op. cit., p. 126.
128. J. Foster, op. cit., p. 132; D. Thompson, op. cit., pp. 152, 163–9; D. J. V. Jones, *Chartism and the Chartists*, op. cit., pp. 30–32.
129. D. Thompson, op. cit., p. 172.
130. For such methodological concerns see N. Kirk, 'The Myth of Class? Workers and the Industrial Revolution in Stockport', *Society Study Labour History Bulletin*, 51, 1 (1986).
131. M. Jenkins, op. cit., Chs. 6 and 7; R. A. Sykes, 'Early Chartism and Trade Unionism', op. cit., pp. 152–4.
132. N. Kirk, 'In Defence of Class', op. cit., p. 35.
133. Ibid., p. 36.
134. Ibid., pp. 41–2.
135. J. A. Epstein, *The Lion of Freedom* (1982), p. 273.
136. T. C. Smout, *A Century of the Scottish People 1830–1950* (1988), pp. 234–6, 243–4.
137. G. Crossick, op. cit.; R. Q. Gray, op. cit.
138. P. F. Taylor, 'Popular Politics and Labour-Capital Relations in Bolton, 1825–1850' (D. Phil., University of Lancaster, 1991), Ch. 3; D. S. Gadian, 'Class Consciousness in Oldham and Other North-West Industrial Towns, 1830–1850', *Historical Journal*, XXI, I (1978), pp. 161–72; and the convincing criticisms of Gadian offered by R. A. Sykes, 'Some Aspects of Working-Class Consciousness in Oldham, 1830–1842', *Historical Journal*, 23, 1 (1980), pp. 167–79.
139. R. A. Sykes, 'Popular Politics and Trade Unionism in South-East Lancashire, 1829–1842' (D.Phil., University of Manchester, 1982), Ch. 10; D. Walsh, *Operative Conservatism in Lancashire 1833–1846: Some Comments on a Changing Political Culture*, University of Salford, Department of Politics and Contemporary History, Occasional Paper no. 11 (Salford, 1987); R. N. Soffer, 'Attitudes and Allegiances in the Unskilled North,

1830–1850' *International Review of Social History*, X, I (1965); D. Thompson, *The Chartists*, op. cit., pp. 237–8.

140. D. Thompson, op. cit., p. 28.

141. C. A. N. Reid, 'The Chartist Movement in Stockport' (M.A. thesis, University of Hull, 1976), pp. 282–99, 352.

142. P. F. Taylor, op. cit., Ch. 3. See also the splendid Ch. 10 ('Radicalism and Middle-Class Politics') in R. A. Sykes, 'Popular Politics and Trade Unionism in South-east Lancashire, 1829–1842', op. cit.

143. R. A. Sykes, thesis, op. cit., pp. 485–501; P. F. Taylor, op. cit., Ch. 3; A. J. Kidd and K. W. Roberts (eds.), *City Class and Culture: Social Policy and Cultural Production in Victorian Manchester* (1985); J. Seed, 'Unitarianism, Political Economy and the Antinomies of Liberal Culture in Manchester, 1830–50', *Social History*, vii, 1 (Jan. 1982).

144. D. Thompson, op. cit., p. 237; J. Cole, 'Chartism in Rochdale', (unpublished M.A. dissertation, Manchester Polytechnic, 1986).

145. D. Thompson, *The Chartists*, op. cit., pp. 257–70; N. Kirk, *The Growth*, op. cit., pp. 64–5.

146. N. Kirk, 'In Defence of Class', op. cit., p. 37.

147. D. Thompson, op. cit., p. 253.

148. N. Kirk, op. cit., pp, 42–3.

149. N. Kirk, *The Growth*, op. cit., pp. 54–66; J. Belchem, *Industrialization and the Working Class*, op. cit., Ch. 6.

150. G. S. Jones, 'Rethinking Chartism', in his *Languages of Class*, op. cit.; N. Kirk, 'In Defence of Class', op. cit., pp. 37–9; D. Thompson, 'The Languages of Class', *Society Study Labour History Bulletin*, 52, 1, (1987), pp. 54–7.

151. J. Saville, *1848*, op. cit., pp. 217–29.

152. D. Thompson, *The Chartists*, op. cit., pp. 82–3.

153. Ibid., p. 83, Ch. 13.

154. N. Kirk, *The Growth*, op. cit., pp. 58–9; J. Belchem, 'English Working-Class Radicalism and the Irish', op. cit.

155. I. Wilks, op. cit., pp. 146, 148, 152–5, 231, 248–9; D. J. V. Jones, *The Last Rising*, op. cit., p. 208.

156. G. S. Jones, 'Class Struggle and the Industrial Revolution', in his *Languages of Class*, op. cit., pp. 60–2; D. S. Gadian, op. cit.; R. A. Sykes, 'Some Aspects of Working-Class Consciousness', op. cit.; A. E. Musson, 'Class Struggle and the Labour Aristocracy, 1830–1860', *Social History*, 3 (1976).

157. E. D. Genovese, *Roll Jordan Roll*, op. cit., p. 587.

158. B. Laurie, *Artisans into Workers*, op. cit., p. 77.

159. S. Wilentz, *Chants Democratic*, op. cit., p. 243 (especially note 45).

160. B. Laurie, op. cit., p. 91.

161. S. Wilentz, op. cit., p. 300.

162. B. Laurie, op. cit., p. 92.

163. Ibid., pp. 92–4; S. Wilentz, op. cit., pp. 306–14; T. A. Murphy, 'Labor, Religion and Moral Reform in Fall River', op. cit., Ch. 5.

164. D. Thompson, *The Chartists*, op. cit., p. 260; D. J. V. Jones, *Chartism and the Chartists*, op. cit., pp. 49–57; T. A. Murphy, op. cit., pp. 165–209; T. A. Murphy, 'Religious Authority and Labor Protest Among Ante-Bellum Working People', paper presented at the AHA convention (Dec. 1986). I am grateful to the author for a copy of the paper.

165. T. A. Murphy, 'Labor, Religion and Moral Reform', op. cit., pp. 87–90.
166. B. Laurie, *Working People*, op. cit., p. 123.
167. S. Wilentz, op. cit., pp. 266–9.
168. Ibid., pp. 315–24.
169. D. Montgomery, 'The Shuttle and the Cross', op. cit.
170. S. Wilentz, op. cit., p. 316.
171. P. S. Foner, *Organized Labor and the Black Worker 1619–1981* (1982), Ch. 1.
172. B. Laurie, *Artisans into Workers*, op. cit., pp. 62, 91–2.
173. B. Laurie, *Working People*, op. cit., p. 124.
174. S. Wilentz, op. cit., pp. 263–4.
175. T. A. Murphy, 'Religious Authority and Labor Protest', op. cit., pp. 144–9.
176. B. Laurie, op. cit., p. 139.
177. B. Laurie, *Artisans into Workers*, op. cit., pp. 91–9; S. Wilentz, op. cit., Ch. 8.
178. S. Wilentz, op. cit., pp. 335–43.
179. T. Dublin, *Women at Work*, op. cit., Ch. 7.
180. T. A. Murphy, 'Religious Authority', op. cit., pp. 9–17.
181. A. Bridges, *A City in the Republic*, op. cit., Ch. 8.
182. S. Wilentz, op. cit., pp. 326–35.
183. Ibid., p. 333.
184. Ibid., pp. 334–5.
185. Ibid., pp. 343–9; B. Laurie, *Working People*, op. cit., pp. 168 ff.
186. S. J. Ross, op. cit., pp. 148–9.
187. B. Laurie, *Artisans into Workers*, op. cit., pp. 100–1; S. Wilentz, op. cit., pp. 353–6.
188. S. Wilentz, op. cit., p. 353.
189. Ibid., pp. 270–1.
190. S. J. Ross, op. cit., pp. 100–4, 107–15, 131–5, 151.
191. Ibid., pp. 186–8; B. Laurie, *Working People*, op. cit., pp. 194–7.
192. A. Bridges, op. cit., Ch. 8; id., 'Becoming American', op. cit., pp. 167–8, 190–6.
193. A. Bridges, *A City in the Republic*, op. cit., pp. 123–4.
194. I. Bernstein, *The New York City Draft Riots: Their Significance for American Society and Politics in the Age of the Civil War* (1990), pp. 90–1.
195. S. J. Ross, op. cit., pp. 186–8.
196. A. Dawley, *Class and Community*, op. cit., pp. 99–104.
197. S. J. Ross, op. cit., p. 149.
198. A. Bridges, 'Becoming American', op. cit., pp. 175–82; S. Wilentz, 'The Rise of the American Working Class, 1776–1877: A Survey', in J. C. Moody and A. K. Harris (eds.), *Perspectives on American Labor History: The Problems of Synthesis* (1990), pp. 110–11, 114–17; T. Dublin, op. cit., p. 205.
199. A. Dawley, op. cit., pp. 78–89.
200. P. S. Foner, *History of the Labor Movement*, Vol. 1, op. cit., p. 222; M. H. Blewett, 'Work, Gender and the Artisan Tradition in New England Shoemaking, 1780–1860', *Journal of Social History*, 18 (1984); id., *Men, Women and Work: Class Gender and Protest in the New England Shoe Industry 1780–1910* (1988), pp. 136–41.
201. C. Stansell, *City of Women*, op. cit., pp. 149–152.

202. B. Laurie, *Artisans into Workers*, op. cit., p. 103; S. Wilentz, *Chants Democratic*, op. cit., pp. 394–5.
203. S. Wilentz, op. cit., pp. 363–86; B. Laurie, op. cit., pp. 102–3; A. Bridges, op. cit., pp. 183–4.
204. T. Dublin, op. cit., pp. 6–7, 203–7; P. Scranton, op. cit., pp. 241, 259, 264–5.
205. B. Laurie, op. cit., p. 104; B. Fields, *Slavery and Freedom*, op. cit., pp. 58–60.
206. S. J. Ross, op. cit., pp. 182–92.
207 B. Laurie, op. cit., pp. 106–9; I. Berlin and H. G. Gutman, 'Natives and Immigrants', op. cit., pp. 1195–8; B. Fields, op. cit., p. 38; E. D. Genovese, op. cit., pp. 22–5.
208. S. and B. Webb, *The History of Trade Unionism* (1920), especially III, IV, V.
209. A. E. Musson, *British Trade Unions*, op. cit., especially Ch. 6.
210. R. Harrison, *Before the Socialists: Studies in Labour and Politics 1861–1881* (1965), Ch. 1 – for a lucid account of the issues involved. E. J. Hobsbawm, 'Debating the Labour Aristocracy', in his *Worlds of Labour*, op. cit., id., 'Trends in the British Labour Movement since 1850', in his *Labouring Men*, op. cit., especially pp. 316–23.
211. E. J. Hobsbawm, 'Trends', op. cit., pp. 337–8.
212. N. Kirk, *The Growth*, op. cit., pp. 174–82, 211–12, 220–2.
213. E. H. Hunt, op. cit., pp. 250–1, 267–8.
214. Ibid., Ch. 8.
215. J. Zeitlin, 'Engineers and Compositors: A Comparison', in R. Harrison and J. Zeitlin (eds.), *Divisions of Labour: Skilled Workers and Technological Change in Nineteenth Century Britain* (1985), pp. 200–1.
216. K. McClelland and A. Reid, 'Wood, Iron and Steel', in ibid., p. 168.
217. Two of the most notable examples of this 'turn', Stedman Jones' 'Rethinking Chartism' (op. cit.) and P. Joyce's *Visions of the People: Industrial England and the Question of Class* (1991), do largely fail to explore the complex meanings of words within specific and changing historical contexts, and to adequately engage language and social structure. In addition, these authors all too easily accept words and meanings at their face values. The result – at least in *Visions of the People* – is a very partial view of reality which fails to adequately examine what people do in addition to what they say. We are caught in the trap of self-justifying ideology.
218. For cotton trade unionism see N. Kirk, *The Growth of Working Class Reformism*, op. cit., Ch. 6.
219. J. Benson, *British Coalminers in the Nineteenth Century: A Social History* (1989), pp. 189–213.
220. N. Kirk, op. cit., pp. 149–52.
221. E. H. Hunt, op. cit., p. 287.
222. N. Kirk, op. cit., pp. 149, 154.
223. E. J. Evans, *The Forging of the Modern State*, op. cit., Ch. 39.
224. E. J. Hobsbawm, 'Trends', op. cit., p. 336.
225. N. Kirk, op. cit., pp. 220–31.
226. Ibid., pp. 145–8, 198–201.
227. Ibid., p. 24. Chapter 3 of Volume Two examines mid-Victorian popular Liberalism and Conservatism in some depth.
228. E. J. Hobsbawm, 'Trends', op. cit., p. 323.

229. N. Kirk, op. cit., p. ix.
230. Ibid., p. 157; S. Pollard, 'Nineteenth-century Cooperation: From Community-Building to Shopkeeping', in A. Briggs and J. Saville (eds.), *Essays in Labour History*, Vol. 1 (1960).
231. K. McClelland, 'Time to Work, Time to Live: Some Aspects of Work and the Re-formation of Class in Britain, 1850–1880', in P. Joyce (ed.), *The Historical Meanings of Work*, op. cit.
232. R. Harrison, op. cit., p. 21.
233. H. Cunningham, 'The Language of Patriotism', *History Workshop Journal*, 12 (1981).
234. N. Kirk, *The Growth*, op. cit., pp. 215–20; S. O. Rose, 'Gender Antagonism and Class Conflict: Exclusionary Strategies of Male Trade Unionists in Ninteenth-century Britain', *Social History*, 13, 2 (May 1988); W. Secombe, 'Patriarchy Stabilized: The Construction of the Male Breadwinner Wage Norm in Nineteenth-century Britain', *Social History*, 21 (1986); E. Gordon, 'Women's Spheres', in W. H. Fraser and R. J. Morris (eds.), *People and Society in Scotland*, II, op. cit.; id., *Women and the Labour Movement in Scotland 1850–1914* (1991), pp. 73–101.
235. N. Kirk, op. cit., pp. 152–4.
236. Ibid., p. 222.
237. Ibid., pp. 335–47, and Ch. 3, Volume Two below.
238. Quoted in N. Kirk, op. cit., p. 184.
239. K. Marx, F. Engels, *On Britain* (1953), pp. 491–2.
240. T. Cooper, *The Life of Thomas Cooper Written by Himself* (1877), p. 393.
241. H. G. Gutman and I. Berlin, 'Class Composition and the Development of the American Working Class', in their *Power and Culture*, op. cit., pp. 380–94.
242. D. Montgomery, *The Fall of the House of Labor*, op. cit., p. 46.
243. D. Montgomery, 'Gutman's Agenda for Future Historical Research', *Labor History*, 29, 3 (Summer 1988), p. 307.
244. Ibid., p. 307.
245. B. Laurie, *Artisans into Workers*, op. cit., p. 27.
246. E. J. Hobsbawm, 'The Formation of British Working-Class Culture', in his *Worlds of Labour*, op. cit., pp. 177–84.
247. R. A. Church, *The Great Victorian Boom* (1975), p. 71.
248. B. Laurie, op. cit., pp. 58–9.
249. See R. Q. Gray, (*The Aristocracy of Labour*, op. cit.) for a good discussion of the labour aristocracy thesis.
250. D. M. Gordon, R. Edwards and M. Reich, *Segmented Work Divided Workers*, op. cit., pp. 13–14.
251. M. H. Blewet, *Men Women and Work*, op. cit., pp. 115–41, Ch. 6.
252. D. M Gordon, R. Edwards and M. Reich, op. cit., pp. 77–99.
253. S. Thernstrom, *Poverty and Progress*, op. cit.; id., *The Other Bostonians: Poverty and Progress in the American Metropolis 1880–1970* (1973).
254. B. Laurie, *Working People*, op. cit., pp. 198–200.
255. J. A. Henretta, 'The Study of Social Mobility: Ideological Assumptions and Conceptual Bias', *Labor History*, 18, 2 (Spring 1977).
256. J. K. Walton, op. cit., pp. 179–80; M. Anderson, op. cit.
257. E. Foner, *Free Soil Free Labour Free Men: The Ideology of the Republican Party Before the Civil War* (1971), p. 33.
258. S. J. Ross, op. cit., pp. 78–81, 115–18.

259. S. Thernstrom, *Poverty and Progress*, op. cit.; H. G. Gutman, 'The Reality of the Rags to Riches "Myth": The Case of Paterson, New Jersey Locomotive, Iron and Machinery Manufacturers, 1830–1880', in his *Work Culture and Society*, op. cit.

260. H. G. Gutman and I. Berlin, *Power and Culture*, op. cit., p. 394.

261. E. H. Hunt, op. cit., p. 278.

262. Ibid., p. 279; E. J. Hobsbawm, *Labouring Men*, pp. 274, 296.

263. E. H. Hunt, op. cit., pp. 279–81.

264. E. J. Hobsbawm, op. cit., p. 324.

265. N. Kirk, *The Growth*, op. cit., pp. 133–48; A. V. John, 'The Chartist Endurance: Industrial South Wales, 1840–68', *Morgannwg/Journal of Glamorgan History*, XV (1971), especially pp. 36–9. I am grateful to the author for a copy of this article. J. F. C. Harrison, 'Chartism in Leeds', in A. Briggs, *Chartist Studies*, op. cit.; T. C. Smout, op. cit., pp. 239–47.

266. E. P. Thompson, 'The Peculiarities of the English', in his *The Poverty of Theory* (1978), p. 71.

267. N. Kirk, *The Growth*, op. cit., pp. 182–9, 220–31; T. R. Tholfsen, *Working Class Radicalism in Mid Victorian England* (1976); id., 'The Intellectual Origins of Mid-Victorian Stability', *Political Science Quarterly*, LXXXVI, 1 (March 1971).

268. R. Harrison, *Before the Socialists*, op. cit., pp. 34–9.

269. For cotton employers' attitudes towards trade unionism see N. Kirk, op. cit., pp. 284–91; P. Joyce, *Work Society and Politics*, op. cit., pp. 148–52.

270. This section on paternalism is based upon P. Joyce, *Work Society and Politics*, op. cit., Ch. 4; N. Kirk, *The Growth*, op. cit., pp. 291–300. See also Chs. 2 and 3 in Vol. 2 below.

271. N. Kirk, *The Growth*, p. 292.

272. G. S. Jones, 'Rethinking Chartism', op. cit., pp. 176–8.

273. Ibid., pp. 177–8; J. Saville, *1848: The British State and the Chartist Movement*, op. cit.; N. Kirk, 'In Defence of Class', op. cit., pp. 43–6; R. McKibbin, *The Ideologies of Class: Social Relations in Britain 1880–1950* (1990), pp. 18, 24–5, 28–9, 38.

274. P. Scranton, *Proprietary Capitalism*, op. cit., pp. 241, 259, 264–5; B. Laurie, *Artisans into Workers*, op. cit., pp. 118–22.

275. A. Bridges, 'Becoming American', op. cit., pp. 189–92.

Index

Compiled by Terry Wyke